Theorising Irish
Social Policy

edited by
Bryan Fanning
Patricia Kennedy
Gabriel Kiely
Suzanne Quin

University College Dublin Press
Preas Choláiste Ollscoile
Bhaile Átha Cliath

First published 2004
by University College Dublin Press
Newman House
86 St Stephen's Green
Dublin 2
Ireland

www.ucdpress.ie

ISBN 1-904558-31-3

Cataloguing in Publication data
available from the British Library

ACKNOWLEDGEMENTS
The editors would like to thank Ruairí Óg Ó Brádaigh
for his excellent copy editing and the UCD President's
Publication Scheme for grant assistance.

Typeset in Ireland in
Adobe Garamond and Trade Gothic
by Elaine Shiels, Bantry, Co. Cork
Text design by Lyn Davies
Index by Jane Rogers
Printed on acid-free paper
in Ireland by ColourBooks

This book is dedicated to the
memory of Cora Fanning
2000–2004

Contents

Contributors to this volume

ALASTAIR CHRISTIE is Professor of Applied Social Studies in the Department of Applied Social Studies, National University of Ireland, Cork, and previously lectured in the Department of Applied Social Science at Lancaster University, England. He is the editor of *Men and Social Work: Theories and Practices* (Palgrave, 2001) and has written articles on the social work profession's response to asylum seekers and refugees; international issues in social work education; the implications of specific social policy initiatives for social work; and the gendering of the social professions. He is currently writing a book on *Social Theory and Social Work: Rethinking the 'Social'*.

ANNE COAKLEY is a lecturer in sociology at the National University of Ireland, Maynooth. Her most recent publications include *Mothers and Poverty* (2004) and *Children and Food in a Global Economy* (2004). She has published on mothers and social welfare, on work and social welfare, and on food and diet in low income households. Her teaching and research interests include citizenship and social policy, childhood and society, risk and the environment, food and globalisation and gender and poverty.

BRYAN FANNING is a lecturer in the Department of Social Policy and Social Work at University College Dublin. His most recent research has been on racism, ethnicity and poverty in Ireland. He is the author of *Racism and Social Change in the Republic of Ireland* (Manchester: Manchester University Press, 2002) and the co-editor of *Ireland Develops: Administration and Social Policy 1953–2003* (Dublin: IPA). He is the co-author of a number of studies of asylum seekers in Ireland; *Regional Resettlement of Asylum Seekers: A Strategic Approach* (Cork: Irish Centre for Migration Studies, 1999), *Asylum Seekers and the Right to Work in Ireland* (Dublin: Irish Refugee Council, 2000) and *Beyond the Pale: Asylum Seeking Children and Social Exclusion in Ireland* (Dublin: Irish Refugee Council, 2001).

PATRICIA KENNEDY is a senior lecturer in social policy at the Department of Social Policy and Social Work, University College Dublin. She co-founded the Irish Social Policy Association in 1997. Her most recent publications include *Motherhood in Ireland, Creation and Context* (2004) and *Maternity in Ireland: A Woman Centred Perspective* (2002). She is co-editor of *Contemporary Irish Social Policy* (1999) and *Irish Social Policy in Context* (1999). Since 1998 she has been a director of (WOVE) Women Overcoming Violent Experiences. She was the Irish representative on the EU COST A13 Working Group on Gender Issues.

GABRIEL KIELY is Professor of Social Policy and Social Work at University College Dublin. From 1996 to 2002 he held the Jean Monnet Chair of European Family Policies. He is the Irish member of the European Observatory on the Social Situation, Demography and the Family. His books include *Finding Love: Counselling for Couples in Crisis* (1989); editor, *In and Out of Marriage: Irish and European Experiences* (1992); joint author, *The Cost of a Child* (1994); and joint editor, *Family Policy: European Perspectives* (1991), *Contemporary Irish Social Policy* (1999) and *Irish Social Policy in Context* (1999). He is a contributor to the *International Encyclopedia of Marriage and Family*. He has also served on numerous national and international committees dealing with social work, social policy and family policy.

PEADAR KIRBY is a senior lecturer in the School of Law and Government at Dublin City University and was previously a journalist with *The Irish Times*. He has written extensively about globalisation and development, in theoretical terms and in relation to Ireland and to Latin America. Recent books include *The Celtic Tiger in Distress: Growth with Inequality in Ireland* (Palgrave, 2002), co-editor of *Reinventing Ireland: Culture, Society and the Global Economy* (Pluto, 2002), of *Rich and Poor: Perspectives on Tackling Inequality in Ireland* (Oak Tree/Combat Poverty Agency 2001), and of *Poverty Amid Plenty: World and Irish Development Reconsidered* (Trócaire/ Gill & Macmillan, 1997). His latest book is *Introduction to Latin America: Twenty-First Century Challenges* (Sage, 2003)

JO MURPHY-LAWLESS has lectured in the Department of Social Policy and Social Work, University College Dublin and in the Department of Sociology and the Centre for Gender and Women's Studies in Trinity College, Dublin. She has published extensively in the area of health research, including *Fighting Back: Women and the Impact of Drug Abuse on Families and Communities* (Liffey, 2002), *The Maternity Care Needs of Refugee and Asylum-seeking Women* (2002 with Patricia Kennedy), *Hacia un modelo social del parto: debates obstétricos interculturales en altiplano Bolivia. Con D. Arnold y otros.* (La Paz: ILCA, 2001). *Prevalence, Profiles and Policy: A Case Study of Drug Use in Inner City Dublin* (Dublin: North Inner City Drugs Task Force, 1999).

SUZANNE QUIN is a senior lecturer in the Department of Social Policy and Social Work, University College Dublin. She has worked as a social worker in St Vincent's Hospital Elm Park, the Eastern Health Board and as Head of the Social Work Department in the National Rehabilitation Hospital. She is the author of *Uncertain Lives, Untimely Deaths* (Avebury, 1996). She has co-edited *Contemporary Irish Social Policy* (1999), *Irish Social Policy in Context* (1999), *Disability and Social Policy in Ireland* (2003) (all published by

University College Dublin Press, 1999 and 2003) and *Understanding Children* vols 1 and 2 (Oak Tree Press, 2001).

MICHAEL RUSH has lectured in the Department of Social Policy and Social Work in University College Dublin for several years. His published work includes articles on comparative family policy, reproductive work and labour market policy. His research in the field includes a recent evaluation of the *Hill Street Family Resource Centre* and the report *Including Children: Disability, Diversity and Additional Needs* for the County Waterford Childcare Committee. His PhD research is a comparative investigation into the political economy of reproductive work, fatherhood, and child well-being in the USA, Sweden and Ireland

GERRY WHYTE is a Fellow of Trinity College, Dublin and Head of the Law School there. He is an acknowledged expert in constitutional law. He has worked closely with a number of NGOs including the Coolock Community Law Centre Ltd, the Free Legal Advice Centres Ltd, the Irish Commission for Justice and Peace and People with Disabilities in Ireland Ltd. His publications include *Social Inclusion and the Legal System: Public Interest Law in Ireland* (Dublin: IPA)

Abbreviations

ABP	area-based partnerships
AFDC	Aid to Families with Dependent Children
CDB	City and County Development Board
CE	community employment
CORI	Conference of Religious in Ireland
CSO	Central Statistics Office
CWO	Community Welfare Officer
DCU	Dublin City University
DJELR	Department of Justice, Equality and Law Reform
ESRI	Economic and Social Research Institute
EU	European Union
FDI	Foreign Direct Investment
FRM	Fathers Responsibility Movement
GDP	Gross Domestic Product
GNP	Gross National Product
HDR	Human Development Report (of the United Nations)
HFEA	Human Fertilisation and Embryology Authority
IDA	Industrial Development Agency
IPA	Institute of Public Administration
NAPS	National Anti-Poverty Strategy
NESC	National Economic and Social Council
NESF	National Economic and Social Forum
NGO	Non-government organisation
TANF	Temporary Aid to Needy Families
TCD	Trinity College, Dublin
UCD	University College Dublin
USFI	The Unmarried and Separated Fathers of Ireland
USI	Union of Students in Ireland
WHO	World Health Organisation

Introduction

Bryan Fanning, Patricia Kennedy, Gabriel Kiely and Suzanne Quin

This book appears as part of the University College Dublin Press series of social policy texts. These are *Contemporary Irish Social Policy* (1999), *Irish Social Policy in Context* (1999) and *Disability and Social Policy in Ireland* (2003). A considerable amount of literature has emerged in the three decades since social policy emerged as an academic discipline in Ireland. Most existing textbooks focus predominantly on the historical development of welfare in Ireland or are primarily descriptive and empirical in focus (Barrington, 1987; Burke, 1987; Curry, 2003; Healy and Reynolds, 1998; Kaim-Caudle, 1967). At the same time, such texts have reflected the shifting ideological and theoretical preoccupations of Western academia and the broader societal shifts of which these were part. For example, the emergence of a focus on gender inequalities in the 1970s reflected concurrent debates in other Western countries (Curtin et al., 1987; Nolan and Watson, 1999; Byrne and Leonard, 1997; Byrne and Lentin, 2000; Kennedy, 2002). In another example, some texts draw upon international debates and Irish research about racism and multiculturalism (Fanning, 2002a; MacLachlan and O'Connell, 2000). Similarly, academic social policy texts on poverty and social exclusion draw both on international theoretical literature and Irish social research (Nolan and Callan, 1994; Pringle, Walsh and Hennessy, 1999). However, none focuses primarily on the relevance of theoretical debates for the study of Irish social policy. *Theorising Irish Social Policy* seeks to address a gap in the existing literature on Irish social policy.

The influence of international theoretical debates on Irish social policy is a central theme to a number of chapters. At the same time contributors have sought to emphasise the specific Irish context within which such theoretical approaches are applied. In the Irish context there has always been a degree of tension between 'off the shelf' appropriations of the literature of other countries, in particular those of the United Kingdom, and claims of Irish exceptionalism. Both are arguably manifestations of the under-theorisation of Irish society, at least in the area of social policy. Perhaps more so than in some larger countries there are gaps in the existing social policy literature. That said, writing about Irish social policy could be located within identifiable 'indigenous' and international ideological and theoretical accounts of society and social problems. *Theorising Irish Social Policy* is an initial attempt to locate a number of Irish social policy debates within such theoretical contexts.

O'Brien and Penna (1998) argue that to understand social policy we need to be conscious of theory in two senses. These they outline as theories and assumptions, which affect how policy is formulated. Different theories highlight the effects and consequences of different policies. Social policies and welfare are built on theoretical assumptions. These include theories on relationships between the individual and the state and the role of organisations in social and economic development. As such, theorising Irish social policy necessitates theorising about social life and places the welfare system in the context of wider social and political struggles. The editors have selected some of the major themes in Irish social policy today and invited some respected authors in these fields to develop theoretical accounts of these within their specific social and political contexts. *Theorising Irish Social Policy* offers divergent perspectives aimed at informing the study of twenty-first century Irish social policy and society. Inevitably, these accounts are partial ones that reflect the preoccupations of their authors. They are to be viewed as contributions to a series of broader debates.

In chapter 1, Bryan Fanning emphasises the centrality of perspectives on modernisation within ideological and theoretical accounts of Irish social policy. In this context ideologies such as those associated with Catholicism, liberalism and feminism are seen to offer critiques of social change with implications for the study of Irish social policy. In the first part of the chapter, he identifies a number of distinct ideological, theoretical and historiographical debates within the broader Irish literature that have informed understandings of Irish social policy. In the second part of the chapter he locates Irish social policy within comparative theoretical perspectives that emphasise welfare convergence as an expression of modernity and those that emphasise the central role of ideology.

In chapter 2, Peadar Kirby examines the relevance of theories of globalisation for theorising Irish social policy. He suggests that theorising the impact of globalisation on social policy in Ireland requires far closer attention to the specifics of Ireland's development trajectory, the nature of its political economy institutions, its political culture, and the productive base of its economy than has been evident in existing literature. He argues that the failure to adequately engage with these aspects has allowed an inflated and benign social policy discourse to emerge amongst policy makers that is ever more out of touch with the reality of major social problems.

In Chapter 3, Bryan Fanning explores theoretical approaches to the study of social change and power within Irish social policy with reference to international and Irish debates on communitarianism, social capital and subsidiarity. He argues that debates about each of these can be seen to converge in discussions of the consequences for Irish social policy of modernisation and social change. In particular, secularisation, urbanisation and the individualisation of life have become associated with a perceived decline in social cohesion. Fanning situates a number of present-day Irish social policy debates about law and order, alcohol policy and the role of social capital within a dominant moral communitarian critique of social modernisation. He argues that present-day communitarian and social capital perspectives can be understood in the Irish case as a set of critiques of late modernity centring on a concern about the apparent decline of community.

In Chapter 4, Gabriel Kiely critically examines the use of the concept of individualisation as a discourse about equality, within debates about Irish taxation and welfare systems. He locates Irish social policy within international trends towards individualisation of welfare systems. He argues that individualisation is construed in terms of meeting goals of equality between men and women, yet does not address an objective of equality between all individuals because it does not take family responsibilities into account. He challenges the capacity of individualisation to meet stated policy objectives of equality between individuals and suggests that security and not equality should be the driving force behind welfare reforms.

In chapter 5, Patricia Kennedy theorises on personal autonomy and bodily integrity by focusing on one's ability to survive outside the labour market, often referred to as de-commodification. Theories of citizenship have been drawn on to explore civil and political rights which are an essential prerequisite to the attainment of social rights. Feminist writers have challenged more mainstream writers in this area for lack of attention to women's unpaid work – caring work. This is related to the notion of relational autonomy; women are generally linked to and responsible for others. Personal autonomy has often been presented as the ability to create an independent household. Kennedy argues that the most essential aspect of personal autonomy is control over one's own body, one's reproductive capacities and sexuality. Her focus is primarily on non-national women, working in Ireland as cleaners, childminders and prostitutes.

In chapter 6, Michael Rush locates societal debates about biological fatherhood in Ireland and social policy debates about male breadwinners within a comparison between debates in the United States and Sweden. The chapter identifies the emergence of a new conservative politics of fatherhood in Ireland. It locates these politics within comparative social policy conceptualisations of male breadwinner welfare systems. It compares and contrasts the new politics of fatherhood in Ireland with those in the United States and Sweden in an analysis of current Irish policy debates.

In chapter 7, Anne Coakley examines the reproduction of poverty, risk and social exclusion in twenty-first century Ireland and the ideological reconstruction of discourses about poverty in the era of the 'Celtic Tiger'. She argues that this era has been characterised by a fragmentation, dilution and increasing spatialisation within social policy responses to poverty. She explores how state policy has facilitated growing inequalities in Irish society, particularly within the low-paid job sector whilst an official discourse maintains that poverty has declined as a result of the Celtic Tiger. She contests such perspectives in an exploration of Irish and international research that emphasises broader conceptualisations of well-being and the structural causes of poverty.

In chapter 8, Jo Murphy-Lawless and Suzanne Quin explore the disjunctures between goals of equity and fairness and goals of efficiency within the Irish healthcare system. They locate current efforts to restructure the healthcare system within an ideological discourse of managerialism. Here, a number of commonalities with the United Kingdom can be identified. In both cases, managerialism seeks to reformulate the relationship between providers and users of the healthcare system from that of patient to that of consumer. Issues about citizen involvement in decision making about health services are raised in the context of the increasingly individualised and fragmented nature of society. The authors explore the particular challenges facing healthcare professionals in trying to reconcile core values of caring with the realities of the everyday context within which they work.

In chapter 9, Alastair Christie explores the significance of understandings of difference for theorising multiculturalism in Ireland and social policies aimed at addressing inequalities. He first locates shifting social policy discourses about Travellers since the 1960s within theoretical debates about difference, recognition and representation. He then offers a critique of conceptualisations of difference in recent social policy reports by the Equality Authority. He argues that social policy, as a set of discourses and practices, constructs differences and similarities *between* and *within* particular groups.

In chapter 10, Gerry Whyte examines the impact of rights-based approaches to social policy upon conceptualisations of and responses to Irish social problems. He defends the constitutional and political legitimacy of using public interest litigation to establish socio-economic rights. He argues that the Irish Constitution does not preclude the judicial enforcement of socio-economic rights. He offers a critique of current Irish debates on the role of the courts in defining justiciable social rights and examines the implications of the recent decisions by the Irish Supreme Court in eschewing this role. Whyte's chapter suggests that, in common with other countries, the Irish courts have become a crucial site of ideological conflict about social policy issues. In effect, a range of potential interpretations of the constitutionality of justiciable social rights can be identified. These range from the libertarian perspectives of writers such as Hayek to those of advocates of social rights to welfare such as Rawls or Dworkin.

The themes that emerge within *Theorising Irish Social Policy* are the result to some extent of conscious editorial intent. There are also elements of happenstance in the overlapping preoccupations that emerge. We commissioned chapters by asking contributing authors to address selected themes. Individual thinkers inevitably have their own theoretical and empirical preoccupations. Yet these inevitably reflect time and place. Collectively the chapters in *Theorising Irish Social Policy* provide a snapshot of thought about Irish social policy. The chapters reveal a number of crosscutting themes. A number are concerned with the impact of modernisation and globalisation upon Irish society. Chapter 3 (on communitarianism and social capital) and chapter 4 (on individualisation) are preoccupied in different ways with theorising shifts in social solidarity resulting from social change. Chapters 4, 5 (on women and personal autonomy) and 6 (fathers) engage with the interrelationships between gender and the body, the market and social change. In twenty-first century Ireland these become intertwined with debates about racism and difference. Chapters 1, 2, 4, 6, 7 and 8 consider in different ways the impact of neo-liberalism upon Irish social policy. Chapters 1, 2 and 7 (on poverty) critically examine ideological claims made about the 'Celtic Tiger'. Chapters 7 and 8 (on health) emphasise how conceptions of well-being interrelate with ideological debates about the nature and extent of welfare provision. Chapters 8 and 9 (on difference) engage with approaches to well-being and identity central to critiques of the British Welfare State by social constructionist academics inspired by Foucault. Chapters 1, 4 and 8 emphasise the specificity of what social constructionists would refer to as the Irish welfare settlement. Chapters 3, 5 and 9 offer critiques of past and present-day racialised inequality. These respectively locate such inequalities within theory about moral community, welfare stratification and the politics of difference and recognition. Chapters 4, 5, 6, 7, 8 and 10 (on judicial activism) engage in different ways with conceptual, political and policy debates about welfare rights and social justice in present-day Ireland.

Chapter 1

Locating Irish social policy

Bryan Fanning

Introduction

The purpose of this chapter, in part, is to set the scene for the subsequent chapters in *Theorising Irish Social Policy*. It has two main aims. The first is to provide a contextual overview of ideological influences on Irish social policy and on the study of Irish social policy. The second is to briefly locate understandings of Irish social policy within international debates. With respect to the first aim the chapter locates current preoccupations with neo-liberalism – a recurring theme in a number of subsequent chapters – within past inter-relationships between liberalism and Catholicism in Ireland. Emphasis is placed upon the role of historiography in interpreting the ideological history of social policy.

From one perspective, liberalism as a colonialist ideology was part of a British project of nation building that shaped many Irish welfare institutions and societal understandings of social problems. From another it has been central to the making of present day 'Celtic Tiger' Irish society. It has been interpreted as an ideology that successfully vied with a moribund 'Irish-Ireland' conception of nation from the mid-twentieth century. Liberalism and Catholicism have long been ideological bedfellows within the processes of modernisation, nation building and social reproduction that have moulded Irish social policy and social citizenship. The former, in the guise of neo-liberalism, now appears to be hogging the bedclothes. Both, as dominant ideologies, have provided ideological lenses through which other ideologies, such as nationalism, feminism and multiculturalism, have influenced social policy. For instance, both liberal feminist and Catholic feminist thought have contributed to Irish social policy debates.

With respect to the second aim of locating Ireland within international debates, a number of comparative frameworks might be summarised according to the way in which they embody a tension between two conflicting arguments in sociology. These relate to consensus and conflict theories of social order. Attempts to categorise Ireland within comparative models of western welfare systems have principally focused on measuring the extent of welfare provision and upon examination of the effect of ideological and economic factors on levels of state provision. These emphasise a number of influences including Catholicism, liberalism, past underdevelopment, the legacy of colonialism and international convergence of welfare systems. Within the literature on Irish social policy a range of theoretical perspectives and ideological positions can be identified. These can be seen to have shifted over time in common with international debates and to some extent around specific 'indigenous' issues and political cleavages.

Historiography, ideology and theory

Shifting accounts of Irish 'social problems' with implications for social policy can be identified throughout various kinds of literature on Irish society. A range of important texts can be identified but these are not always focused on questions of theory *per se*. In the absence of a distinct canon of theoretical works on Irish social policy it becomes necessary to draw upon the works of modern historians, sociologists, economists, geographers and political scientists to piece together the equivalent of the theoretical debates usual in larger societies with larger academic and intellectual communities. A 'loose' social policy canon might be fashioned, if one felt it was prudent to do so, from a mixture of influential texts which have shaped academic accounts of Irish social policy, texts which reveal evolving ideological debates about Irish social policy and texts that reveal shifting understandings of social problems. The 'texts' in question range from academic studies in the first and second instances and key policy documents in the second and third cases. They also include popular discourses about social change that have informed thinking about social policy in Ireland. For example, discourses about women's reproductive rights and about the politics of abortion reveal ideological shifts and continuities that have influenced social policy.

A range of preoccupations can be identified within such materials and debates. Again and again the problem of modernisation is posed, whether as a response to a perceived crisis of national decline, underdevelopment and emigration or as a threat to 'traditional' social and religious solidarities. Accounts of Irish modernisation are central to the Irish narratives within which understandings of social policy must be located. Irish social policy emerged in the shadow of nineteenth-century, often radical, Catholic and liberal projects of modernisation that became, to a considerable extent, problematic conservative legacies after independence in 1922. The Catholic, rural, Gaelic, 'Irish-Ireland' national ideal of the decades after independence was consciously reformulated in response to a perceived social crisis by a state-driven programme of economic expansion from the 1950s. Economic modernisation supplanted a post-colonial isolationist emphasis on frugality (Lee, 1989: 335). Within this context many social policy goals were subordinated to goals of growth and development. It is perhaps useful to compare the Irish economic project of national salvation (a commitment to growth without a commitment to universal security) to those of other countries that encountered the spectre of population decline. The Swedish response to declining population size included pro-natalist and universalist welfare policies. The advocacy of contraception was influenced by neo-Malthusian ideas about limiting family sizes to combat poverty (Myrdal, 1945: 121). Social consensus on the population question fostered, to a considerable extent, ideological support for social democratic policies (Ginsburg, 1997: 190). By contrast, emigration became central to Irish social modernisation and nation building. In the aftermath of the Famine it was constructed as inevitable and even desirable within rhetoric tinged with determinism, fatalism and social Darwinism.

The subject of history dominates the Irish social policy 'loose cannon' to a considerable extent. Historiography, the bedrock of Irish history theory, remains predominantly focused on the national question with ongoing debates between 'green' (nationalist, post-colonialist) and 'revisionist' readings of the present and the past (Boyce and O'Day, 1996: 3). Its theoretical relevance to Irish social policy as a tool for exploring the social construction of social policy can be seen in the relationship between nation building and social citizenship. The independent Irish state emerged with specific ideological understandings of belonging and social membership. For at least the first half of the twentieth century the social construction of social policy was dominated by 'Irish-Ireland' understandings of citizenship (Fanning, 2003: 8). This advanced a doctrinaire formulation of 'Irishness' grounded in claims about the exclusive authenticity of a Gaelic-Catholic Ireland. It dominated official rhetoric and, more pervasively, the symbols and statutes of the Irish state from the 1920s to, perhaps, the 1960s (Ó Tuathaigh, 1991: 58). Yet the courts, the civil service and state welfare institutions tended to persist in their pre-independence form. The red postboxes of the Crown were painted green, and official documents were now also published in Irish.

Historiography
A brief historiography of Irish social policy debates could include a number of strands. One obvious strand adheres closely to the cleavage between 'green' and 'revisionist' readings of modern Irish history. A revisionist critique of social policy might emphasise how nationalist ideologies, as institutionalised with the nation state, emphasised a narrow construction of social membership that excluded indigenous minorities such as Travellers, Protestants and Jews (Fanning, 2002a: 30–57). It might emphasise how the forms of ideological

closure associated with such nation building partially unravelled following a failed experiment in economic isolationism during the 1930s. Fennell suggests that the Irish-Ireland project could only have succeeded if the Irish state had been sufficiently isolationalist (like the Soviet Union which prohibited immigration and had a language barrier, censorship, and a radio-jamming apparatus to exclude information about the outside world) for low standards of living not to matter. However, because the Republic of Ireland was an English-speaking liberal democracy, standards of living mattered so much that it became necessary to improve the economy by any means (Fennell, 1993: 57). Hence, the argument goes, Ireland came to pursue from the 1950s a conformist modernising project while retaining some opposition, through censorship, church censure and legal barriers, to an accompanying liberal social project. By and large these barriers have dissipated. Yet narrow constructions of 'Irishness' have obtained a new lease of life in some responses to immigration. One example was the government's determination to challenge the residency rights of the Irish-born children of immigrant parents and their families (*Lobe* v. *Minister of Justice*) in the Supreme Court (2003).

Another strand might focus on the impact of secularisation and of shifts within Catholicism on social policy issues over the last several decades. Contestations of Catholic authoritarianism and intellectual contributions to secularisation have included academic critiques such as *Church and State in Modern Ireland* by John Whyte (1971). Retrospective critiques into the legacy of Catholic authoritarianism have been generated by inquiries into clerical child abuse (Raftery and O'Sullivan, 1999). A longstanding emphasis on vocationalist and natural law Catholic social teaching in the university social policy curriculum was gradually displaced in the post-Vatican Two era in favour of an emphasis on social justice. The former was exemplified by *The Manual of Social Ethics* by James Kavanagh, a cleric appointed as head of social science in University College Dublin by Archbishop McQuaid (Kavanagh, 1966). McQuaid effectively controlled appointments to five academic chairs in the moral or social sciences; 'all funded at taxpayers expense' (Garvin, 1998: 309). In 1984, Whyte became the first twentieth-century lay chair of politics in UCD. The first lay professor of sociology in the Republic of Ireland, Damien Hannon, was appointed to University College Cork in 1971.

According to Tovey and Share (2000), 'Catholic sociology' emphasised the study of civil society (institutions outside the state such as the family, community and parish). It coexisted with a nineteenth-century legacy of statistical inquiry epitomised by the Statistical and Social Inquiry Society (SSIS). The SSIS influenced the remit of key twentieth-century bodies which served the state such as the Economic Research Institute which became the Economic and Social Research Institute (ESRI) in 1966:

Both discourses tended to be positivistic and rather uninterested in theoretical issues and debates. Each took for granted that they could easily identify the proper objects of sociological research in the 'real world' (social problems) and tended to encourage empirical research rather than theoretical or conceptual development. (Tovey and Share, 2000: 29).

Tovey and Share argue that the perceived remit of 'official' and 'Catholic' research were different from each other. The former addressed the state and its agents. The latter sought to influence civil society. In the post-Vatican Two era, the latter has included 'social justice' critiques of government polices in areas such as social welfare and asylum (CORI, 1993; Irish Commission for Justice and Peace, 1997).

Arguably, quantitative research methods have been privileged over qualitative methodologies in social policy research. One example of this lies in the area of poverty research where an emphasis on income poverty (use of a poverty line calculated by the ESRI against an annually adjusted average industrial wage) persists despite endorsements within the National Anti-Poverty Strategy (NAPS) of more sociologically complex concepts such as social exclusion (Government of Ireland, 1997: 4; ESRI, 2000). In this context qualitative studies of the dynamics of poverty (such as within-household studies grounded in feminist methodologies) tend to carry less weight or even be denigrated. For example, a peer-reviewed qualitative study of poverty amongst asylum-seeker children was criticised by the Taoiseach who suggested that the findings could be disregarded because the sample was too small (Fanning, Veale and O'Connor, 2001; Dáil Debates, 15 November 2001).

A further strand of historiography can be identified with respect to shifting critiques of Irish modernisation from the 1970s and 1980s to the era of the 'Celtic Tiger'. This centres to some extent on academic accounts of the technocratic role of the state in pursuing economic development since the 1950s and the relationship between such development and the expansion of welfare goods and services (Fanning, 2003: 3). Many accounts typically refer to the role of key officials and politicians (notably T. K. Whitaker and Sean Lemass) in mobilising the state (Lalor, 2003: 90; Murphy, 2003: 115). The 1980s witnessed a resurgence of emigration after a few decades of relative prosperity and growth. The preoccupations of a number of historical and sociological works published at that time reflected a perception of crisis that has, to some extent, been superseded by the feel-good (or triumphalist) lens of the 'Celtic Tiger' era. Within these shifting accounts an emphasis on structural inequalities has partially lost out to explanations that emphasise liberal conceptions of agency. Accounts of Irish modernisation during the 1980s emphasised the role of fatalism and deterministic beliefs in blocking enterprise. An underdevelopment narrative has been replaced by a neo-liberal one that emphasises individualism and agency. Sweeney suggests that for many Irish people the past is indeed a foreign country in noting, by way of comparison with previous generations, 'several hundred thousand young Irish adults have only known prosperity' (Sweeney, 1999: xii).

A number of authors writing in the 1980s depicted ideological consequences of underdevelopment in psychological terms. Lee in *Modern Ireland: 1912–1985* emphasises the emergence of a 'zero sum' mindset in which people saw the advancement of others as possible only at their own expense:

> The size of the cake was more or less fixed in more or less stagnating communities and in small institutions. In a stunted society, one man's gain did tend to be another man's loss. Winners could only flourish at the expense of losers. Status depended not only on rising oneself but on preventing others from rising. For many, keeping the other fellow down offered the surest defence of their own position (Lee, 1989: 647).

He argued that such begrudgery severely hampered the emergence of meritocracy and an 'enterprise culture'. In Lee's account an essentially liberal project of modernisation found itself in contestation with deterministic thinking about social problems. Lee's concern in emphasising such factors was to account for the economic crisis of the 1980s where high levels of emigration evoked memories of the 1950s. His panacea against this prosperity-blocking fatalism was a liberal mindset adept at enterprise. Moving forward to the present time, such qualities are routinely valorised in politics, social partnership and the media, within what Coulter calls hagiographies of the 'Celtic Tiger' (Coulter, 2003: 10).

Lee's perception of determinism and fatalism was borne out to some extent in academic accounts of Irish underdevelopment during the 1980s. For instance, Raymond Crotty's *Ireland in Crisis: A Study in Capitalist Colonial Underdevelopment* described the effects of emigration in lurid terms:

> It is at least conceivable that this rigorous systematic selection has altered the genetic character of the resulting population. It is conceivable that the Irish population now is genetically more cautious, less disposed to change, than the population of 1920. Neither can it be discounted that Ireland now has a 'fat cat' population, with a genetically induced propensity for conservative caution. (Crotty, 1986: 70)

Whilst Crotty's assumptions about national character are problematic, his analysis of social regulation had much in common with that of Lee. Crotty argued that systematic social selection had occurred, generation by generation, since the Famine. Over six generations fewer than 40 per cent of Irish-born people had married and reproduced. Distributional conflicts in post-Famine Ireland shaped emigration. Those driven into emigration were not the only losers. They were often 'relatives assisting', unable to marry, maybe inheriting property too late in life to gain much from it, unable to lead independent lives in a society unable to create sufficient work to provide even for a dwindling population (Crotty, 1986: 70). This of course impacted on social policy. For example, emigration was extolled as a useful economic safety valve. A 1958 analysis in the *Irish Banking Review* held that emigration began when the 'supply of labour' exceeded the capacity to absorb it locally. The prevailing assumption that no more could be done meant that it was better for the unemployed surplus to move abroad rather than to be condemned to chronic unemployment. (Lee, 1989: 227). Such fatalism also found expression in the Malthusian argument that emigrants were a manifestation of overpopulation. An increase in population was not to be condoned because under zero sum 'rules' it would mean a decline in living standards for the rest. The fact of emigration itself became the criterion of population excess. Emigration dispensed with the need to do anything about its causes. In this context the unemployed 'surplus' rather than the problem of unemployment was con-structed as a social problem.

Ideology

The role of religion, specifically Catholicism, in the social reproduction of post-Famine Ireland, is emphasised by sociologists. Inglis's landmark analysis of the regulatory role of the Catholic Church in post-Famine Irish society helps place in context both Crotty's determinism and Lee's critique of the role of fatalism in the regulation of Irish society. Sociological accounts of the role of religion emphasise how religious control of sexuality has major conse-quences for the distribution of wealth and authority (Turner, 1999: 8). Inglis describes how the Catholic Church, no longer hampered by penal laws, attained an effective moral monopoly in post-Famine Ireland (1998: 107–28). In this context, social Darwinism became intertwined with body politics. Changing patterns of inheritance and of sexual regulation consigned the landless and jobless to emigration or celibacy and lesser status at home. The ideological role of the Church with regard to social and sexual reproduction was complemented by its institutional contributions to nation building. Nineteenth-century political activism was centred on the parish as a unit of organisation. So too was the denominational education system that was part of the post-Catholic Emancipation political settlement. In the late nineteenth century, with the establishment of the Gaelic Athletic Association (GAA), cultural nationalism also became centred on the parish as did revolutionary nationalism which used the GAA as an organisational base. The Catholic Church was central, therefore, to the modernisation of Irish society within mass education, culture and politics.

The ideological legacy of liberalism warrants analysis in an era when neo-liberalism has proved to be a strong influence on social policy. Welfare provision at the time of independence had been influenced by a nineteenth-century colonialist liberal project of modernity characterised by belief in progress and reason. According to Bellamy, nineteenth-century liberalism had broad cultural roots that ultimately amounted to an ideological hegemony in nineteenth-century Britain. These

> incorporated a variety of heterogeneous political languages, and evolved piece-meal over a long period of social change. Intellectual sources as diverse as natural rights doctrines, Whiggism, classical political economy, utilitarianism, evangelical Christianity, idealism, and evolutionary biology all played a part in liberal ideology, modifying its understanding of, and emphasis on, the market mechanism and property ownership (Bellamy, 1990: 2)

They shaped as well as reflected the economic and social interests of the middle classes, informing their attitude towards the role of the state and the management of the economy (Bellamy, 1990: 2). A liberal hegemony found expression in the construction of social norms as well as in economic behaviour, notably with the social construction of poverty as a moral problem. It was evident in Friedrich Engels's accounts of the Irish poor as 'dissolute, unsteady, drunken' and as having a 'strong degrading influence on their English companions in toil' (Engels, 1844: 122).

Yet nineteenth-century liberalism was also a component of the ideological, social and institutional processes of Irish nation building (Breuilly, 1994: 234; Boyce, 1992: 44). Preston argues that stereotypes of the Irish Catholic poor – which depicted them as immoral, licentious, thriftless, criminal, in short uncivilised – within British philanthropy achieved a similar status within urban Irish Catholic and Protestant philanthropy (1998: 110). Liberalism, no less that Catholicism, contributed to the social and sexual regulation of Irish society. It offered a discourse of moral responsibility that regulated the domestic sphere as well as the workplace. Liberalism ideologically confined women to the domestic sphere and shaped a welfare system that linked benefits to paid employment even though Ireland was, for the most part, not an industrial society (see Kennedy in chapter 5). Liberal conceptions of welfare had considerable affinity with Catholic social teaching. Both held that the state should only act when the male breadwinner was proven to have failed to provide for his dependants. Both contributed to an official ideology of the privatised family. The link between welfare and work within early twentieth-century legislation remained consistent with the exclusion from the remit of social policy of 'surplus' population. Post-independence Ireland was in many respects a privatised nation of providers and dependents.

The ideological settlement between liberalism and Catholicism became destabilised as a result of technocratic modernisation and a degree of secularisation. Increased social liberalism, in areas such as sexuality and gender roles, has impacted in various ways upon social policy. Secondly, accounts of economic 'success' have emphasised possibilities for individual agency at the expense of an emphasis on structural barriers and inequalities. In this context, Lee's fatalism has arguably been superseded by what Galbraith terms a culture of contentment. Galbraith, like Lee, has emphasised the importance of understandings of social problems and the social construction of welfare possibilities. He suggested that social policy priorities came to accommodate the beliefs of the contented in society who form an electoral majority. This majority consists, for the most part, of those who have benefited from the welfare solidarities and social policies of an earlier generation yet no longer feel dependent upon these. They attribute their success to their own intrinsic qualities (Galbraith, 1992: 23). Galbraith suggests that neo-liberalism in valorising individual agency has resuscitated the old (Poor Law) liberal emphasis on poverty as a moral problem of individual failing:

> The problem is not economics; it goes back to a far deeper part of human nature. As people become fortunate in their well-being, and as countries become similarly fortunate, there is a common tendency to ignore the poor, or to develop some rationalisation for the good fortune of the fortunate. Responsibility is assigned to the poor themselves. Given their personal disposition and moral tone, they are meant to be poor. Poverty is inevitable and, in some measure, deserved. The fortunate individuals and countries enjoy their well-being without the burden of conscience, without a troublesome sense of responsibility (1998).

Thirdly, neo-liberalism has taken much credit for growth and prosperity at the expense of an emphasis on the role of welfare goods and services. The role of free secondary education from the 1960s in the growth of wealth and productivity in Ireland can be seen as one example of the latter. However, the 1990s boom tends to be attributed in popular discourse to subsequent neo-liberal policies such as privatisation and to 'responsible' fiscal policies (O'Hearn, 2001: 190).

Theory
Interpretations of Irish social policy are inevitably influenced by broader theoretical debates. The use of dependency theory in accounts of Irish modernisation is one example. Economic and social changes since the 1980s have reformulated the question for left theorists from explaining social problems in terms of dependency and underdevelopment to accounting for wealth and inequality in an era of globalisation (Allen, 2000; O'Hearn, 1998). Allen's

critique of the inequalities in 'Celtic Tiger' Ireland depicts corporatist 'social partnership' mechanisms as articulating a neo-liberal hegemony (2003: 120). Against this perspective must be set contestations of inequality *within* social partnership arrangements as these widened to include a 'Community Pillar' of voluntary organisations, community development partnerships and NGO representatives who have been 'the main voices of state criticism or opposition' (Rush, 1999: 167). These critiques are to some extent rooted in the afore-mentioned Catholic conceptions of civil society that influenced Irish sociology. However, Irish civil society and Catholic voluntarism are no longer one and the same. In recent years voluntary sector groups and new social movements relating to gender, ethnicity, disability and sexuality have campaigned for rights-based approaches to social policy in opposition to a strong resistance from successive centre-right (Fianna Fáil–Progressive Democrat) governments. For example, some Community Pillar submissions to the revised National Anti-Poverty Strategy in 2001 were critical of government asylum policies (Goodbody, 2001). The campaigns of such organisations for rights-based approaches to disability have played a pivotal role in recent debates about justiciable social rights (see Whyte in chapter 10).

The role of social policy in reproducing social inequalities on the basis of class has been emphasised by a number of writers, notably in the area of education (Clancy, 1995; Drudy and Lynch, 1993: 149). These studies, in common with those in other countries, suggest the importance of cultural capital in the maintenance of structural inequalities (see Fanning in chapter 3). The work of Bourdieu has been central to a number of explorations of power and social reproduction in Irish society. For example, Peillon, in one of the few books explicitly focused on theorising Irish social policy, employs Bourdieu's notion of interconnected social fields to examine the use and exchange of symbolic, economic, cultural and political capital between the Catholic Church, the state and other actors within Irish social policy (Peillon, 2001). Peillon describes Irish society as being shaped by a range of social forces each with their own particular projects for society. He argues that some projects have acquired dominant positions in that they constitute what he refers to as 'pillars of State action' while others are placed in a subordinate position. Thus the 'project of the State is structured, and this structure reveals the differential relation of social forces to the State'. (Peillon, 1995: 363). Peillon views the project of the state as heavily influenced by the interests of the economic elite who are concerned with promoting economic develop-ment based on private enterprise. The corporatist state may play one force off against the other but it will be responsive to comparatively powerful forces to the detriment of other groups in society.

Gender narratives, ideology and theory

A significant body of academic work exists on gender inequality in Ireland.
Generally this has been empirical in focus though informed by international
feminist debates. Feminist critiques of the Irish state and of Irish social policy
are evident in texts such as *Women and Irish Society* (Byrne and Leonard,
1997) and in a range of empirical studies of social problems and social policies
(Daly and Leonard, 2002; Murphy-Lawless, 2002; Kennedy, 2002, 2004).
These have contributed significantly to the study of social policy in Ireland. A
feminist critique of social inequality, expressed though a women's movement,
was central to reforms of welfare and employment legislation following the
establishment of the Commission on the Status of Women in 1970 (Beere,
2003: 241; Yeates, 1997: 156). This critique has, in particular, emphasised the
institutionalisation of gendered social citizenship within *Bunreacht na hÉireann*,
the 1937 Irish Constitution. This prescribed specific roles for women within
society in stating in Article 41.2.1 that; 'the State recognises by her life within
the home Woman gives to the State a support without which the common
good cannot be achieved'. Feminist thought is central to understandings of
gendered labour commodification in Ireland and of the gendered welfare
stratifications resulting from the differential access of women to paid employ-
ment that confers welfare entitlements (see Kennedy in chapter 5).

However, feminism in Ireland can be seen to include a heterogeneity of
ideological positions ranging from those which emphasise the need for
individual equality to those which challenge the premises of liberal individ-
ualism within which mainstream feminism is grounded. In Ireland, women's
bodies have become metaphorical and material sites of ideological debates
about modernisation and secularisation. This is most evident in ideological
conflicts over the last two decades about abortion. To some extent these
reflected challenges to Catholic authoritarianism, evident in welfare institutions
such as the Magdalene laundries, as part of a broader critique of gender
inequality. On the other hand the 1980s 'pro-life' activism that led to the
constitutional prohibition on abortion can be read as a response to a perceived
crisis of 'traditional' Catholic hegemony. The 'ethical hornet's nest' of
abortion remains central to ideological critiques of gender, citizenship, rights
and power in Ireland (Dooley, 1998: 131). Yet a cleavage can be identified
within Irish feminisms where advocacy of a woman's 'right to choose' has
come into conflict with the views of 'pro-life' women who also describe them-
selves as feminist (Connolly, 1997: 564; Kennedy, 1997: 2). Here some parallels
can be noted with conflicts between liberal feminism and Muslim feminists
who argue that adherence to tradition cultural and religious practices, such as
in relation to attire, must be viewed as the legitimate expression of the agency
of some Muslim women. Irish feminisms can be located, as in the cases of

other ideologies, along divergent paths between so-called traditional and individualist 'modern' conceptions of Irish society.

Locating Irish social policy

Accounts of modernisation can be seen as central to the conceptualisation of Irish social policy. Kennett, writing about the role of theory and analysis in cross-national social policy research emphasises the question of relationships between forms of economic and social modernisation and social policy. As she puts it, 'the coming of the welfare state is one more aspect of a more wide-spread process of modernisation' (2001: 64). The question as to what sort of 'welfare state', or more accurately 'welfare regime', will be engendered by modernisation processes is central to comparative social policy analysis. A 'welfare state' can be understood as one potential ideal type against which the actual mixed economies of countries might be examined. Any exploration of the impact of modernisation on Irish social policy would need to take account of different domains of modernisation such as religion, the economy and the state. The development of social policy in Ireland occurred through the state, the (initially) religious voluntary sector and the market (Fanning, 1999: 52). Each of these sectors can be understood as responding to overlapping forms of modernisation. Each contributes to the social and ideological reproduction of Irish society.

Welfare convergence as an expression of modernity

A convergence thesis holds that welfare systems are principally shaped by levels of economic development. It is argued that welfare systems tend to become more like those of richer countries as GNP rises. For example, Wilensky compared social security spending as a proportion of GNP in 64 states from 1966. He concluded that 'economic levels', i.e. GNP per head of population, count more than 'regime type' as a predictor of social security effort over the long term. In other words differing welfare ideologies and political regimes amongst nation states are much less significant than different levels of economic development, and related differences in demographic structure, in explaining differences in social security spending (Wilensky, 1975). Such convergence approaches are bound up with 'consensus' theories of social order. These presuppose a model of society which is based upon consensus around central or core values such as those embodied within the structural functionalist theories of Talcott Parsons. Structuralist function-alism is a theory of social order which sees power as a facilitative tool in society, as 'power to' rather than 'power over'. This view of power is related to an argument that social control and socialisation in society are expressions of an underlying consensus in society. By contrast, Marxist perspectives could be described as social conflict theories of social order as these examine power and social order in terms of processes of exploitation (Ritzer, 1992: 233–9). Structural functionalist perspectives support a theory of welfare convergence. These understand the growth of the role of states in the provision of welfare in terms of social consensus. Convergence theorists argued that all industrial societies, by virtue of their use of similar technologies, were developing similar social structures. It was argued that the role of nation states in the production of welfare similarly grew to meet the requirements of economic growth. More recently, globalisation is seen to have produced other forms of convergence (see Kirby in chapter 2). Commonalities have been identified in the restructuring of the mixed economies of welfare of a number of countries since the 1970s (Gould, 1993: 10).

Convergence theories offer some explanation of divergence between Irish and British welfare approaches after independence in 1922. Different levels of GNP accounted for lower levels of welfare expenditure in Ireland after independence (Fanning, 1999: 55). It accounts to some extent for differences between the massive expansion of welfare provision in Britain after the Second World War and the incremental extension of state provision in Ireland. Of course other factors need to be taken into consideration. There was an ideological resistance to extending the role of the state in the provision of welfare. This was bound up with post-colonial Irish-Ireland isolationism as much as Catholicism. This fundamentalism was displaced by a conventional western capitalist national project of modernisation in the late 1950s after which it might be seen that institutional development in Ireland was driven by similar economic orthodoxies as other Western countries.

However, there are caveats. These aspirations emerged within a context of economic underdevelopment. It is important to note that structural functionalist arguments that welfare systems are the product of levels of development do not address the reasons for underdevelopment or offer a critique of the forms of modernity that these express. For some theorists underdevelopment itself has been the key factor in explaining the nature and extent of welfare provision. Theories of underdevelopment share the assumptions of convergence theories that the extensiveness of welfare regimes depends upon levels of capitalist industrialisation. From this perspective distinctions have been made between developed or core European countries and underdeveloped countries, including Ireland, Greece, Spain and Portugal, which have been labelled as semi-peripheral (Peillon, 1995: 184).

In the Irish case underdevelopment was bound up with colonialism (Peillon, 1995: 193). Both shaped the very societal base from which welfare consensus and welfare possibilities might be understood to emerge. Clientelism, authoritarianism, a weak civil society and a hollowed-out class structure might be understood as consequences of colonialism with the result that where the welfare systems of a more economically developed country were transplanted they took root in a different form. The administrative legacy of colonialism can be seen in shared patterns of public administration with Britain before independence that persisted after 1922. Examples of institutional similarity prior to independence included local government, health and social welfare. However, as part of the British Empire, Ireland also had a separate colonial administration characterised by paternalism and emphasis on military security which resulted in the centralised administration of policing and education (Chubb, 1993: 213). Even before independence it had a different mixed economy of welfare from other parts of the British Isles notably owing to the political settlement with Catholicism that resulted in denominational education. As such, to continue with the Irish-British example, differences in GNP did not solely account for differences in levels of state welfare provision.

Welfare diversity as an expression of ideology

In contrast to the structural functionalist position, other analysts have emphasised the relationship between politics and welfare approaches. Here a comparative analysis of welfare regimes seeks to establish a quantitative relationship between welfare spending and the political composition of governments. It is argued that party politics have been the main influence on welfare state development and comparative political differences account in large measure for differences in welfare expenditure between countries. In simple terms, the extent of state welfare provision has been linked to the power of parties of the left. Such a view is sometimes described as the class mobilisation thesis. This suggests that the development of 'welfare states' is closely linked to the extent of mobilisation of working-class parties of the left. The 'partisan control of government' was an important factor in determining social expenditure in the 1960s and the 1970s, with strong parties of the right curtailing the expansion of welfare expenditure and social democratic and other parties serving as a stimulus to such expenditure. For example, Alber (1983) compared social security expenditure of the political complexion of governments in 13 Western states over the years 1949 to 1977. He found that left cabinets tended to increase social expenditure more than cabinets which excluded socialist parties or centre-left coalitions (Alber, 1983: 166). This, he argued, suggests that the development of 'welfare states' is closely linked to the extent of mobilisation of working-class parties of the left.

Arguably, the class mobilisation thesis presumes a level of industrialisation which was absent in Ireland for much of its development. Even other forms of welfare ideology, such as expressed within Catholic social theory, fell on fallow ground. Fahey argues that the impact of Catholic social thought on social policy in Ireland was limited because it emerged to counter extremes of *laissez-faire* capitalism and state socialism which were not to be found in Ireland. 'Outside the industrialised north-east of the Island, capitalism had failed to take off and the socialist movement scarcely developed beyond the embryonic stage. The main targets of attack for Catholic social teaching were thus either weak or absent in Ireland' (Fahey, 1998b: 418).

Western modernity has emerged through a number of religious and secular traditions. Protestant individualism, liberalism and secularism challenged the *anciens régimes* which dominated Europe before the enlightenment with varying degrees of success in different countries. The resultant liberal democracy with its emphasis upon market-based freedoms was subsequently challenged by socialist and social democratic notions of the good society. Liberal and socialist traditions of modernity coexist with a third tradition of European etatist conservative reformism often referred to as Catholic conservatism. These three traditions of modernity or, as put by Esping-Anderson, three worlds of welfare capitalism, might be seen in themselves to represent distinct welfare typologies (1990). However, the welfare systems of states are to be understood as historic accommodations between various traditions of modernity even if it is argued that specific traditions dominate the welfare systems of some countries.

Esping-Andersen's conservative typology described the corporatist welfare systems seen as characteristic of countries where Catholic political parties and church influences remained strong, where the political left was weak and where there has been a history of absolutism and authoritarianism (Cochrane and Clarke, 1993: 8). Within this typology corporatist or vocationalist welfare structures are preferred to state provision of welfare. Ideologically, Catholic social teaching viewed the state as a functional necessity with an important role of ensuring social order but opposed state encroachment on voluntary welfare and charity that would challenge its influence. It held that the state had no right to interfere within the family as long as the family fulfilled its responsibilities and cared for its members (McLaughlin, 1993: 206). This typology was seen to fit European countries such as Germany, Austria and France but not Ireland. Esping-Anderson argued that Ireland was seen to exhibit a medium degree of conservative characteristics, a low degree of liberal characteristics and a low degree of socialist characteristics (1990: 53). Certainly, the Irish welfare economy is considerably different from Esping-Andersen's essentially Christian Democratic typology. Irish welfare institutions have been more influenced by liberal prohibitions on the kinds of mandatory social insurance typical of European Catholic conservative welfare regimes. Esping-Andersen arguably underestimates the importance of liberalism within Irish social policy. Liberalism can be seen as an ideological legacy which became embedded in the political and social institutions of Ireland prior to independence. Many contemporary welfare institutions are derived from the Poor Law of 1838 and the neo-liberal welfare legislation of the early twentieth century. The introduction before independence of a liberal system of state benefits linked to paid employment accounts in part for differences between the Irish welfare economy and those of *ancien régime* countries where vocationalist welfare schemes were built around various status groups. Such interest groups were not so well developed in Ireland. Vocationalism was popular within the Catholic ideological rhetoric particularly during the 1930s in the aftermath of the papal encyclical *Quadragesimo Anno*. However, this encyclical and its 1891 predecessor *Rerum Novarum* focused on the politics of welfare-developed industrial countries (see Fanning in chapter 3 and Kiely in chapter 4).

Conclusion: relocating Irish social policy

An emphasis on globalisation has come to the fore in accounts of modernisation in Ireland. At least one comparative index identifies Ireland as the most 'globalised' country in the world. Yet, as Kirby emphasises in chapter 2, globalisation like modernisation is a contested term. It suggests, as does the term modernisation, a potential range of ideological accounts of social change. These interpretations will arguably be grounded in established ideological traditions from which social policy options will be identified. The social policy choices facing Ireland in the twenty-first century are often represented in the media as those between Boston and Berlin. Whilst this crude dichotomy does not hold up to close scrutiny, the suggestion of a choice between neo-liberalism and a presumed European Union project grounded in social democrat and Christian democrat traditions is not unreasonable (see Rush in chapter 6). However, Ireland is neither Boston nor Berlin. Elements of both these crude typologies potentially coexist within Irish social policy. Liberal institutions prevail within the collectivist part of the Irish welfare economy (examples include two-tiered benefit and health systems). At the same time, Ireland is perhaps awkwardly placed, both institutionally and ideologically, to reform existing welfare institutions along European (corporatist or vocationalist) lines. A case in point has been the lack of popularity of proposals by the Irish Labour Party to reform the existing liberal two-tier system of access to health care by means of a Christian Democrat compulsory universal system of health insurance (Labour Party, 2002; Quin and Lawless in chapter 8).

This chapter suggests that debates on the future development of Irish social policy are likely to be situated within or in opposition to existing prevalent ideological and theoretical narratives about social change. Thus positions on abortion cannot be reduced to preferences for either authoritarian Catholicism or secular liberalism. Yet the emergence of abortion as a pivotal social issue signals the existence of broader ideological cleavages relating to modernisation that continue to inform social policy choices. Similarly, reformulations of social citizenship in an era of immigration will occur against the backdrop of past constructions of nation (see Christie in chapter 9). Present-day contestations of racism can be seen to vie with 'zero sum' perspectives on asylum policies and immigration that echo the 'zero sum' ideological drivers of past Irish emigration (O'Connell, 2003: 130). Debates on social capital and community, in an era of neo-liberal challenges to conservatism, are likely to occur with reference to previously dominant Catholic traditions of social solidarity (see Fanning in chapter 3 and Rush in chapter 6). Left critiques of capitalism and development remain prominent within academic literature on the 'Celtic Tiger' and its aftermath (Allen, 2000; O'Hearn 2001). Critiques of power relevant to Irish social policy can, though, be potentially drawn from a range of sources. These are central to the explorations of Irish social policy in a number of subsequent chapters. It has been argued in this chapter that the task of theorising Irish social policy is incomplete. Yet the narratives discussed in this chapter remain crucial to locating Irish social policy within broader theoretical debates.

Chapter 2

Globalisation

Peadar Kirby

The 'great globalization debate' identifies some of the most fundamental issues of our time. It poses key questions about the organization of human affairs and the trajectory of global social change. It also raises matters which go to the centre of political discussion, illuminating the strategic choices societies confront and the constraints which define the possibilities of effective political action.

Held and McGrew, 2002: 118

The concept 'globalisation' has come into widespread use in both the social sciences and in public discourse over the course of the 1990s in an attempt to capture some of the immensely complex changes that are reshaping our personal and social worlds. Waters (1995: 2) traces its usage since the early 1960s but states that it was not recognised as academically significant until the early or mid-1980s. Even by the mid-1990s, he found the term was relatively rare in the title of journal articles. By the early 2000s, there was an avalanche of social science books with the word in the title, as a glance at the catalogues of leading publishers would attest. Yet though no consensus exists as to its meaning, and even its very existence is contested, its widespread reception and the coining of terms for it in languages around the world[1] indicate that people find it useful to make sense of the world around them. The importance of the term for Ireland is indicated by the fact that the country emerged as the most globalised in the world in the second and third editions of the globalisation index published by the prestigious US magazine *Foreign Policy*, a fact that received widespread publicity worldwide (Kearney, 2002, 2003).

Theorising social policy in Ireland, therefore, requires consideration of how the processes of change that the concept 'globalisation' seeks to identify may impact on the nature, mechanisms and outcomes of social policy. That is the purpose of this chapter. It begins in its first section by interrogating what the concept 'globalisation' means, mapping different interpretations of the significance and impact of the processes described by the term. Section two surveys the implications of globalisation for social policy, focusing broadly on the welfare of society and not just on the institutional form of the welfare state. Having drawn conclusions from an overview of the international literature, the third section applies them to Ireland. The factors that help mediate the social impact of globalisation in the Irish case are identified and their logic and role critically interrogated. This discussion is presented as a contribution to the task of theorising social policy in today's Ireland.

Globalisation: flows, structures and meaning

Though the term globalisation may be recent, it is widely accepted that flows of trade, information and migration linking distant parts of the world have existed for thousands of years, with ever growing intensity. Certainly since the integration of the Americas into a transatlantic trading system linking North and South America with Europe and Africa from the sixteenth century onwards, we can speak of a transnational system being in operation. Yet the first phase of globalisation is usually dated to the impact of technological innovations such as the steamship, the railways and the telegraph which, from around the 1870s onwards, led to the emergence of a truly global economic system, integrating more and more regions into it (though with many parts of Asia and Africa still excluded). This sparked a huge growth in worldwide trade, financial flows and migration, with Irish people playing a major role in the last of these. Damaged by the First World War, this first phase is reckoned to finish with the Great Depression of 1929 and the retreat into protectionism that followed it. The Second World War sparked a new commitment to ensuring that a more stable world system might emerge, underpinned with global institutions such as the World Bank and the International Monetary Fund. This second phase of globalisation which lasted until the oil crisis of 1973 was characterised by intensifying trade flows but strong national restrictions on financial and labour flows, so that its dynamic was much more under the control of nation states; in this it underpinned the historical compromise between capital and labour that led to this period being known as the golden age of welfare capitalism. The third and present phase of globalisation gathered pace gradually from the mid-1970s 'characterized by an ever greater mobility of capital, by the considerable expansion of trade worldwide . . . by the increasing similarity or homogenization of development models in all parts of the world (the triumph of neoliberalism), by the growing global dominance of transnational corporations in the production of goods and services, and by continuing restrictions on labour mobility' (Kirby, 2003a: 186–7).

As a description of fundamental processes shaping, with ever greater intensity and extensity, our world order over the past 150 years or so this account of globalisation would, I expect, be widely accepted. After all, it limits itself to an empirical description of what has happened. Yet it raises the obvious question: if these processes have been going on for so long, why all the fuss about globalisation? What, if anything, is new? It is in answering these sorts of questions that the disagreements begin. In their authoritative account of the 'the great globalisation debate', Held and McGrew survey a range of approaches towards theorising globalisation, identifying three dimensions of the 'significant transformation of the organizing principles of social life and world order' that proponents of globalisation claim is happening – the transformation of traditional patterns of socio-economic organisation, of the territorial principle, and of power (Held and McGrew, 2002: 7). These dimensions – the economic, the cultural and the political – provide a framework to order a discussion of the nature of the transformations that the term 'globalisation' seeks to analyse.

The growing interconnectedness of economic activities across borders is probably the dimension of globalisation that is most evident to many people. As is immediately obvious, the nature and functioning of the Irish economy has, to an ever greater extent, come to depend on global flows of investment, trade and migration. While this may be more obviously true of a small economy, data given in Held et al. show the extent to which even large economies like the US, Britain, France and Germany have become much more deeply enmeshed in global economic flows (Held et al., 1999). As a result, more people's livelihoods depend on events and decisions beyond their borders and beyond the effective influence of national decision makers. Some analysts, dubbed the hyperglobalists by Held et al., hail this as marking a new era of global prosperity as a single global market, unfettered by state interference, delivers ever more high-quality goods and services to consumers. One of the most frequently quoted hyperglobalists, Kenichi Ohmae, sees Ireland as 'a harbinger of the coming shift in national economies' (2000: 119). Irish economists Clinch, Convery and Walsh (2002: 59) broadly agree that globalisation is vital for Ireland's prosperity though they acknowledge that it involves a 'Faustian bargain' as it comes 'at a price in terms of domestic economic autonomy'. In this view, therefore, globalisation is primarily a process of growing market integration at a global level that offers immense benefits to those societies which accommodate themselves to its inevitable dynamic. This view found expression in mainstream interpretations of the 'Celtic Tiger' boom that equated high levels of economic growth with permanent economic and social transformation (Kirby, 2002a: chapters 4–5).

However, such a view is countered by those who see a continuing role for politics in shaping the nature and impact of globalisation. Among these are the so-called sceptics who argue that the extent of today's global market interconnectedness is greatly exaggerated and that, instead of a global market, what exists is closer integration between the economies of North America,

Western Europe and Japan (often called the Triad) with most of the rest of
the world marginalised (Hirst and Thompson, 1999). For them, therefore,
globalisation is largely a 'myth' used to prise open national economies and
submit their citizens to the disciplines of the global marketplace. Such a view
is articulated in the Irish case by Allen, who argues that 'globalisation myths
systematically disempower people' and provide 'a powerful alibi for those
who want to discourage resistance and militancy' (2000: 185–6). Apart from
the sceptics, however, others argue that states play a crucial role in shaping the
extent to which national economies can benefit from the dynamics of the
global economy. For example, Ó Riain (2000) proposes that Ireland is a 'flexible
developmental state' as the state has been deeply involved in establishing the
conditions for economic success through winning high levels of foreign
investment, through actively helping foster an indigenous software industry,
and through maintaining wage competitiveness through social partnership.

'Resituating of the state'

The international political economy (IPE) literature has helped throw light
on how power is being reconfigured. It is not that states are standing against
capital, nor that they are being cast aside by capital, rather they are estab-
lishing a new relationship that is defined essentially by its facilitation of the
market, though pockets of strong state regulation still remain. Cerny sums up
this new logic of state actions in his description of the move from the national
welfare state to the competition state:

> Rather than attempt to take certain economic activities *out* of the market, to
> 'decommodify' them as the welfare state in particular was organized to do, the
> competition state has pursued *increased* marketization in order to make economic
> activities located within the national territory, or which otherwise contribute to
> national wealth, more competitive in international and transnational terms
> (Cerny, 2000a: 122–3; emphasis in original).

Paradoxically, therefore, globalisation is not resulting in a reduction of
state activity but rather in its splintering or fragmentation as the priority of
international competitiveness takes precedence over the welfare of citizens,
thereby 'undermining [states'] overall strategic and developmental capacity'
(Cerny, 2000b: 34). As Falk (1999: 49, 50) sums up this 'resituating of the
state', it is 'being subtly deformed as an instrument of human well-being by
the dynamics of globalization, which are pushing the state by degrees and to
varying extents into a subordinate relationship with global market forces'.
This, then, helps pinpoint the key way state structures (embodying public
authority) are being reconfigured by market flows (embodying private autho-
rity), the intensification of which so defines this present phase of globalisation.

The resituating of the state also draws attention to cultural features of the transformations associated with globalisation. For the national welfare state rested on, gave expression to and constantly reinforced a strong sense of belonging to a national community. In this way culture and the economy served one another. However, as Touraine (2000: 2) has perceptively recognised, in this globalised world 'culture and the economy have become divorced from one another'. For the ever more globalised production and distribution of goods stand in contrast to and drive a process of ever more fragmenting and multiple cultural identities. There are many dimensions to these cultural transformations. Bauman notes that 'localities are losing their meaning-generating and meaning-negotiating capacity and are increasingly dependent on sense-giving and interpreting actions which they do not control' (1998a: 2–3). This dynamic was well applied to Ireland by Cronin, thereby highlighting its dynamic of inclusion and exclusion:

> Stasis is stigma. Those who are grounded by poverty, disability or prejudice are keenly aware of an isolation that is both social and geographical. They are the Irish locals who can watch the Irish globals riverdancing from Paris to Paraguay but who find themselves trapped in the slow land of neglect and indifference (2002: 62).

Those in the slow lane may be excluded from many of the benefits of globalisation but that does not mean that they are not actors in the process. Bauman rightly identifies their responses as an integral part of globalisation, something impossible to ignore after 9/11: 'Neo-tribal and fundamentalist tendencies, which reflect and articulate the experience of people on the receiving end of globalization, are as much legitimate offspring of globalization as the widely acclaimed "hybridization" of top culture – the culture at the globalized top' (Bauman, 1998a: 3). Meanwhile, the 'globalized top', what Sklair (2002: 98) characterises as the 'transnational capitalist class (TCC)', being less firmly rooted in their national societies, may find ways of minimising their contributions to those societies, as illustrated by some high-profile Irish 'tax exiles'.

In these ways, therefore, as Touraine puts it, 'the state, defined as the central agency for growth and justice, is under attack from the internationalization of the economy, on the one hand, and the fragmentation of cultural identities, on the other' (2000: 11). This helps identify some of the key features of what is regarded as being new about this phase of globalisation, features that have major implications for social policy. To these implications we now turn.

Implications for social policy

Most attention in the social policy literature has been devoted to the effects of economic globalisation on welfare states. Focusing on such elements as international financial mobility, trade openness and mobility of production as companies move location, one hypothesis foresees a 'race to the bottom' as international pressures force states to reduce welfare provisions. This view is summarised by Gray:

> The effect of competition from countries in which a regime of deregulation, low taxes and a shrinking welfare state has been imposed is to force downwards harmonization of policies on states which retain social market economies. Policies enforcing a deregulated labour market and cuts in welfare provision are adopted as defensive strategies in response to policies implemented in other countries. Tax competition among advanced states works to draw in public finances and make a welfare state unaffordable (1998: 87–8).

Thus, 'as states become powerless to make "real" policy choices, governments will be forced to adopt similar economic, fiscal and social policies. This is expected to entail the abandonment of comprehensive state welfare and redistributive policies and their replacement by deregulation, privatization and welfare residualization worldwide, leading to some form of convergence' (Yeates, 2000: 22). Yet, more detailed empirical studies have failed to support such apocalyptic scenarios. Not only do they not show any marked reduction of welfare effort, instead they show a general picture of public sector expansion in response to the pressures of globalisation (Garrett, 2000: 124) lending support to the 'compensation thesis', namely that social programmes 'have expanded to protect populations whose incomes and employment have been adversely affected by globalization' (Swank, 2002: 275). Furthermore, far from a convergence towards reducing taxes and spending, Garrett finds that 'capital market integration has been associated with increasing divergence in most facets of tax and spending policies' (2000: 108).

The picture that emerges, therefore, is far more complex than that presented by the 'race to the bottom' hypothesis and shows the continuing resilience of welfare effort in response to the pressures of globalisation. In analysing the changing nature of welfare states, a range of positions can be identified. At one end of the spectrum lie analysts whose position mirrors those of the sceptics referred to in the previous section. For example, Pierson argues that 'to focus on globalization is to mistake the essential nature of the problem' which derives from national pressures on the welfare state (quoted in Yeates, 2000: 16). Esping-Andersen takes a similar position: in identifying the causes of the 'profound crisis' faced by all welfare state models today, he places much more emphasis on the pressures posed by population ageing and declining fertility, and by family change and the new economic role of women, than he does on globalisation. Indeed, he concludes that 'the view that ambitious welfare aims are incompatible with the new global order is not persuasive' (Esping-Andersen, 2002: 219). This sceptical position can be summarised in the words of Kvist and Meier Jaeger: 'Globalization remains little more than a "buzz"-concept, mainly because its existence and impact on welfare states has so far not been established convincingly in the literature' (2003: 10).

However, many social policy analysts draw more nuanced conclusions that do identify important ways in which globalisation is impacting on welfare policy and provision at national and international levels. Since the national state is still the level at which most welfare activity is organised and funded, analysts have focused on the constraints posed by globalisation on both state capacity and room for manoeuvre. Scharpf summarises these by examining the effects at national level of increased international competition, mobile firms and mobile capital:

> As a consequence, the terms of trade between capital, labour and the state have shifted in favour of capital interests, national powers to tax and regulate have become constrained, and governments and unions wishing to maintain employment in the exposed sectors of the economy must seek ways to increase productivity rather than redistribution. At the same time, welfare state revenue is constrained by international tax competition, by the need to reduce non-wage labour costs, and by the need to avoid public sector deficits – while welfare state retrenchment is encountering massive political opposition (2000: 224).

This comes closer to expressing some of the constraints associated with the competition state as outlined by Cerny in the previous section. Mishra goes further, including in his analysis such features as the erosion of social citizenship, the retreat from universality and the public sphere, the strengthening of the hand of capital as against labour, and the dropping of redistribution as an objective of the welfare state (1999). In these ways, he identifies how globalisation is eroding some of the cultural underpinnings of a strong and robust welfare state. He concludes that, under these pressures, the welfare state is at best a holding operation: 'True, many European nationals have inherited a large welfare state from the golden age and, for the moment, seem to be able to hold on to them. But can they hold out against global pressures?' (1999: 70).

Resisting pressures
This more nuanced acknowledgement of the impact of globalisation by social policy theorists leads them to identify two principal means through which these pressures are being resisted. The first relates to national-level institutions

and politics, the second to international or global social policy. Some analysts are specific in identifying the factors at national level which have best enabled states to resist the pressures of globalisation on welfare regimes. For Garrett, these are what he calls 'left-labour regimes' with strong corporatist wage-setting institutions, particularly those in the Nordic countries. In his analysis, these are the necessary elements which allow countries to combine the benefits of market integration with the ability to shield their most vulnerable citizens. 'In contrast,' he adds, 'under more "market liberal" regimes, the insulating effects of the public economy against market-generated risk and inequality are being eroded' (Garrett, 2000: 129). Swank largely agrees, though he adds that Continental European corporatist conservative systems have also been successful in limiting retrenchment of social protection and providing modest extensions of welfare provision. His findings point to an unravelling of the compromise of embedded liberalism in the 'Anglo-Saxon' liberal welfare regimes (Swank, 2002: 286). Scharpf (2000: 222) also identifies two problems with the Continental systems – insufficient employment deriving from the excessive burden of non-wage labour costs, and an over-committed transfer system combining redistribution and contribution-related insurance in a single scheme that 'is resented as a (highly regressive!) form of taxation'. The 'Anglo-Saxon' liberal regimes, while avoiding both of these problems through deregulated labour markets and lean welfare states, are less successful at reducing poverty and inequality. However, he identifies in measures used by Australia and Switzerland to invest in education and assist low-paid workers gain upward occupational mobility, the potential for liberal regimes to mitigate the socially disintegrative consequences usually associated with them while not endangering their economic efficiency (Scharpf, 2000: 219). Though there may not be final agreement on exactly which regimes are most successful in combining growth with equity, this debate underlines the continuing importance of domestic politics and institutions in the era of globalisation.

Some social policy theorists move beyond the focus on the national state to examine the globalisation of social policy itself. This includes both social regulation and provision at international or even global level (EU directives and structural funds are examples of international social regulation and provision, while organisations like the World Trade Organisation or the International Labour Organisation lay down global regulations in their respective areas of competence), and social policy making at global level (through the OECD or the World Bank, for example). While the former (regulation and provision) are binding on member governments, the latter (policy making) is confined to advising national governments. These activities highlight the emergence of global policy-making fora as another source of influence on social policy at national level (for a comprehensive overview, see

Deacon, 1999). Yet, as Yeates has emphasised in her survey of global policy discourse among intergovernmental organisations, 'the range of welfare alternatives backed by these institutions is currently confined to variants of liberalism, and there is a marked absence of any international institutions advancing a social democratic or redistributive agenda' (Yeates, 2000: 29). Analysts who see in global social policy another means of securing robust welfare provision through public means tend to be critical of the existing orientation of such global policy and point instead to the potential of inter-governmental organisations, states and NGOs to establish and enforce funda-mental social standards worldwide. Mishra (1999: 114) argues that the present mix of 'global *laissez-faire*, entrenched welfare states and electoral democracy are an unstable combination which could prove to be explosive' if electoral support for ultra-nationalism and protectionism continues to grow. Instead, he advocates the formulation of global social standards (linked to economic standards, so that some governments could not avoid them on the basis that they were too expensive) and their implementation through intergovernmental organisations (under pressure from global civil society). Though he is not very hopeful of the prospects for such standards, he writes that 'basic social stan-dards – applicable globally – are of the utmost importance today in that they can provide a degree of stability and continuity for human communities in the context of global economic competition and technological change' (1999: 131).

With its more inductive methodological approach – examining in detail the nature of social policy and provision – the social policy literature offers rich empirical evidence to test the more deductive theoretical approach of the international political economy literature on the nature of globalisation. As has been argued in this section, it offers no consensus on the implications of globalisation for social policy, though a central (and perhaps dominant?) strand in the literature marshals evidence that, in general outline, confirms the hypothesis of the competition state and the erosion of some of the foun-dations of the national welfare state. In doing this, it provides at least two important correctives to a tendency in the globalisation literature towards a structural determinism, namely the view that the erosion of social provision is an inevitable consequence of globalisation. One corrective highlights the fact that welfare states have by no means been dismantled by globalisation and, while under pressure, many are adjusting quite successfully. The second draws attention to the vital importance of national (and transnational) politics and institutions in securing social outcomes.

It can be concluded, therefore, that while globalisation may constrain national governments, it by no means makes them irrelevant. As George and Wilding conclude in their survey of the impact of globalisation on human welfare, 'nation states can, and do, respond differently to the pressures which globalization imposes. The impact of globalization is mediated by history, politics and economics. States matter even in a more global world' (2002: 44). However, only an examination of each national state can tell us *how* it mediates global forces and what the outcomes are for human welfare. To do this in the case of Ireland is the objective of the next section.

Ireland's response: model or mirage?

If, as the A. T. Kearney/*Foreign Policy* index finds, Ireland is the most globalised country in the world, then the issues raised in the previous sections take on a major significance for the theorising of Irish social policy. The demands these make on the work of Irish social policy analysts can be grouped under five headings: the political economy context; the ambiguities of social activism; theorising society; the nature and logic of state actions; and the demands on social policy. The purpose of this section is to identify the tasks to be undertaken if we hope to develop a theoretical framework adequate to explaining how and why the Irish state is mediating the social impact of globalisation, that helps identify the underlying logic and institutional responses, and how different elements of these responses interconnect (especially how the economic and the social interconnect). Until such a theoretical framework is elaborated, the formulation and implementation of social policy will lack any clear understanding of the constraints within which it operates, of the dilemmas facing it, and of the choices available to actors (whether state, market or civil society actors).

1   The political economy context
Between 1994 and 2000, Ireland achieved some of the highest economic growth rates in the world (it was in a league with China, Singapore, Vietnam and Mozambique), rates that far surpassed anything it had known in its history. The particular combination of state and market that helped deliver such high growth attracted widespread interest from policy-makers around the world who saw Ireland as 'a showpiece of globalization' (O'Hearn, 2000: 73). Yet, initial emphasis on the success of the Irish state's growth model (see Kirby, 2003b for a discussion of the nature of this model), has given way to a recognition of what the National Economic and Social Council (NESC) calls the 'undoubted vulnerabilities' of Ireland's 'type of economic development' (NESC, 2002: 12). While the NESC emphasises vulnerabilities deriving from loss of competitiveness, increased prices and policy failures in the areas of fiscal policy and regulatory regimes, other analysts point to structural vulnerabilities inherent in the model itself.

Two major types of vulnerability can be identified. The first is economic and derives from the structural nature of Ireland's productive economy.

While ever higher percentages of Ireland's manufacturing employment, output and exports depended on foreign firms over the period of the Celtic Tiger, economists debate the extent to which the long-term decline in indigenous industry has been reversed. O'Donnell sees a 'significant improvement in the capabilities and performance of indigenous firms in both manufacturing and services' (2002: 14); however, other economists point to the continuing dualism between foreign and indigenous industry, even at the height of the boom (Gallagher et al., 2002) and the assistant director general of the Irish Central Bank, Dr Michael Casey, was quoted in late 2003 as describing indigenous industry as the Irish economy's 'Achilles heel' (*The Irish Times*, 3 October 2002). Focusing on the importance of high levels of foreign direct investment (FDI) to Ireland, Barry highlights that 'external shocks to our ability to attract FDI might have serious long-term consequences for the economy' (Barry, 2002: 99).[2] In a report on EU enlargement, Goodbody stockbrokers (2003) also predict growing pressure on Irish public finances as the country becomes a net contributor to the EU in 2007 and receives lower receipts, especially in agricultural supports. The Irish growth model is therefore highly vulnerable to shifts in flows of foreign direct investment and of EU funding.

The second type of vulnerability results from this and has major implications for social policy. Ireland's productive success has been based centrally on a strategy of using low taxes on manufacturing profits to gain a competitive edge in attracting FDI, a policy described by the former managing director of the Industrial Development Agency (IDA), Padraic White, as 'the unique and essential foundation of Ireland's foreign investment boom' (MacSharry and White, 2000: 250). Furthermore, wage competitiveness under social partnership has been maintained by a policy of trading moderate wage rises for cuts in income taxes. As a result of this policy mix, Ireland has fallen further and further behind all other EU states in social spending and in tax receipts. Between 1993 and 2000, Irish government expenditure on social protection fell from 20.2 per cent of GDP to 14.1 per cent, while the average EU expenditure has fallen from 28.8 per cent to 27.3 per cent over the same period. Meanwhile, Irish government current tax and non-tax receipts decreased from 38.6 per cent of GDP to 33.8 per cent over this period while the EU average increased from 43.2 per cent to 43.9 per cent (Kirby, 2003b: table 17, p. 41). The Irish state has become a low-tax, low-spend state ever more dependent on market forces to achieve social outcomes and with a greatly weakened ability to provide quality infrastructure or services, or to counteract with any effectiveness the polarising impact of market forces. It finds itself caught amid contradictory pressures: economists tell policy makers that they must further reduce spending and taxation to maintain competitiveness (Sachs, 1997: 62) while those concerned with social problems call for increased social spending (Nolan, O'Connell and Whelan, 2000: 352). The evidence points to the fact that the former have more influence over policy than the latter.

2 The ambiguities of social activism

Accompanying economic success in the 1990s, Conroy identifies 'a marked shift in social policy' as it moved 'directly into the mainstream of national policy making by incorporation into negotiated centralized collective bargaining' (Conroy, 1999: 45). The expansion of the partnership model, through the establishment of the National Economic and Social Forum (NESF) in 1993 and the inclusion of the community and voluntary sector as social partners in 1996, and through its extension to different levels of policy making and execution such as the area-based partnerships (ABPs) and the city and county development boards (CDBs), indicated a wave of what Sabel called 'productive and formative ferment . . . to extend the circles of social and economic participation locally, and guide reform of public administration nationally' (Sabel, 1998: xi). This ferment has found expression in extensive activism and institutional innovation, through such key mechanisms as gender mainstreaming, poverty and equality proofing, benchmarking against best practice, and monitoring outcomes. The National Anti-Poverty Strategy (NAPS) has led to a National Action Plan against Poverty and Social Exclusion (NAPs/incl) for the period 2003–5 while a wide range of targeted supports and initiatives exists to address continuing challenges in areas such as employment, children, health, drugs, rural development, adult education and homelessness (see Annexes 3 and 4 in Office for Social Inclusion, n.d.: xix–xl).

On the other hand, this extensive innovative effort has gone hand-in-hand with reinforcing a residual welfare state with declining percentages of GDP/GNP devoted to social expenditure. As Timonen sums up, while Irish social expenditure increased in real terms throughout the 1990s, as a proportion of GNP it has fallen steadily from 12.3 per cent in 1992 to 7.8 per cent in 2000, and as a proportion of GDP from 10.9 per cent to 6.6 per cent over the same period. The Irish welfare state

> continues to exhibit the defining characteristics of the residual, or liberal, welfare state model. Many 'old' features – support for family carers, predominance of means-tested payments, relatively low, flat-rate social insurance payments – continue to exist and in some cases have been reinforced recently. While some 'new' elements – improved universal benefits, statement of intention to link benefit increases to wages and inflation, lessening of means-testing, increasing qualified adult allowances – have been introduced, the Irish welfare state still remains focused on poverty prevention and is weak in the area of service provision. This is reflected in the allocation of social expenditure between cash

transfers and services: Ireland spends a comparatively low proportion of its total net social expenditure on services (Timonen, 2003: 21).

While many lofty claims have been made for what has been called an 'emerging Irish model of economic and social governance' (Laffan and O'Donnell, 1998: 165), much more attention has been paid to the innovative nature of the mechanisms created than to their effectiveness in delivering robust social outcomes or to the contradictions between such activism and the residualisation of the welfare state. Until we know a lot more about the actual difference public policies make to improving social outcomes, especially for the most vulnerable, the weight of evidence points to the conclusion that the much vaunted Irish model is more a mirage obfuscating the relative power-lessness of the state to achieve robust social outcomes.

3   Theorising society

In this context, it is important that social policy analysts achieve a greater critical distance from the hectic torrent of activities that characterises the Irish state's social activism today. For a crucial role such analysts have to play is to resist the seduction of activism and to ask sharp and insistent questions about the effectiveness of state policy in achieving its stated outcomes. Furthermore, this role goes beyond assessing existing policy; there is an urgent need for theorising society, identifying how it is changing under the impact of market forces, and the challenges this poses for social policy.

In assessing outcomes, the main successes have been the increase in employment, the growth of jobs, the upskilling of sectors of the labour force, the increase in women's employment and the reduction of long-term unemployment. These are largely attributable to market forces though state programmes have undoubtedly played a role. In the context of Ireland's traditional employment problems, they are major achievements. However, they must be set against marked failures in areas traditionally identified as the province of social policy. Among these is the significant increase in income inequality and in relative poverty (see Nolan, 2003a, for the former and Whelan et al., 2003 for the latter); the effective exclusion of ever growing percentages of the population from the housing market owing to rising prices (see Drudy and Punch, 2001); the inexorable rise in homelessness (from 2,371 in 1992 to 5,581 in 2002 (Simonnews, 2003: 2); the persistence of profound structural inequalities in the health system (see Wren, 2003) and in the edu-cational system (see Smyth and Hannan, 2000); and tax and welfare systems that 'are serving to widen not to narrow the gap between rich and poor' (Fitzgerald, 2001: 192). At the very least, this evidence points to a marked disjuncture between high levels of economic growth and its social outcomes, what Kirby has called 'a stark contrast between economic success and social failure' (Kirby, 2002a: 5) and it raises major questions about the effectiveness of so much social activism.

Beyond these issues, Ireland's recent social change is resulting in what has been referred to as 'a breakdown in society' (Neill, reported in *The Irish Times*, 15 October 2003). Evidence of very high levels of alcohol and drug abuse (by international standards), of high rates of suicide among young males, of significant increases in violent assaults and sexual offences, and of a sharp rise in the homicide rate has led one leading professor of psychiatry to conclude that 'there are worrying trends to suggest that the civic order is in disarray' (Casey, 2002). This raises important questions about social well-being and its constitution that are largely neglected by social policy theorists in Ireland. Not only is it giving rise to major challenges for social policy but it suggests that the larger theoretical questions about society itself raised by Touraine (2000) are manifesting themselves also in Ireland. Indeed, the apparent paradox of growing dislocation and alienation in the midst of a successful economy with high levels of employment and income appears to vindicate the central insights of Karl Polanyi who highlighted the social dislocation that results from the imposition of the self-regulating market on society since it leads to 'the running of society as an adjunct to the market' (Polanyi, 1957: 57, 58), requiring that 'the individual respect economic law even if it happened to destroy him'. These questions raise urgent challenges for Irish social scientists.

4   The nature and logic of state actions

The ambiguities highlighted in the previous sub-sections point to the importance of identifying the central logic that informs the actions of the Irish state. One way of explaining them would be to accept the benign social rhetoric of the state at face value (reducing inequality, supplying quality services, etc.) and conclude simply that it is grossly inefficient in fulfilling most of the social goals it sets itself. If this is true, then it raises other questions about how the state can be so efficient in the economic sphere (warranting it being characterised as a 'flexible developmental state' by Ó Riain, 2000), but so inefficient in the social sphere. However, if instead we characterise the Irish state as a competition state, this offers a logic that explains why the state might prioritise goals of economic competitiveness over those of social cohesion and welfare. Such a logic flows from a recognition of the constraints imposed by globalisation, constraints that operate in a particularly acute way in such a small, open and vulnerable economy as the Irish one. It involves the move from a national welfare state to the competition state, as outlined by Cerny earlier in this chapter, involving the reduction of government spending to minimise the 'crowding out' of private investment, the deregulation of economic activity, and the elevation of competitiveness over welfare as the state's overriding priority. It is therefore a very good example of Falk's resituating of the state as it is pushed by degrees to a subordinate relationship to global market forces. This is the logic of the Irish state's actions identified by Taylor in his examination of the apparent contradiction between the state's commitment to social partnership (such concertative mechanisms involving the social partners are associated elsewhere with the effort by strong social democratic states to maintain high levels of social services and standards) and the residualisation of the Irish welfare state. For Taylor, the Irish state's benign social rhetoric obfuscates a fundamental political shift in which 'free market solutions to public policy problems have moved increasingly to the fore' (Taylor, 2002: 521). Instead of the confrontational imposition of neoliberal restructuring that has characterised this policy shift in countries like Britain, Irish governments have used forms of wage and policy concertation as 'a vehicle for imposing a neoliberal political agenda' (Taylor, 2002: 504) with the result that 'this transition has been almost seamless' (Taylor, 2002: 523).[3]

Accepting such a logic raises another question about *why* Ireland has responded in this way. For if Ireland is presented as a state which is managing successfully to combine market openness with social welfare under the pressures of globalisation, as O'Donnell claims (O'Donnell: 2000), then it would contradict some of the essential conditions identified in the social policy literature for this correlation. As outlined above, this literature points to the importance of 'left-labour' regimes with strong corporatist wage-setting institutions as providing the conditions which most successfully combine market integration with strong redistributive welfare states. The literature also points to the high-spending universalistic Nordic welfare states as the most successful. Furthermore, analysts who have identified in some programmes initiated by liberal welfare states the possibility of combining market efficiency with equitable outcomes, point to the fact that such programmes are expensive (Pearson, 2003). Ireland contradicts most of these conditions. Left-wing parties are weak and, anyway, a government coalition marked by a strong neoliberal policy orientation has been in power since 1997. Instead of maintaining high levels of social spending, Ireland has become an outlier among EU states for the low percentage of its GDP/GNP it devotes to social protection. While social partnership may appear similar to social democratic corporatist institutions, it has also been identified as a form of 'competitive', 'supply-side' or even 'lean' corporatism which prioritises national competitiveness over social welfare, emphasising deregulation and flexibility over income distribution or elimination of want (Roche and Cradden, 2003: 72–3). Explaining why Ireland has responded as it has requires examining its history, economy, and political culture and institutions. Central to such an account must be the populist, non-ideological and catch-all nature of Irish political culture and the weak policy-making role of politicians within the Irish political system. The post-colonial nature of Irish society within which class divisions are hidden behind a discourse with strong emphasis on the national community, and the profound economic crisis of the 1980s, all combined to reinforce a consensual response to the crisis, through a host of 'partnership' institutions with little involvement by politicians, other than those in government. As a result, as Ó Cinnéide (1998: 47) has pointed out, social partnership has 'represented a major shift in power from elected representatives to full-time officials in the civil service and the organisations of the major interests'. The highly dependent nature of Ireland's strategy of economic development and the dualism of its industrial base (foreign versus indigenous industry) further reinforce the reasons why Ireland responded as it did.

5   Demands on social policy

The foregoing sub-sections have highlighted some major challenges facing Irish social policy and the context within which these challenges need to be addressed. Social policy is the field of activity through which public authorities seek to ensure economic processes are translated into social goods, not just individual or sectoral ones. Social policy as a disciplinary field is therefore itself challenged to offer a more holistic, critical and robust response to the changed situation in which it finds itself operating. The discussion here limits itself to two dimensions of this challenge: discourse and market/state.

Instead of social policy elucidating and addressing the complex dilemmas that flow from the resituation of the Irish state, most social policy discourse is complicit in the official obfuscation of the shift taking place and its implications for the welfare of vulnerable citizens. Irish social policy documents are peppered with benign discourse about 'social inclusion', 'poverty elimination', 'equality' and 'quality public services', while apparently blind to the growth in relative poverty and income inequality, and the widespread perception of crisis in key public services (especially health and social supports to the most vulnerable). Key terms like 'social inclusion' and 'equality' are lifted from social science discourse without any thorough examination of the demands they would make on state capacity and on the public purse were any serious attempt to be made to implement them. Extensive attention is paid to the goal of 'equality' in Irish policy discourse but this is limited entirely to anti-discrimination measures for nine categories of named 'minorities' (including women). The Irish state has no policy for addressing socio-economic inequality, and apparently suffers from the 'confusion' identified by Barry when he said that 'a government professing itself concerned with social exclusion but indifferent to inequality is, to put it charitably, suffering from a certain amount of confusion' (1998: 32). The dangers of, and the dubious theoretical basis for, the policy of asking members of the nine identified 'minorities' to make themselves known for the purposes of 'equality proofing' has merited

remarkably little critical attention.[4] The NESC adopts the term 'develop-
mental welfare state' while neglecting entirely the different types of states to
which these terms refer and the extensive literature on how globalisation is
eroding even the most successful of them, much less the fact that the Irish
state has shown neither the political will nor administrative capacity to shape
social outcomes in any robust way (NESC, 2002: 51–8). Institutional
innovation is celebrated while far less attention is paid to the resultant
institutional fragmentation and the apparent inability of state authorities to
reform public institutions in a coherent and effective way (the glaring failures
of local government reform are just one example).

Furthermore, much policy discourse rests on a belief about the adequacy
of the national state on its own to provide for the welfare of its citizens,
whereas social policy analysts are increasingly highlighting the need for global
social policy (see George and Wilding, 2002). Yet Ireland is at best lukewarm
and at worst obstructionist in its support for stronger measures of inter-
governmental or global social regulation and provision, and Irish social policy
pays scant attention to this dimension. For these reasons, social policy is
losing credibility as a field of discourse that can articulate robust social goals
on behalf of citizens (especially the most vulnerable), highlight the requirements
necessary to achieve such goals, identify the changing social needs arising
from the impact of the vulnerabilities associated with globalisation, and foster
public debates adequate to the dilemmas and choices involved.

Irish social policy also needs to devote much closer attention to distin-
guishing the contribution of market and state to social outcomes, specifying
the effectiveness of state agency in ensuring the market serves the social good.[5]
Two examples highlight the issues at stake. Nolan has made the claim that
'individual countries retain a great deal of scope to influence the distribution
of income (and wealth)' (Nolan, 2003a: 140). However, in examining in
another paper the reasons for a decline in earnings inequality between 1997
and 2000 (Nolan, n.d.), he points to the tightness of the labour market as
playing a more important role in achieving these positive outcomes than did
the minimum wage, widely seen as a key policy instrument for this purpose.
In this case, therefore, the market is the principal agent responsible for the
positive social outcome. However, in a situation of increasing unemployment
it is unlikely that the market will continue to operate in this way, raising the
question of whether public policy intervention can intervene in an effective
way to influence outcomes. Ó Riain provides another example when he
identifies features of Ireland's political economy as generating social tensions
that are overwhelming state institutions:

> This model of development . . . turns out to be Janus-faced. Its success, based on
> a profound internationalisation of social and economic life through flexible state

institutions, turns out to be the major threat to its sustainability as these multiple globalisations generate an inequality and enormous political tensions that the decentralised state institutions have great difficulty containing (2000: 183).

In this case, the market is again the agent which is generating outcomes with the state in a relatively less powerful position. This identification of the relative power of market and state to determine social outcomes raises major challenges for social policy, both as a disciplinary area of study, and as a practice of public intervention to achieve goals in the public interest.

Conclusions

This chapter has examined the impact on social policy of the processes of change we label 'globalisation'. In the first section, it identified shifts in economic, political and cultural power that are pushing the state into a subordinate relationship with market forces. Examining the implications for social policy, the second section concluded that these shifts are increasing pressure on welfare regimes, but that the responses of national states can still make a big difference in influencing outcomes. The third section analysed the response of the Irish state, identifying the globalised nature of the Irish economy and the nature and logic of the state's response to this. It concluded that the task of theorising Irish social policy in the context of globalisation requires a critical distance from its subject enabling it to ask sharp and insistent questions about the effectiveness of public action in achieving social outcomes, and to highlight both empirically and theoretically the impact on society of market forces. In addition, it argued that social policy analysts need to attend more carefully to the nature and logic of the Irish state's social policy, and it identified two particular analytical challenges – to deconstruct the content of social policy discourse, and to analyse the ways market and state interact in contributing to social outcomes. In these ways, the chapter has mapped an agenda for both academic analysis and for political action, illuminating the strategic choices Irish society confronts and the constraints defining the possibilities of effective political action.

Notes

1   For example, in Irish two terms vie for acceptance. DCU's Irish-language unit, Fiontar, coined the term *forchríochú* to express the fact that globalisation is a process that transcends (thus *for-* which is a prefix meaning over- or super-) territories (thus *críoch*, a boundary or a territory). However, I notice the term *domhandú* also being used, a direct translation of the French term *mondialisation*. To me, the former is a far superior term, but popular usage will ultimately determine which endures.

2   Data on the changing destinations of inward investment to Europe over the period 2000–2 show that central European countries like Poland, Hungary, the Czech Republic and Slovakia are overtaking Ireland as favoured destinations for certain types of manufacturing investment. Ireland has been most successful in pharmaceuticals, customer contact centres and software investments (see IDA, 2003).

3   For a more detailed examination of theoretical and empirical problems associated with the concept of Ireland as a 'flexible development state' and a more substantial treatment of Ireland as a competition state, see Kirby (forthcoming).

4   The policy gives rise to at least two grounds for major concern. The first is the practice of asking people to identify themselves as belonging to any of the specified categories thereby reinforcing their sense of being different and even, perhaps, abnormal. Can the Equality Authority guarantee that such lists could never fall into the hands of people who might use them to scapegoat people who had so categorised themselves? The second is the erosion and fragmentation of wider social solidarities which could be an unintended side effect of such a practice.

5   In an example of this sort of analysis, Kirby (2002b) draws on both quantitative data and qualitative evidence from Latin America to show how the liberalisation of the labour market is increasing people's vulnerability to poverty (through the growth in non-permanent employment, and in the percentage of the workforce who lack both a formal work contract and state social security cover). As a result, even if employment is increasing and poverty is decreasing, more people are at risk of falling into poverty owing to market pressures (greater competitiveness driving down wages, sudden unemployment without the safety net of social security). This highlights ways in which greater resort to the market and the erosion of state benefits and protections increase the risk of poverty and reduce people's security. The lack of equivalent data and evidence from Ireland makes it much more difficult to reach conclusions about how these mechanisms are operating in the Irish case. However, since in the World Bank's Voices of the Poor survey the poor themselves identified vulnerability as one of the most important features of poverty for them (the other was powerlessness), then growing vulnerability must in itself be seen as undermining people's welfare (see Narayan, 2000).

Chapter 3

Communitarianism, social capital and subsidiarity

Bryan Fanning

Introduction

This chapter considers the study of social cohesion, social change and social exclusion within Irish social policy with reference to international debates on communitarianism, social capital and subsidiarity. Each of these domains of social policy debate can be related, in turn, to distinct ideological claims about the nature of society and of social problems. They are often linked to prescriptions aimed at the renewal of social cohesion and the retrieval of presumed 'traditional' communal values or attributes as a response to social change. All three emphasise the importance of 'community' within social policy. At the same time these suggest divergent understandings of the nature of community that have been linked to different social policy prescriptions.

The chapter begins with an account of the ideological role of subsidiarity within the Irish mixed economy of welfare. In essence the principle of subsidiarity was evoked to oppose state encroachment on the community as institutionalised within the religious voluntary sector and religious communal structures. Subsidiarity therefore stood for a set of claims about the viability of religious social solidarity and moral community in Ireland. The chapter argues that until recent decades dominant Catholic welfare prescriptions were characterised by a conservative moral communitarianism and that present-day Irish social policy debates can be usefully located within a moral communitarian critique of social modernisation. Similarly the chapter emphasises the relevance of current international debates about social capital in the Irish case. In this context, subsidiarity refers to a longstanding welfare settlement about the role of the state and the voluntary sector in the production of welfare. Preoccupations about the role of the state, or more correctly with limiting the role of the state, are central to both communitarian and social capital debates in Ireland. In part, debates about the necessity for state engendered forms of social capital and about a greater role for the state in the moral regulation of Irish society have been prompted by concerns about the relative decline of traditional social institutions, notably those associated with religiosity. This communitarian critique of social change can be seen in Irish debates on alcohol policy and law and order. It also influences, to an extent, Irish debates about the need to promote social capital.

Debates about communitarianism, social capital and subsidiarity can be seen to converge in discussions of the consequences for Irish social policy of modernisation and social change. In particular secularisation, urbanisation and the individualisation of life have become associated with a decline in social cohesion. The ideological emphasis in Catholic social thought upon pre-modern forms of community – what Emile Durkheim refers to as 'mechanistic solidarity' or Ferdinand Toennies refers to as *Gemeinschaft* – is central to some forms of communitarianism. Durkheim provided a conceptual account of the unravelling of traditional forms of social solidarity by modernity. He employed two archetypes of social order: mechanistic solidarity where individual members of society resembled each other because they cherished the same values and held the same things sacred; and organic solidarity which referred to the social diversification and interdependence resulting from the modernisation of Western society (Ritzer, 1996: 80). Similarly Toennies used the concept of *Gemeinschaft* to refer to traditional forms of community and social relationship, characterised by shared values and goals, threatened by industrialisation. Toennies's ideas have underpinned a modernisation thesis that assumes the decline of community as a 'key fact' about the modern world (Tovey and Share, 2000: 337). At one level the communitarian search for *Gemeinschaft* is a manifestation of nostalgia (Bellah, 1995: 1; Etzioni, 1993: 116). At the same time idealisations of supposedly past forms of community, be it a Norman Rockwell white picket fence image of the American past or its Catholic equivalent, have ideologically influenced social policy.

The emergence of Catholic social doctrine in the late nineteenth century as a response to industrialisation and its accompanying ideologies of liberal individualism and socialism has many parallels with the rise of communitarian thought almost a century later. Present-day communitarian perspectives too can be understood as a set of critiques of late modernity centring on a concern about the apparent decline of community. Similarly, a growing emphasis on promoting social capital in recent years has been prompted by the apparent weakening of what Robert Putnam refers to as the sociological superglue of traditional community bonds (2000: 23).

Subsidiarity, modernisation and Irish social policy

The papal encyclical that initially outlined Catholic social thought on modernity, *Rerum Novarum* (1891), harked back to a time before the Enlightenment when liberalism and individualism did not exist. At one level, Catholic social teaching faced the challenges of twentieth-century modernisation with a static thirteenth-century panacea. At the same time, it offered the industrial age a vision of the good society that drew upon a coherent intellectual legacy stretching back to Aristotle via Thomas Aquinas, one that contested both liberalism and Marxism. Like Marxism, Catholic social doctrine proposed a general plan for the whole world. In particular, it emphasised the interdependence of individuals and society and stood opposed to secular individualism and socialism. In a subsequent encyclical, *Quadragesimo Anno* (1931), Pius XI proposed a reconstructed social order based on corporatist principles and subsidiarity as an alternative to capitalism and socialism.

The concept of subsidiarity refers to a normative principle of social association that has been articulated in various religious and intellectual traditions and is implicit in much classical and medieval political thought (Hochschild, 2002: 1). It is much used, in the Irish context, to refer to principles within Catholic social thought concerning the relationship between the 'lower order' institutions of family and community and the higher order institutions of the state. As reiterated by Pope John Paul in *Centesimus Annus* in 1991:

> A community of a higher order should not interfere in the internal life of a community of a lower order, depriving the latter of its functions, but rather should support it in case of need and help to coordinate its activity with the activities of the rest of society, always with a view to the common good.

Subsidiarity, as outlined in various papal encyclicals, was a strategy to ameliorate the worst features of capitalism while resisting state interference in civil society. It held that the state should not usurp the relationship between Catholic institutions and the family. These included Catholic schools, hospitals and welfare services. The collectivisation of such services by the state was opposed. Such institutions provided a means of transferring the faith from one generation to the next. They were also infrastructure owned and controlled by the Church. As explained by Peillon, 'In defending the family unit and independence of voluntary organisations, the Church was seeking to consolidate its own authority and influence' (1982: 95).

The principle of subsidiarity in Ireland came to be used to refer to opposition to encroachment by the state on Catholic voluntary provision. However, it was not just a question of maintaining a demarcation between the voluntary sector and the state in the provision of welfare. The principle of subsidiarity was concerned with the maintenance of a 'traditional' Irish society that was constituted after the Famine by specifically modern means. Or to put it another way, post-independence Catholic conservatism (and the radicalism it took to embed it within the new state) was the product of a nineteenth-century Catholic social modernisation. Debates in twentieth-century Ireland about modernisation were not challenges to some primordial *Gemeinschaft* but involved struggles over sophisticated mechanisms of social control and social reproduction. Yet, insofar as the Church insisted on mono-poly control of such mechanisms, it can be seen to have opposed subsidiarity autonomy to families and individuals.

The development of a role for the state in Irish social policy was not necessarily opposed by Catholicism. In effect, the nineteenth-century Poor Law administration and a subsequent 'New-Liberal' system of social insurance linked to paid employment coexisted peacefully before and after independence with voluntary controlled forms of social policy, in the areas of education and health, seen to be crucial for the reproduction of Catholicism (Fanning, 2003: 7). In this context, subsidiarity became a watchword for a specific Catholic/liberal welfare settlement. Insofar as this welfare settlement was characterised by a limited role for the state, the principle of subsidiarity related to forms of communal solidarity rooted in nineteenth-century Catholic modernisation (Whyte, 1971: 69). The Catholic welfare, community and familial structures encompassed by subsidiarity in the Irish context were strongly authoritarian. After Independence the norms and values of post-Famine ultramontane Catholicism became enshrined in restrictive legislation on divorce (1925), film and publication censorship (1929) and alcohol (1924 and 1927). Lay Catholic organisations, most conspicuously the Knights of Columbanus, 'controlled official and unofficial censorship systems and acted as what might be termed paraclerics' (Garvin, 2004). In particular there was a huge emphasis on the control of sexuality whether in the home or in Catholic workhouses for sexual transgressors such as the Magdelene laundries. Whyte quotes Episcopal advice to fathers in one 1925 statement; 'if your girls do not obey you, if they are not in at the hours appointed, lay the lash upon their backs' (1971: 26).

Garvin notes a contrast between European and American social and eco-nomic modernisation (2004). In the European case, and here we can include Ireland, such modernisation was accompanied by a decline in religious faith not apparent in America. Crucially in Europe there had often been an intimate relationship between ecclesiastical organisations and political power. This contrasted with America where a strong separation between church and state pertained. This contrast has considerable potential implications for civil society. In effect civil society has become declericalised – owing to an overall decline in numbers of clergy, lay participation and church attendance – and less authoritarian because of the decline of Church power within civil society. Prior to the watershed of Vatican Two (1965), which coincided with a degree of secularisation in Irish society, subsidiarity could be equated with a distinctly restrictive and conservative moral communitarianism. The emergence of liberal Catholicism and a decline in authoritarianism are arguably at odds with such forms of communitarianism. However, such reforms, in themselves, are not predicated upon the unravelling of Catholic ideological subsidiarity. For example, the Education Act (1998) represented a new settlement within Irish education, which took account of declining numbers of clerical teachers and demands for greater lay teacher and parental involvement in the management of schools, whilst protecting the schools' religious ethos.

Communitarian ideologies

The central premise within communitarian conceptions of social order is that communities and societies should limit selfish individualism. There exists a range of communitarian perspectives but in general these stand opposed to libertarianism. They are generally grounded in metaphysical conceptions of human nature derived from some strands of ancient Greek philosophy and from some strands of Old and New Testament religious thought (Etzioni, 1999: 144). Rorty argues that communitarian perspectives share a 'picture of the self' in common with Greek metaphysics, Christian theology and Enlightenment rationalism (1994: 204). This is the idea of human nature. The belief that there is such a thing as a human nature has informed secular conceptions of inalienable human rights (Dworkin, 1978: 198). To some extent, this is countered by a pessimistic view of human nature, common to the thought of Plato, Augustine and Calvin that has legitimised the suppression of human desire and behaviour. This strand of conservative moral communitarianism rejects the individualistic rationalism of the Enlightenment and the privileging of individual rights over collective responsibilities. Rorty identifies this perspective with contemporary thinkers such as Robert Bellah, Alastair McIntyre, Micheal Sandel and Charles Taylor (1994: 177). In effect, moral communitarians consider that the sort of human being produced by liberal institutions and culture is undesirable. Arguably, this strand has come to dominate social policy debates influenced by American communitarian thought, notwithstanding efforts of influential communitarians such as Amitai Etzioni and Robert Bellah to distinguish their prescriptions from those of the 'moral majority' religious right.

A further strand of communitarian might be identified within the liberal philosophical tradition of social contract theorists such as Locke, Rousseau and Kant. Social contract theory, currently dominated by the work of John Rawls, relates to the notional norms and values of justice that citizens hypothetically share (Rawls, 1973: viii). In common with other strands of communitarian thought, Rawls emphasises some degree of subordination of the individual pursuit of self-interest to the common interests of human beings. He shares much with the first strand of human rights communitarianism insofar as both emphasise human liberty. As summarised by Hess: 'Only respecting the liberty of other individuals – fair play in other words – enables us to achieve justice. Yet in order to play a game called "society", it is necessary that all players have roughly equal means before entering the "game" – a precondition that justifies the labelling of Rawls's approach as a model of "distributive justice"' (Hess, 2000: 81).

Communitarianism has been espoused left and right alike in the wake of neo-liberal challenges to collective welfare. To some extent, the attraction of communitarian ideas to Clinton Democrats or New Labour was in their capacity to signal differences from the new right. On the one hand communitarian ideas offered a formula for addressing the right-wing critique that the welfare state had undermined society. A resultant emphasis on linking social rights to obligations can be understood as a re-moralisation of social policy aimed at re-legitimatising state-produced welfare. On the other hand, communitarian ideas became intertwined with a privatisation of risk resulting from neo-liberal policies. Examples here include John Major's conception of 'active citizenship' and George W. Bush's proposals to replace state welfare by faith communities. In short, the take up of communitarian ideas can be understood as part of and as a response to the rightward shift in welfare politics in a number of western countries in recent decades.

The influential 'democratic communitarianism' espoused by Amitai Etzioni and Robert Bellah has sought to distinguish itself from the American religious right or 'moral majority' in calling for a 'moral revival without puritanism' (Etzioni, 1993: 1). Etzioni considers that both have shared concerns and a shared agenda of 'family values, community and morality' yet says that the 'moral majority' 'although they raised the right question they provided the wrong, largely authoritarian and dogmatic answers' (Etzioni, 1993: 13). His solution is to enforce reciprocal obligations within 'moral communities' or to achieve a moral reconstruction of social norms (1993: 12). This softer sociological emphasis on the social control role of social norms has much in common with the consensual structural functionalist model of power developed by Talcott Parsons (Ritzer, 1996: 271–4). This held that social order was the product of consensual social norms. Arguably, Etzioni underrepresents the authoritarianism implicit in his project.

Stier identifies a distinction between 'Augustinian' or authoritarian and 'Aristotelian' or non-authoritarian forms of American communitarianism

(Stier, 1998). The political project of 'Augustinian' communitarianism is the 'revival' of the moral community through a repressive conservatism. The later works of Saint Augustine, with their emphasis on a sinful mankind seeking assurances of salvation, prefigured the centrality of the doctrine of predestination within Calvinism (Brown, 2000: 422). Calvinists could not aim for personal salvation. The goal instead was the glorification of God through active labour. Good works alone were not enough but they were indispensable signs of salvation. The elect were spurred into an active life of individual agency yet one of intense moral prescription and communal regulation (Tawney, 1926: 193). Weber, amongst others, identified this Protestant ethic as an important contributing factor to the development of capitalism (Tawney, 1926; Weber, 1904; Troeltsch, 1931: 810). The resultant individualism had an anti-civic side that could be distinguished from other forms of communitarianism rooted in Christian thought. As explained by Bellah et al.:

> The state and the larger civil society are considered unnecessary because the saved can take care of themselves. Even more problematic is the tendency in this same strand of Protestantism to exclude those who are considered morally unworthy – unworthiness often being determined by their lack of economic success (the undeserving poor) – from the social body altogether. This attitude is countered by other Protestants and particularly by the Catholic tradition in which an emphasis on the common good precludes the exclusion of anyone from society's care and concern (2002: 277).

A second type of metaphysical communitarianism is derived from Aristotelian conceptions of natural law which, as adapted by Thomas Aquinas, have had considerable influence on Catholic social thought. Aquinas took from Aristotle an emphasis on the social nature of mankind and on the necessity of mutual co-operation. Government was recognised as a natural necessity if the activities of all were to be organised so that the good and sufficient life could be realised for everyone. As summarised by Lewis:

> The compelling logic of his own characteristics made man a social and political animal and inclined him to associate himself with his fellows under a coordinating government; but it was his own reason that devised the institutions that his nature sought. Thus the authority of governments was immediately based on human institution though it was ultimately based on the will of God, who was the cause both of the need and of the reason that found the answer to the need (1954: 150).

Aquinas viewed the state as natural, necessary and good. Its purpose was to direct people to the common good and their own good. This was a very different perspective from that offered by Lutheran theology with its strong emphasis on sin and the need for a coercive state to hold sinful humans in check: 'God instituted the state as an order of preservation to keep sinful human beings from killing one another' (Curran, 2002: 139). Both perspectives suggested different understandings of human nature and community and potentially different responses to social change.

Communitarianism in Irish social policy

Post-Famine Irish Catholicism fostered a coercive moral communitarianism centred on the regulation of sexuality. By the 1990s this had unravelled although it had arguably been in decline since the 1960s. One key milestone was the introduction in 1973 of the Unmarried Mother's Allowance whereby the state accepted, for the first time, their right to public support. Changes in the name of this category of benefit entitlement to Lone Mother's Allowance and subsequently to Lone Parent's Allowance by 1990 reveal a destigmatisation of sexuality in social policy over time. This has coincided with ongoing revelations, scandals and debates about punitive and authoritarian social policies such as the Magdalene Laundries, the secret foreign adoption of 'illegitimate' babies and widespread institutional sexual abuse obscured by a climate of authoritarianism and sexual repression (Millotte, 1997; Raftery and O'Sullivan, 1999). Arguably, the intense critical scrutiny of the legacy of Catholic moral communitarianism in recent years has partially exempted Ireland from some aspects of the renascent moral communitarian ideologies that have emerged within American and British social policy.

Communitarian accounts of present-day social problems in Ireland tend to emphasise anomie caused by the decline of 'traditional' values and ways of life. One such example was a Dáil debate on a report by the European Monitoring Centre for Drugs and Drug Addiction in 1997. As put by Roisin Shortall TD:

> Another factor is the declining influence of the Catholic church and the fact that its influence has not been replaced by anything else so that once people stop practising their religion they are left with little in term of points of reference for themselves regarding standards of behaviour. I am aware that there would be huge reluctance on behalf of the Government to become involved in this area, but we have no choice other than to address the moral agenda. For many years we depended on the Catholic Church to provide moral education. Clearly that is no longer happening in the case of vast numbers of people (Dáil Éireann, 13 November 1997)

Recent Irish communitarian debates have been characterised by a shift in emphasis from the regulation of sexuality to a concern about anti-social behaviour, particularly in relation to alcohol. Historically, responses to alcohol-related social problems were largely driven by religious social movements. For example, the Pioneer Total Abstinence Association of the Sacred Heart, founded in 1898, played a pivotal role in discouraging the consumption of alcohol. In 1959 it claimed a membership of nearly 500,000 registered members (Ferriter, 1999: 191). The decline of the Pioneers was, to some extent, a symptom of secularisation and an increase of social liberalism and materialism in Irish society. Social liberalism, in turn, in Ireland and elsewhere, has been blamed by communitarians as a reason for social decline.

The development of a role for the Irish state in regulating the consumption of alcohol has occurred within the context of a communitarian critique of moral decline and in the context of religious anti-alcohol activism. The Irish government established a Strategic Task Force on Alcohol in 2000. The report emerged within the context of growing alarm about alcohol-related public order offences and alcohol-related road accident fatalities (Department of Health and Children, 2002: 6). In recent years television advertisements aimed at discouraging drink driving and other forms of dangerous driving have depicted car crashes in extremely graphic terms and employed the slogan 'can you live with the shame?' Yet the report concluded that public education and persuasion measures were generally ineffective (2002: 17). In effect, the Task Force endorsed measures that punished 'anti-social' behaviour.

A growing emphasis on 'law and order' communitarianism might paradoxically be understood in terms of a decline in authoritarianism. Irish society prior to independence and in the post-colonial era was characterised by authoritarian deference to political and Church power and a mistrust of authority that undermined the legitimacy of public institutions and the legitimacy of law (Peillon, 1982: 124). Schmitt argues that this resulted in a popular ambivalence to legal rules and regulations (1973: 45). The apparent popularity of legal sanctions such as penalty points to curb 'deviant' motorist behaviour suggest a decline in such ambivalence. Similarly, only in recent years has an emphasis on honesty in public life and financial affairs, evidenced by a plethora of corruption tribunals, crept onto the political agenda (Ó Cinnéide, 2003: 336).

Exclusionary communitarianism

The emergence of a new role for the state as moral arbitrator is evident in a degree of emphasis on stigma and social control within state strategies to address alcohol-related social problems. In another example, Fianna Fail ministers at the Party's 2003 *Ard Fheis* (conference) endorsed polices of heavily fining parents of young offenders within a discourse that blamed irresponsible parenting for juvenile crime. This followed the implementation of the Children's Act (2001) that allowed the courts to prosecute the parents of young offenders and to impose curfews on children guilty of offences. The mobilisation of stigma in social policy is nothing new. Nor is the emphasis on punitive social policies aimed as a corrective to the perceived moral failing of clients. Such an emphasis was evident in Poor Law understandings of poverty and the oppression of 'fallen women' in institutions such as the Magdalene Laundries.

Moral communitarians tend to view individuals and groups perceived as deviant as deserving of social exclusion. In the introduction to *The Spirit of Community: The Reinvention of American Society*, Etzioni describes his own personal communitarian epiphany when a neighbour pressed him to maintain his lawn so that neighbourhood would not decline (1993). Etzioni's communitarianism may not be puritanical (that is preoccupied with personal asceticism) but it does allow for the exclusion of those who do not conform to the norms of dominant groups to be accused of moral failure. Its problematic nature can be illustrated in the Irish case using the example of community responses to Travellers. Anti-Traveller racism can be understood as an exclusionary communitarian ideology that justifies the displacement of Travellers from Irish society on the grounds of their presumed deviance from dominant communal norms (MacLaughlin, 1995: 24). Anti-Traveller communitarianism is grounded in racialised stereotypes insofar as it presumes that all Travellers are intrinsic 'bad neighbours'. The social exclusion of Travellers, in common with other 'underclass' racialised groups such as African Americans, is justified by their presumed moral failure to meet dominant social norms. Notwithstanding the specific inclusion of Travellers within Irish equality legislation during the 1990s, hostility towards Travellers has influenced local and national politics. In the case of the former, local authorities find it difficult to contest trenchant opposition from residents' groups to the provision of accommodation for Travellers. The Housing (Miscellaneous Provisions) Act (2002) criminalised those Travellers without access to designated halting sites. The Act permitted local authorities to respond to political pressure from anti-Traveller community groups (Fanning, 2002b: 327).

Moral communitarian 'gated community' responses to drugs problems are also evident to some extent in Ireland. The Housing Act (1997) allows local authorities to evict tenants for anti-social behaviour. However, statutory responses to anti-social behaviour co-existed during the 1990s in some urban areas with vigilante expulsions of suspected drug dealers and users from their homes. Populist protest against drug users was, to a considerable extent, protest against perceived inaction by the Gardaí and the government. It had some impact on policy. For example, 'law and order' responses to the drugs problem (such as Operation Dochas) were stepped up in the late 1990s. Other forms of anti-drug activism, such as punishment beatings, echoed paramilitary communitarianism in Northern Ireland and in themselves constituted a law and order problem. Collectively these responses placed drugs users outside the moral community and claimed that drugs problems could be resolved by authoritarian means. As expressed by a Portlaoise Town Commissioner at a meeting that resolved to evict any local authority tenant convicted of dealing in illegal drugs, there was no anti-social behaviour that could not be stamped out if 'the powers that be want to do it' (*Laois Nationalist*, September 1999).

Moral communitarian responses to Travellers and drug addicts have similarly defined social problems in terms of a need to exclude undesirable groups. The Traveller problem is understood as the problem of the existence of Travellers rather than problems facing Irish society as a result of inequalities, discrimination and social exclusion encountered by Travellers. The drugs problem is similarly defined as the problem of the presence of addicts. Yet such perspectives are contested within debates about social problems. For example, understandings of the drugs problem as a law and order problem vie with those which regard it as a health problem (necessitating responses to addictions and HIV) and as a problem caused or perpetrated by social inequality and poverty. These latter explanations have had an increasing impact on social policy in recent years and have contested anti-civic forms of communitarianism. As outlined in the policy statement of one community project, 'Addicts are not aliens from outer space, who have suddenly appeared out of nowhere. They are our brothers and sisters, sons and daughters, our neighbours. As a community we need to take ownership of the issue in a rational, democratic and peaceful manner' (Greater Blanchardstown Response to Drugs, 2003).

Social capital

According to Robert Putnam, the concept of social capital was independently invented at least six times during the twentieth century (2000: 1920). It was used in the late 1970s by Glenn Loury to refer to the cognitive and social dispositions that enabled individuals to acquire the skills needed for gainful employment. In the 1980s the idea was popularised by the French sociologist Pierre Bourdieu, who argued that educational systems were mainly devoted to the reproduction of social capital and, by extension, social status. Both Bourdieu and the German economist Ekkehart Schlicht used the term to underline the social and economic resources embodied in social networks (Putnam, 2000: 19–20) The notion of social capital is bound up with the view that human reproduction is both a biological and a social process. Human biological reproduction occurs, of course, within a social context. It is affected by material resources, relationships and interdependencies. As employed by

Bourdieu, reproduction refers to the political, social and cultural processes that transmit the social structure and culture of a society over time (Bocock and Thompson, 1988: 2). This includes, for example, the social policies that transmit education and skills from one generation to the next.

Putnam distinguishes between individual and collective forms of social capital. Individuals form ties and connections and develop skills that benefit their own interests. They may network to secure employment or promotions. As Putnam puts it, 'most of us get our jobs because of whom we know not what we know' (2000: 20). At the same time, individual social capital is seen to be dependent upon the state of the wider community. Networks involve mutual obligations and reciprocity. Well-connected individuals may not thrive where social cohesion is poor yet poorly connected individuals may benefit from living in a well-connected community. Social capital is therefore a private good and a public good.

The relationship between the idea of social capital and communitarianism can be illustrated by Max Weber's account of American Protestants in North Carolina at the turn of the twentieth century:

> When I asked him after the ceremony, 'Why did you anticipate the baptism of that man?' He answered, 'because he wants to open a bank account in M'.
>
> 'Are there so many Baptists around that he can make a living?'
>
> 'Not at all, but once being baptised he will get the patronage of the whole region and he will outcompete everybody' (1969: 305).

Here the interviewee identified membership of the Baptist community as an important form of individual social capital. Membership depended on the internalisation of specific norms of behaviour and demeanour. Possession of these was another form of social capital that enabled the bearer to become accepted as a member of the Baptist community. Those without the right social capital could be excluded. In any given case such social capital is a currency fixed to a specific society. While the unequal distribution of economic capital divides society into the 'haves' and the 'have-nots', the uneven distribution of social capital divides society in the 'knows' and the 'know-nots' (Miller, 1987: 151–2).

Putnam's general thesis is that fostering social capital is good for society. Yet he clearly identifies possibilities for both good and bad forms of social capital. He distinguishes between inclusionary or 'bridging' forms of social capital and exclusionary or 'bonding' forms of social capital. For example, he describes how power elites, terrorists, the mafia, urban gangs, racist organisations and middle-class NIMBY (not in my back yard) movements are each sustained by forms of reciprocity that exclude others. The consequences of bonding social capital can include sectarianism, ethnocentricism or corruption.

An increase in bridging social capital has the potential to destroy certain exclusive non-bridging forms of social capital. For example, the American civil rights movement challenged racially homogeneous schools and neighbour-hoods (Putnam, 2000: 362). Putnam's emphasis on bridging social capital signals a vital difference from many communitarian perspectives. He identifies a need to challenge forms of communitarianism characterised by exclusionary bonding forms of social capital by means of civil rights and rights to welfare.

Etzioni, by contrast, in his 1993 book, *The Spirit of Community*, opposed the expansion of individual rights because these allowed individuals to recklessly disengage from their moral obligations to one another (1993: 5). Moral communitarians, including 'democratic communitarians', prioritise bonding forms of social capital that have the wherewithal to exclude those who do not adhere to group norms and values. That is not to say that Putnam is hostile to bonding social capital. He notes that some communal bonds are characterised by both bonding and bridging forms of social capital. For example, Church groups may bond along religious lines but bridge across ethnic ones. As such, the question for social policy makers is how to minimise the exclusionary consequences of bonding social capital and to maximise the positive consequences of bridging social capital (Putnam, 2000: 23). He depicts social capital as a tool against social exclusion potentially available to marginal groups who lack other forms of capital (Putnam, 2000: 359).

Education inequality and social capital

Education is a source of individual and collective forms of social capital but access to a good education or educational success may be determined by access to other forms of social capital (Bocock and Thompson, 1988: 3). The reproduction of education as a form of cultural capital may be affected by parental socio-economic status. Cultural capital may be understood as a form of intellectual capital that affects the life chances of individuals even as it reproduces a specific social order. This is because valued forms of social capital promote the status of specific forms of knowledge, norms and habits that confer social acceptance. The unequal distribution of social capital results in cultural hierarchies alongside material ones (Bocock: 1998: 147). For example, going to the right school may translate into subsequent access to elite net-works. Bourdieu identifies a 'hidden curriculum' loaded in favour of certain social groups and against others on the basis of class (Bourdieu, 1974: 32). Others suggest that similar inequalities may pertain on the basis of gender, ethnicity or religion (Whitty, 1998: 280). Social inequalities may thus be embedded in social capital. Norms and networks that serve some groups may exclude others (Putnam, 2000: 358).

Bourdieu's thesis is arguably borne out in the Irish case by research findings that indicate that access to third-level education is stratified on the basis of social class. Some Irish research suggests that norms, linked to educational success, of seeking voluntary extra tuition and choosing to spend an additional (optional) year of secondary education are skewed on the basis of social class. Research has also indicated that a sense of alienation amongst 'working-class' communities from the education system (as distinct from education itself) has been transmitted from parents to their children (Drudy and Lynch, 1993: 162).

Clancy, in his 2003 survey of access to higher education in Ireland, describes education as 'a crucial mechanism of social exclusion' because of the role it plays in the status attainment process and reward structure of Irish society (2003: 15). He identifies an emphasis in Irish education policy upon 'human capital' goals and objectives of addressing social disadvantage since 1965 when an influential report, *Investment in Education*, paved the way for universal free secondary education. He argues that access to third-level education has become an increasingly important determinant of life chances. With the contraction of employment opportunities for those who lack advanced education and training-education qualifications have become the currency for employment. Access to third-level education in Ireland was found to be stratified on the basis of the socio-economic status of the fathers of students. For example, a disproportionate number of third-level students in 1998 had fathers who were employers and managers, professionals and farmers whilst the children of agricultural workers, manual skilled, semi-skilled and unskilled workers were underrepresented in third-level education (Clancy, 2003: 49). Clancy argues that social group differentials in participation in third-level education originate in patterns of participation and performance in second-level education. Stratifications in third level reflect those in second-level education attainment on the basis of parental socio-economic status (2003: 67). Furthermore, he noted that participation in third-level education is skewed spatially so that relatively deprived localities are underrepresented. For example, in Dublin an overall participation rate of just eight per cent was found compared with rates in excess of 50 per cent in five relatively advantaged districts in the south side of the city (2003: 121).

Social capital and Irish social policy

Central to Putnam's argument is the notion that social capital can be fostered. He identifies several distinct sites of bridging and bonding social capital. These include political, civic and religious forms of social participation, connections in the workplace, family, informal social connections, volunteering and philanthropy (Putnam, 2000: 115). If social capital is viewed as an asset, the apparent decline of various forms of social capital offers a distinct critique of late modernity that has points of commonality with Catholic perspectives about social cohesion. Putnam links a decline of some forms of shared social capital to the pressures of present-day capitalism and is critical of the capitalist individualisation of life. However, unlike those communitarians who identify modernity as a crisis, Putnam can point to periods of relative growth and relative decline in different domains of social capital (2000: 57, 71, 125).

The advantage of the social capital perspective, compared to the purely ideological perspectives about the good society embodied in debates about subsidiarity and communitarianism, is that it lends itself to measurement. For example, individual and collective social capital can be operationalised within policies aimed at addressing social exclusion and community development. Cremer-Schäfer et al. (2001), in a study of strategies for coping with and avoiding social exclusion in a number of EU countries, offer a definition of social exclusion which focuses on the resources necessary to secure participation:

> 'Social exclusion' is, in an adequately broad sense, to be understood as *being deprived of aspects of full social participation* in different fields and with different consequences for other fields. Participation, in turn, has discernible levels: the most basic level being the ability to reproduce a person's own life on a daily basis, the highest level determining and bringing about the future, better state of society (2001: 3).

The focus of their study was upon marginal groups such as immigrants. Their findings suggest that the capacity to participate in society will be stratified on the basis of rights and access to various material and cultural resources.

An implicit emphasis on individual and collective social capital is also evident in the Revised National Anti-Poverty Strategy (NAPS) (2002). It restated a definition of poverty from the NAPS (Government of Ireland, 1997) that identified poverty as a cause of social exclusion, and thus the goal of combating poverty as promoting social inclusion:

> As a result of inadequate income and resources people may be excluded and marginalised from participating in activities which are considered the norm for other people in society (Government of Ireland, 2002: 6).

Some forms of participation engender others. Conversely, the absence of opportunities to participate in some areas (such as education), may have a detrimental impact on other areas (such as employment). The interrelationship between various fields of participation is mirrored in forms of exclusion where multiple or cumulative forms of deprivation can also be noted. Policies aimed at promoting social inclusion can also usefully take into account the distinction between bonding and bridging social capital. For example, existing forms of community development may be poor at developing bridging social capital that benefits new immigrant communities. Policies aimed at addressing racism, lesser social rights and institutional barriers encountered by ethnic minorities, potentially engender bridging social capital. Various definitions of community development by Irish bodies place a strong emphasis on social participation and community empowerment (Combat Poverty Agency, 2000b). For example, a rights-based approach to social inclusion has been emphasised by some community development partnerships in multi-ethnic areas. As stated in one community development plan, 'Local citizenship should not be graded on the basis of inter-generational family links with the area' (North West Inner City Area Network, 1999: 42).

Similarly, social policy responses to child poverty in Ireland have increasingly emphasised child-specific indicators of deprivation that could be viewed as social capital indicators. These include a safe area in which to play with friends and involvement in organised sports or a club and participation in after-school classes (Nolan, 2000: xxiii). In other words, child poverty is seen to diminish the individual social capital of children and the ability of children to participate in society. Policy statements on child poverty in Ireland have been framed to a considerable extent with the rights-based approach of the United Nations Convention on the Rights of the Child that was ratified by Ireland in 1992. For instance, there is a strong implicit emphasis on child social capital in the 'whole child perspective' employed within Ireland's National Children's Strategy (2000). Under the headings of social and peer relationships and social presentation, it refers to developing the capacity of children to engage with others and the development of 'children's ability to learn to pick up messages about the impressions they are creating, while not necessarily feeling that they need to conform' (Government of Ireland, 2000: 27).

In 2003, the National Economic and Social Forum published a report on the policy implications of social capital in Ireland. This distinguished between 'top down' and 'bottom down' approaches to engendering social capital. The identification of roles in promoting social capital for social partnership, public bodies, community development organisations and for direct engagement of citizens by the state pointed to a strong emphasis on the 'top down' approach (NESF, 2003b: 7). The NESF report suggested a communitarian understanding of social capital in defining it as 'networks together with shared norms, values and understandings that facilitate co-operation within or amongst groups' (2003b: 10). It identified a role for such networks and norms in supporting community development and social inclusion. It emphasised a role for the state in the following terms:

Perhaps the greatest contribution the Government and the social partners can make to investment in social capital is through actions that encourage social inclusion, fairness, transparency, and equality of opportunity. It is also evident that the development of social infrastructure from education, health and welfare to employment and training support are needed to provide crucial supports in an era when traditional forms of family and local neighbourhood social capital are weaker. The state can never substitute entirely for these other forms of social capital. But it has an important role to play through a proactive and enabling process with a mobilised and empowered civil society (NESF, 2003b: 14)

The NESF report emphasised the prevalence of a moral communitarian critique of social change in Ireland. It suggested the perception of a crisis in Irish society owing to what might be termed a communitarian critique of social change:

A feature of social change is the often expressed view that there is a growing sense of disconnection from others and a lack of common purpose and values. These comments are often expressed in the context of rising levels of reported crime, drug addiction and youth suicide – especially amongst young men or in the belief in '*me fein*' or self-interested approach to living and engagement. In the absence of solid evidence over time, a claim of generalised decline in civic and moral standards – whether in public or political life or in family or civil society is difficult to substantiate. Certainly, the speed of economic and social change as well as instances of declining standards in political and religious institutions have left many people bewildered, lonely, frustrated and feeling disempowered or let down (NESF, 2003b: 29).

However, it contested this critique to some extent and argued that shifts from traditional mass values and norms need not be interpreted as moral decline (NESF, 2003b: 29). Social capital could potentially counter perceptions of social decline as well as the actual erosion of traditional networks and norms that provided social capital. Here it is useful to draw a distinction between political responses to fears of social decline, crime and deviance (potentially a politics of moral panic) and the suggested use of social capital to bolster existing social policies. The report argued that fears of decline find expression in levels of 'community efficacy' (a sense of community capacity or incapacity to change things for the better). Levels of community confidence and the social norms that inform such confidence may thus matter more than social networks in explaining the prevalence of anti-social behaviour (2003b: 54). This, in essence, was a communitarian model as social capital.

What then of social capital as infrastructure? This too was understood by the NESF to require shared social norms. The report emphasised the potential for many existing models of community development to generate networks based on trust and shared values. It also emphasised the role of social networks and norms in fostering particular types of community development (2003b: 32–3). It argued that *public–private–voluntary partnerships* had the potential to release new civic and community energy especially in relation to care and social services. It identified a range of 'policy malleable' areas including community development, public voluntary partnerships and measures to encourage volunteering and participation in civic life (2003b: 88). In summary, then, the report identified a role for the state in responding to the perceived decline of community. The political context of social capital renewal was a communitarian critique of social decline.

The persistence of subsidiarity

The NESF report suggested a need to avoid a model of social capital development that over-relied on externally provided support for communities. Furthermore it suggested that there were practical and ideological limits to the extent to which social capital could be engendered. It argued that over-reliance on external help could undermine communities and referred explicitly to the principle of subsidiarity:

> Subsidiarity recognises that the main 'doers' of social capital investment include a range of civil society, corporate and informal networks of local actors. Any public support for social capital needs, therefore, to respect the principle of empowerment and facilitation. Too much control, social engineering or provision of external incentives could negate the very principle of an active civil society which is based on voluntary effort and support motivated by a collective desire and endeavour for the common good (NESF, 2003b: 78)

This endorsement of subsidiarity can be understood as a restatement of a longstanding ideological settlement within the Irish mixed economy of welfare characterised by resistance to state encroachment of community and civil society (see chapter 1). Historically, this was characterised by a Catholic 'moral monopoly', to use Inglis's term (1998) and a moral communitarianism that was hegemonic and authoritarian. To some extent, the emphasis on subsidiarity can be understood as an ideological quest for *Gemeinschaft*. One notable articulation of this quest was contained in a speech by de Valera in 1942 that espoused the ideal of a contented anti-materialistic Catholic peasant society. However, this was at odds with the reality of rural decline, high unemployment and high emigration due to economic stagnation (Lee, 1989: 227). From the late 1950s the pursuit of economic growth and modernisation became something of a national religion. Yet a strong ideological emphasis on social cohesion has been evident within Irish social policy. This has been bolstered on an ongoing basis by the European Union through mechanisms such as the Common Agricultural Policy that managed Ireland's transition to an urban society. It continues to be expressed rhetorically within social partnership, the current National Development Plan and its predecessors. However, it is also the case that, in general, social inclusion goals have been subordinated to goals of economic growth since The First Programme for Economic Expansion in 1958 (Fanning, 2003: 3). The resultant hegemonic national project of technocratic and economic modernisation remains subject to communitarian critiques in the present era.

Conclusion

An international neo-liberal critique of the welfare state has emphasised a reprivatisation of risk sustained by moral communitarianism in which individual responsibility is governed, where necessary, by authoritarian social controls in the traditions of Augustine, Calvin and Luther. The resultant gated model of social cohesion, as an archetype, is likely to be strong on bonding social capital but weak on universalist social rights that engender bridging social capital. Outside the gates, the argument goes, will be an underclass consisting of various categories of 'undeserving' social undesirables subject to punitive social policies. In the Irish case such neo-conservative communitarianism has been contested to a degree by a Catholic tradition of social solidarity and by an ethos of social inclusion that implicitly emphasises a need for bridging social capital to foster a universalist social cohesion. Yet exclusionary forms of communitarism are identifiable in Ireland. For example, exclusionary social policy responses to Travellers are driven by populist politics at a local and national level.

The decline of a Catholic 'moral monopoly' in Ireland has not necessarily undermined ideological subsidiarity. One result of a corresponding decline in authoritarianism has been the emergence of rights-based and distributive justice communitarian approaches within secular and religious civil society (Healy and Reynolds, 1993: 40). For example, present-day Irish social inclusion policies can be traced to an alliance between Catholic social justice groups and the Labour Party during the 1970s (Rush, 1999: 168). Another has been the promotion of secular social capital within state-fostered community development and social inclusion policies (NESF, 2003b). Notwithstanding expectations of a state role in promoting social capital, the persistence of ideological subsidiarity can be seen in Irish social capital debates.

This chapter has argued that a communitarian critique of social modernisation can be identified within Irish debates about social capital as well as in those with an obvious communitarian emphasis. In the absence of a clear left–right continuum within Irish politics it is arguably the case that political, ideological and social policy debates in Ireland can be understood as occurring along a continuum characterised by an emphasis upon traditionalism at one end and modernity at the other. The former has included romantic *Gemeinschaft* and authoritarian Catholic moral communitarian ideological conceptions of good society. The latter has included contestations of such traditionalisms by means of secularisation, individualisation and the economic modernisation of Irish society. This modernisation has been pursued from both the left (through an emphasis on social justice and social rights) and the right (through an emphasis on economic rights and the market) within a social partnership model. Arguably, the memory of a recent authoritarian past has impeded the influence of neo-conservative moral communitarian perspectives in Ireland. However, it might also be argued that the moral communitarian critique of social change is gaining ground, for instance in debates about law and order and alcohol. It can be seen to influence Irish social capital debates insofar as these emphasise the role of social norms and social values as well as social networks. Ultimately, debates about social capital and communitarianism can be seen to overlap. The crucial distinction is not between one and the other but between the sorts of values and norms being advocated in both.

Chapter 4

Individualisation

Gabriel Kiely

Introduction

This chapter discusses the concept of individualisation as applied to taxation and welfare systems. The discussion critically examines the relationship between individualism and the ideology of equality and their influence on the policy trend towards individualisation. This trend, however, while meeting the objective of equality between men and women, it is argued, does not meet the objective of equality between all individuals when family responsibilities are taken into account. Official Irish policy is to gradually introduce individualisation into the taxation and welfare systems. The chapter challenges the capacity of individualisation to meet the policy objectives as articulated by the government. It concludes by arguing that while the attainment of equality must continue to be a major policy objective, the driving force behind social policy reforms continues to be the attainment of security.

In its simplest form, individualisation is the term used when referring to a system of social security based on individual entitlement and a system of taxation based on individual assessment of personal income (McLaughlin, 1999). Individualisation is in contrast to systems which are based on aggregation of the means and incomes of more than one person, as – for example – where a couple are jointly assessed or where dependants, such as children, are included in the assessment. 'Individualisation is the process by which the individual rather than the group becomes the key unit of society.' (Pahl, 1999: 182)

It is not a unitary concept, however. There are many different approaches to individualisation. These run from the extreme of total independent treatment in the social welfare and the taxation systems, to what is known as *administrative individualisation* which simply means dividing benefits equally between members of a given group, such as married partners, even though their entitlements may have been assessed jointly.

The policy shift in the direction of the individualisation of the welfare and taxation systems is generally seen as a reflection of a move away from the traditional breadwinner model to one based on the value of equality. An examination of the extent to which this shift has taken place in welfare states across Europe suggests, however, that the shift has been more talked about than acted upon with family membership continuing to be a significant element in both assessment and entitlement in both of these systems. This is particularly evident in such major areas as pensions, health care, unemployment and means-tested supplementary welfare. This chapter critically examines the theoretical debates underpinning this policy shift in the context of recent developments in the Irish taxation and welfare systems.

It begins with a discussion of the theoretical debate about individualisation in the context of rising individualism. It then examines the normative usage of the term 'individualisation' in the Irish social policy debate. The chapter goes on to argue that the underlying principle driving social policy developments is security and not equality, and that this is particularly evident when the family dimension is taken into account.

Individualisation and individualism

The main argument put forward in favour of the individualisation of the social security and taxation systems is that the traditional approach based on the male breadwinner model is not suited either to the current labour market composition or the evolution of new family forms of life. Individualisation, by treating men and women equally, would change the status of many women from that of dependency to that of economic independence. This is also the approach favoured by some feminists. Yeates (1997: 146), for example, in her analysis of the Irish social security system, argues that 'an alternative framework for social policy development based on individual rights is a prerequisite for substantive gender equality'. Individualisation is the articulation of the value of individualism in public policy. As such, it is part of the reform agenda to replace dependency in the social welfare and taxation systems with individual entitlements.

Individualism can be a difficult concept to define as it can have different meanings in different contexts. Individualism associated with the pursuit of self-interest, for example, is quite different from individualism that is associated with exercising greater personal choices. Likewise, individualism as understood in the context of free-market ideologies is not the same as individualism that promotes individual rights. Within this tangle of meanings, individualism can be seen to have two different but interrelated meanings: individualism as understood in the free-market ideologies and individualism as an expression of individual freedoms. Individualism as used in this chapter refers to 'a set of beliefs that puts paramount importance on the rights and freedoms of individuals and the power of free-market mechanisms' (Gray and Jenkins, 1999: 246).

Individualism as understood in the context of free-market ideologies is an essential part of neo-liberalism. This neo-liberalism, at its most extreme, is represented by the 'new right', which has developed since the 1970s and was popularly known as Reaganism and Thatcherism. The driving force behind the 'new right' is the challenge by free-market philosophies to old-style socialism which believed in state intervention in the marketplace to control market capitalism. Giddens, in writing about this in *The Third Way* (1998: 12), says that the state – and particularly the welfare state – is seen by neo-liberals as destructive of the civil order, while markets are not, because markets thrive on individual initiative. The argument is that, if left to themselves, markets will deliver the greatest good to society. Individualism, as opposed to socialist collectivism, is central to the free-market philosophy, as is maximum individual choice in the economy. The theoretical underpinnings of individualism have their origin in the Enlightenment period which promoted individual rights. In recent times, the works of Hayek (1993) have provided an additional theoretical argument, based on his theory of 'spontaneous order' (1993: 65). In other words, society will produce its own order if left on its own without state controls. The market, he argues, is what produces this spontaneous order in society (Kukathas, 1990). This requires minimum or no state intervention and maximum individual freedom.

However, neo-liberalism and the ideology of the free market are not the only factors influencing the rise in individualism. Individualism is also advocated because of its emphasis on new freedoms for the individual. This freedom is to be found in the greater exercise of choice which comes with liberation from the prescriptions of tradition, religion, society or the state. This discourse on individualism is part of the debate on equality, that is, a desire not just for gender equality, but for a more inclusive society. In this context, the expansion of individual rights is seen as central to the notion of social citizenship.

The major report by the National Economic and Social Council (NESC, 1999: 64), for example, states that 'there is now widespread acknowledgement of the crucial importance of social equality as a principle underlying public policy and the associated importance of the recognition and respect for fundamental rights accompanied by appropriate policies'. The report cites several international conventions as evidence of this, e.g. the United Nations Declaration on Human Rights, the Council of Europe Convention on Human Rights and the European Social Charter. For example, the revised European Social Charter of 1996, which came into effect in 1999, guarantees (among a series of other rights) the right of workers with families to equal opportunities and treatment. The Comité des Sages, in its report on fundamental rights in the European Union, emphasised the need to strengthen the sense of democracy in the European Union by treating civil and social rights as indivisible. In recommending the protection of fundamental rights, the European

Working Group on Fundamental Rights (1999), which was established by Directorate General V of the European Commission, also stressed the indivisibility of both civil and social rights.

Powell and Guerin, in their work, *Civil Society and Social Policy* (1997: 53), discuss civil citizenship and state that 'democratic participation is based on the citizen's relationship not with the means of production, but with the means of distribution – with the Welfare State rather than the market economy'. They go on to say that 'in this political order the State has achieved hegemony through regulating the relationship between labour and business and the redistributive systems involving taxation and social welfare benefits'.

The location of the discourse on individualism in the debate on citizenship has its origins in Marshall's theory of citizenship. Marshall (1969) divided citizenship into his well-known classification based on what he called civil, political and social citizenship. Each type of citizenship carried with it certain rights. Thus civil citizenship includes such rights as the right to choose where to live, the right to free speech, the right to own property and the right to equal treatment before the law. Political citizenship is concerned with rights such as the right to elect and to be elected. The third type of citizenship, social citizenship, deals with the right to enjoy a minimum standard of welfare. This includes not only the right to economic security, but also the right to the prevailing standard of living. It is in this context of social citizenship that individualism is most clearly articulated. If all citizens are to have equal social rights, then they must all be treated equally. This challenges the notion of derived rights, especially in the social welfare system. In order to enjoy the status of social citizenship, each citizen must have an autonomous right to a minimum standard of welfare. This is an individual right, not a derived right. A major criticism of social citizenship as it is currently debated in the European Union is that it applies effectively only to those in employment. The same criticism can be made of equality legislation. This then leaves the exercise of social citizenship by large sections of the community somewhat meaningless. The key question is how individualism as an expression of social citizenship can protect people from personal or public dependency, and in so doing bridge the gap between paid and unpaid work, the marketplace and the family.

David Green (1990: 2) challenges the social citizenship argument as a justification for individualism. He seems to argue that notions of social citizenship represent a doctrine which demands that the power of the state should be used to 'equalise' people. He argues that socialists have now shifted from focusing on 'production' (accepting that the market economy delivers prosperity), to 'consumption'. 'They now no longer want to use the power of the state to direct control of industrial production; instead, they hope to use state power to equalise consumption'. He goes on to say that the socialist desire for material equality not only remains, but is being repackaged and advocated with renewed vigour under the rallying cries of 'citizenship', 'social justice' and 'positive freedom'. He believes that pursuing equality is incompatible with a society of free individuals.

The achievement of social citizenship is a complex process and does not involve, as Green argues, a process of equalising people. Equality in civil and political citizenship simply implies treating everyone equally. Social citizenship, on the other hand, implies recognising differences associated with particular conditions or statuses that exclude individuals from the mainstream (NESC, 1999: 78). Rather than being incompatible with a society of free individuals (as Green argues), the liberal debate holds that individualism is an essential component of social citizenship discourse. Individualism is part, then, of what is called the liberal citizenship that argues for equal rights for all, based on the notion of the autonomy of the individual. This discourse on liberal citizenship is in juxtaposition to the discourse on communitarian citizenship which argues that people are dependent on each other and are, therefore, not autonomous.

To some extent, these notions of liberalism and communitarianism are placed in opposition to each other. As a citizen, you are either autonomous, or you are not. This leads to a dichotomy between 'individualism' on the one hand, and 'communitarianism' on the other. However, such a dichotomy – while perhaps useful as a theoretical construct – does not adequately explain what is meant by individualism in current social policy debates or, indeed, communitarianism. As Bussemaker and Voet (1998: 295) in their analysis of discourses on citizenship and gender conclude, 'a clear-cut choice for one specific discourse is probably not possible'. They go on to say that 'within a feminist perspective it is probably to be expected that most thinkers arrive at "amended" versions of citizenship, in which intermediary positions tend to be adopted, combining different aspects of different traditions and linking social values to the effect of political institutions' (1998: 296).

Taking up this feminist critique, it seems that rather than presenting individualism and communitarianism as a dichotomy, they are better represented as two ends of a continuum. Thus one can talk about degrees of individualism and degrees of communitarianism. This is illustrated by Bussemaker and Voet (1998), for example, when discussing some of the difficulties feminists have with individualism, especially as put forward by neo-liberals in the context of the restructuring of the welfare state. They distinguish between economic individualism and social or democratic individualism. Social individualism includes a commitment to the common good, where individual rights and the social and political community in which they are embedded are interrelated (1998: 279). Thus, each of these two types of individualism can be located on different points on the continuum, with economic individualism more towards the individualism end and social individualism towards the communitarianism end.

Individualisation in the Irish context

The 1990s were a period of unprecedented economic growth and social change in Ireland. It was the decade that saw the birth of the so-called Celtic Tiger and the convergence of Irish demographic patterns with the other member states of the European Union. These changes, and in particular the increased participation of women in the paid labour force and the rise of diverse family forms, challenged the long-standing assumption in the welfare and taxation systems that the basic unit of society consisted of a 'bread-winning father', with dependent spouse and children. While the welfare and taxation systems attempted to respond to this challenge, it became apparent that if women were to maintain economic independence and equity were to be achieved between different household types, a more radical change would be required. This led to the articulation in the Budget speech of the Minister for Finance in December 1999, of what he called a 'radical change' towards the individualisation of the taxation system (McCreevy, 1999: 12).

This 'radical change' by the Minister for Finance followed the publication of a number of key reports that included recommendations on the individual-isation of the welfare and taxation system. These included the Report of an interdepartmental committee set up by the Minister for Social, Community and Family Affairs, which examined the treatment of married, cohabiting and one-parent families under the tax and social welfare codes (*Report of the Working Group*, 1999). Although the Group did not reach agreement on which approach to recommend, they did support an extension of administrative arrangements (i.e. administrative individualisation) which would lead to a greater degree of individualisation among social welfare recipients (1999: 141). NESC's influential report, *Opportunities, Challenges and Capacities for Choice*, while supporting the continued expansion of administrative individualisation (1999: 397), empha-sised 'the need for policies and institutions to adapt effectively to changes in economic and social circumstances' (1999: 222) in its discussion of the welfare and taxation systems.

McCashin (1999), in his analysis of the Irish situation, identifies five possible variations of individualisation. The first would confer rights on 'all individuals as individuals without reference to any personal, familial, household or marital status' (1999: 6). The strongest form of the approach would be a basic income scheme. The second variant would link social security rights to the individual experience of the needs and contingencies social security was trying to address. With this approach, there would be no additional payments for dependants. Instead, child benefit would be enhanced and spouses without direct social insurance entitlements would be credited to give them access to social insurance payments. The third variant would 'individualise the resources we allocate to spouses and partners working in the home' (1999: 7). This would involve the introduction of what he calls a home responsibility allowance. The fourth approach, somewhat similar to the first, would involve the 'individualisation of the tax system incorporating a substantial improvement in child income support' (1999: 8). This approach would abolish the transferability of tax bands and allowances between married couples. The current aggregation of the income of married couples for tax purposes results in a higher marginal tax rate on the second earner. This approach would redress this. The fifth approach would be the administrative individualisation of social security payments (1999: 9), which in the Irish case entails the splitting in half of the 'couple rate' and paying it as two separate payments while retaining the couple as the unit of assessment.

However, the report published by the Commission on the Family, *Strengthening Families for the Future* (1998: 61), cautioned against the individualisation of the welfare and taxation systems because of the possible consequence for families. The report made this point strongly when it stated 'that "family incentives", such as the incentive to marry and form a stable relationship, and to provide joint parenthood to children, should be accorded a greater prominence in evaluating the outcomes of social welfare and taxation policy, similar to that at present accorded to mothers such as work incentives and other economic effects of social welfare provision' (1998: 58). The point is further made when it draws the conclusion that the role the state has taken in sharing the costs of raising children across the community 'can be seen as involving an element of redistribution of income over the life-cycle, and in part an element of redistribution as between those with and without children' (1998: 59).

The introduction in the Budget 2000 of new measures to begin the process of bringing about the individualisation of the income taxation system sparked off an intensive debate about the balance between family responsibilities and employment needs. The debate focused mainly on the employment of married women and mothers. With the continued high rate of growth in the economy and near full-employment, the pressure on married women to remain in, or return to, the paid workforce had greatly increased. The changes in the taxation system were seen as putting further pressure on these women and as discriminatory against married women who stayed at home.

The change in the taxation system meant that dual-earner married couples with a combined income of at least €35,553 per annum, and the second earner having at least a taxable income of €7,618, would have a lower taxation liability than single-earner couples on the same income. This came about as a result of the non-transferability of some allowances between married couples, resulting in these dual-earner couples having a lower tax liability of up to €7,618 than their counterpart single-earner couples.

The Government defended the change on the grounds that it was in keeping with the policy of moving to individualisation of the income tax system and that it would rectify what up to then was seen as an unfair tax liability for two-earner couples. However, there was strong public reaction against the change on the basis that it discriminated against one-earner couples, and that there was no benefit in the change for two-earner couples on low incomes. The change was seen as a labour market policy aimed at encouraging married women to remain in employment.

In addition to the perceived inequality of the change, the debate focused on the treatment of mothers who made the choice to stay at home to raise their children. It was argued by lobby groups representing the interests of women who stayed at home that this work, which was already undervalued, was further devalued by this change. For some years, stay-at-home parents had lobbied for financial recognition of their contribution to society in caring for the nation's children. The change in the tax system was therefore seen not only as a rejection of this aspiration, but as discrimination against full-time parenting. There was also some concern that the change was unconstitutional on the grounds that it discriminated against the family.

Following strong public pressure, the Government – while maintaining the change in the tax system – introduced a new home carer's allowance. This was seen as an attempt to appease the public reaction to the tax changes. This new allowance consisted of a tax-free allowance of €3,809 for people who cared for a child, an older person or a person with a disability. (This allowance was in addition to other carers' allowances and benefits.) To qualify for the allowance, a number of conditions applied, including the condition that the carer must be married and jointly assessed for income-tax purposes. The allowance varied according to the income of the carer, which had to be below €6,349, and if the couple took advantage of the higher standard-rate tax band for two-income couples they would not be eligible for the allowance. The allowance was welcomed as a move towards recognition of the work of stay-at-home parents and, in part, a compensation for the change in the tax system.

The move to the individualisation of the income tax system opened up a lively debate on the needs of families. The change essentially attempted to equalise the tax liability for all earners on the same level of income. This may make good economic sense and be a desirable move in simplifying the tax system, but it raised questions about support for families, since the main beneficiaries of the change were two-income couples with high earnings and no children. It also raised questions about equality as a policy objective. If the driving force behind the introduction of individualisation is equality between men and women, then how can equality between individuals be achieved? – that is, equality between those who have family responsibilities and those who do not, and equality between different household types.

Individualism and the family

The rise in individualism is also seen as an aspect of the modernising process that accompanies economic development. Ester et al. (1993), in their comparative analysis of the 1990 European Value System data, hypothesise that as countries advance economically, the values of their populations increasingly shift in the direction of individualism and that in the long run societies will converge in the direction of individualised value systems, including the family.

This approach to changes in the family puts individualism in juxtaposition to family values in a way that equates family values with traditionalism and individualism with modernism. The equation is sometimes negatively expressed so that family values are seen as representing fundamentalism and individualism as representing materialism. Furthermore, some of the public debate on current trends in family patterns by the 'new right' – as, for example, with the political rhetoric of the British Conservative Party's call for a return to basic family values – reflects this negative approach to the presumed dichotomy between family values and individualism. This is, of course, an interesting position, with the 'new right' committed to individual freedom in the marketplace, while opposing individual freedom in the family.

We find, then, a tendency to attribute in a somewhat negative way the changes in family behaviours over the past few decades to growing individualism. For example, the drop in birth rates is seen as reflecting a decision by parents to put their own needs over a desire for more children. This is a particularly popular view expressed in the mass media as for example in a major feature in the *Irish Independent* on 23 October 2003. Likewise, the decrease in marriage rates and the accompanying rise in cohabitation and divorce are seen as indicative of people being unwilling to make commitments that might hinder their own personal fulfilment, a view expressed in a feature article by Garret FitzGerald in *The Irish Times*, 11 November 2000. The collective results of these choices can then be seen as ultimately resulting in a rise in non-marital births and lone-parenthood.

It is hard, however, to see how a rise in individualism can account for all changes in family trends, when demographic data are disaggregated. For example, 61 per cent of lone parents in Ireland are widows. In addition, family behaviours do not always reflect individual family members' aspirations or, indeed, values. In a Danish study the preferred family type by mothers with small children was a family in which both parents work part-time, while the children are in kindergarten (Jorgensen, 1991:104). This preference is not, however, reflected in Danish employment patterns, which has one of the lowest levels of part-time employment in the EU – currently standing at 20 per cent of all employed persons (European Commission, 2000: 15). This divergence between behaviours and aspirations is further illustrated by an Irish study which found that 80.7 per cent of mothers in the study agreed that housework should be shared equally between husbands and wives, though in reality very few husbands shared the burden (Kiely, 1995: 148).

Perhaps the answer to this apparent conflict between values of the family and individualism is best answered by the French sociologists Commaille and de Singly, in the introduction to their book *The European Family* (1998). Drawing on the work of Durkheim, they argue that the modern family is a family of relationships which has to ensure for each of its members the conditions for the construction of each person's personal and social identity. In order to achieve this the family group has to be able to reconcile two principles: that of the respect of the individual and his/her autonomy, and that of communal life (1998: 12). They argue that diversity of family forms reflects a diversity not of family models, but of arrangements between the principles of autonomy and those of the organisation of communal life.

In his analysis of the European Values Study of 1990, Peter van den Akker (1993) concluded that marriage, family and modernisation are not incompatible with one another. He found that family values remain very important, and that modernisation does not proceed at the expense of a family orientation; more individualisation does not necessarily mean less family orientation.

Families therefore continue not only as a basic unit of society, but also as major providers of welfare. The provision of welfare is also, however, shared with the state. Traditionally this sharing was provided through the welfare state, as an expression of the ideals of collectivism. Increasingly this collectivism is being replaced by individualism, with its emphasis on individual rights and entitlements. Individualism, in this context, finds its expression in public policy as a move towards the individualisation of the social welfare and taxation systems. This is not to say that individualisation is in any way necessarily associated with neo-liberalism. Individualisation is promoted, not as a mechanism for cutting back on state welfare systems, although it may have this effect, but primarily as a means of securing greater individual freedom and security.

Individualisation in Ireland

In contrast to most other member states of the European Union, individual-isation of the welfare and taxation system is relatively less developed in Ireland. Some efforts have been made to introduce individualisation into the social welfare system, but this has been primarily confined to insurance-based benefits, and has focused on splitting the benefit, while still using the couple as the unit of assessment. Indeed, as is evident from the changes announced in the Budget for 2004 by the Minister for Finance, very little progress has been made in advancing individualisation in the social welfare system other than with administrative individualisation. The taxation system, in spite of claims that the system is being individualised, still retains most of the element of a non-individualised system, with the transfer of tax allowances and credits between spouses.

In contrast to insurance-based benefits, the individualisation of non-insurance based cash payments – such as supplementary welfare allowances – is virtually unknown in Ireland. The same is true across other member states in the European Union, as an analysis of these payments, detailed in the European Union's report *Mutual Information System on Social Protection* (MISSOC) (European Commission, 2001) reveals. All member states (except Greece, because it does not have a supplementary scheme) include in one form or another household composition, such as the presence of spouse, partner and dependent children as the assessment unit – that is, when determining the need of the applicant. Likewise, all member states (again, except Greece) include all resources in the household when determining the resources of the applicant – that is, partners, dependent children and others depending on the member state. It appears then that two approaches coexist: one which is applied in insurance-based benefits, and one which is applied to non-insurance based benefits. A similar situation applies in the case of some categories of the self-employed, particularly in agriculture where most states include 'helping family members' in their calculations of benefits (European Commission, 2001). Thus, while there is a general trend in Ireland – as across the EU – towards the individualisation of the social welfare and taxation systems, it is by no means a consistent trend.

Further inconsistencies are apparent in other areas of government policy and stated policy objectives. The Tanaiste, Mary Harney, at a seminar in Dublin on ageing as reported in *The Irish Times*, 28 January 2004, proposed that families should be obliged to financially support dependent older people. Similarly, a report commissioned by the Department of Social Community and Family Affairs (2002) recommends that the assessment process to deter-mine the entitlement of older people and people with disabilities to state support when in need of long-term care should include an assessment of the carer's capacity to pay as well as that of the care recipient. These policy proposals are in direct conflict with policy objectives advocating an individualised system of social welfare.

Individualisation is therefore not a straightforward matter, as is apparent from the *Report of the Working Group Examining the Treatment of Married, Cohabiting and One-Parent Families under the Tax and Social Welfare Codes* (1999). The Group did not, for example, reach agreement on the individualisation of the social welfare code. Apart from cost implications, there are other considerations that need to be taken into account, such as the historical and cultural context of the schemes already in existence. For Ireland, the Group's report points out that there is a need to protect the needs of older generations of women who were encouraged, and in some cases obliged, to give up employment following marriage.

As already pointed out, the changed labour-market situation and the existence of new forms of family life pose new challenges – apart from the issue of equality – for any social welfare or taxation system. For example, there is the need to deal with pensions and access to health care for those in the status of dependant. There is also the need to deal with employment disincentives when supplements to employment benefit are lost owing to the take-up of employment by another family member, and in the case of taxation there is the need to counteract the negative impact on dual-earner couples of joint assessment. There is also the problem of how to treat cohabiting couples and to remove disincentives to marriage for lone parents.

McLaughlin (1999) identifies what she describes as three main policy drivers for individualisation. The first relates to the labour market. Current tax/benefit regimes impact on women's autonomy and labour-market opportunities. Individualisation would address this relationship between labour-market participation and equality of opportunity therein. The second policy driver is household formation and composition. While she speculates on the possible impact of individualisation on household formation, she notes that the research evidence is weak and that much of the discussion about these concerns has been ideological. The third policy driver is social inclusion/ exclusion. The concern here is with the concentration of poverty among women and children, largely as a result of women's engagement in domestic and caring labour. Social policies, she argues, need to encourage and facilitate earned income and changes in social security systems to more fully recognise the nature of the social insecurities faced by women.

In their analysis of the various policy options, including individualisation, the Working Group identified a framework of principles to be used in the evaluation of the various options. These included adequacy, equity, positive labour and behavioural incentives, consistency and affordability. Whether one agrees or disagrees with the particular set of principles, the approach has many advantages. This approach implicitly recognises the normative nature of policies – that is, that policies are always a choice between alternatives and involve value decisions. Not all values can be equally met. Moroney (1991: 222) illustrates this in his discussion of the three basic value orientations that underpin social policy: freedom, equality and community. Since all three cannot be simultaneously maximised, he argues that the issue becomes one of determining which value is to be given primacy. 'If we begin with a communitarian first principle, absolute liberty is not possible, because responsibility takes precedence over individual rights. The same happens . . . if we begin with freedom, with its emphasis on individualism . . . and a concern for equality would require some restriction at the expense of some individuals' freedom.' This highlights some of the difficulties involved in whatever policy option one selects. As Moroney puts it, 'social policy is the articulation of the ideology between means and ends' (1991: 29). There is no doubt that the traditional welfare state based on the breadwinner model results in inequalities and discrimination, and that these must be addressed. Individualisation, however, while having the potential to eradicate differences in the treatment between individuals and various household types, has its own difficulties.

Equality or security?

As we have seen, one of the driving forces behind the introduction of individualisation in Ireland has been gender equality. As a policy objective, the attainment of equality is generally undisputed. The attainment of equality, however, and whether individualisation is the best or only means of achieving this objective, is another matter. This can be seen by Hervey and Shaw's (1998) analysis of how the European Court of Justice has dealt with EU sex law as applied to women, in their dual role of employees and family carers. The problem they found was not equality legislation itself, or indeed its enforcement, but with conceptions of equality. These conceptions provide the basic reference point against which the European Court of Justice adjudicates.

Hervey and Shaw (1998) identify two types of equality: formal equality and substantive equality. Formal equality essentially means that there is some universal standard of equality based on the notion of treating 'like with like'. In the context of equality between men and women, formal equality has a number of difficulties. First of all, women and men are not alike as, for example, when a woman is pregnant. A formal model of equality in the labour market is based on male norms and thus assumes that the standard is men, and that women must therefore be like men. Those workers who meet the market definition of a worker are entitled to equal treatment. Atypical workers who are predominantly women (such as part-time workers who combine care giving in the family with labour-market attachment) fall outside this definition. Thus the standard of equality becomes 'equal treatment', not 'treatment as an equal'.

Substantive equality, on the other hand, is based on standards of treatment as an equal. Notions of equality are placed in the context of women's position of historical disadvantage in relation to men and therefore take account of the different situations of women, whether historical, biological, cultural or economic. As such, substantive equality is a context-specific model of equality and therefore it does not operate according to a universalist standard, whether applied to men or women, or to the category of women only (Hervey and Shaw, 1998: 48). There are, of course, some difficulties with the use of such a model, as it can be used to justify detrimental treatment of women. Use of substantive equality as the basic standard of equality must be used only with a guarantee of no adverse treatment. Thus, as Hervey and Shaw (1998: 48) point out, 'the notion of what is required in a particular case by a substantive model is modifiable depending upon the current structures which may operate to women's disadvantage.' In relation to caring in families by women, they conclude that 'the structure of care work is such that women's caring burden needs to be firmly in focus both when constructing equality models and when applying them in concrete situations'.

Taking account, then, of these difficulties with standards of equality, what models of welfare can support families, while also protecting the interest of women and, in particular, mothers? By turning to the Scandinavian models of welfare societies, which, although traditionally seen as based on a commitment to equality, we find that they have other objectives in addition to equality. Abrahamson (1999: 38), citing the Norwegian sociologist Willy Martinussen's analysis of the Scandinavian welfare states, challenges the notion that equality is the central value. Security, and not equality, he claims, is the central value. This view is shared by other Scandinavian commentators, such as Anderson (cited and translated by Abrahamson, 1999: 38), who claims that equality has played a minor role in the development of Scandinavian welfare states since the mid-1960s, except for the improvement of life-chances for women. Anderson bases his argument on the redistributive nature of welfare measures which arise from the interplay between the state and civil society, and not (as is argued by Esping-Andersen, 1990) from the interplay between the state and the market.

Healy and Reynolds (1998) also highlight the importance of security in their discussion of paradigms and policy: 'people want assurance against the future' (1998: 6). This assurance or security is central to any system of social welfare. Is this not what the very title 'social security' itself implies? This shift in focus from 'equality' to 'security' opens up a whole new basis of analysis.

Successive partnership agreements between the government and the social partners have sought to strengthen economic and social cohesion. *Sustaining*

Progress: Social Partnership Agreement 2003–2005 (Government of Ireland, 2003), for example, states that 'a central theme of this Agreement is the building of a fair and inclusive society and to ensure that people have the resources and opportunities to live with dignity' (2003: 8). The Agreement goes on to identify the reduction of poverty and in particular child poverty as a specific target of the Agreement (2003: 35). This objective is clearly located in issues of security not equality. Thus, the starting point of any system of income support must address the income needs of families with children.

It is difficult to see how the aims of the National Anti-Poverty Strategy (1997) can be attained through individualisation without a policy of income redistribution. The Combat Poverty Agency (2003), for example, in its pre-budget submission to the government for the 2004 budget states that ending child poverty requires measures to increase family income. The same submission also highlights the significance of additional payments for spouses and partners to the personal welfare rates as important in determining family living standards. It is interesting to note that the theme of the submission is *Investing in the Future: Ending Child and Family Poverty*. To achieve this objective requires a system of income support for all children which would be independent of the parents' employment, income and marital status. In the context of individualisation this is a separate question from how benefits are paid to the parents. The difficulty facing the policy maker is how to redress inequalities of outcome for men and women within families while continuing to support families. Security and equality cannot both be simultaneously maximised.

Conclusion

One of the most fundamental questions confronting policy makers in reforming the welfare and taxation systems is how to combine social solidarity with individualism. Both policy objectives cannot be equally maximised. Social solidarity implies a transfer of resources between individuals both horizontally and vertically. Individualism implies treating everyone equally. The maintenance of social solidarity is seen as central to a fair society while the advancement of individualism is a hallmark of modern democracies. To treat all people the same, as full individualisation implies, would be to put aside the value of social solidarity. As Sennett (2004: 105, 124) puts it, Durkheim believed that social cohesion occurs because one person is always dependent upon another to achieve a feeling of completeness whilst individualism has come to imply a denial of social cohesion.

The argument put forward in this chapter is that rather than focusing on the opposition of these two values that the debate should focus on the need for security. This would not only overcome the somewhat sterile argument that equality can only be attained through individualisation, but would provide a more productive approach to solving the question of how to combine social solidarity and individualism. The provision of an equitable welfare and taxation system that provides security for all must be the driving force for any policy reform. This is an undisputed objective of all welfare states including Ireland.

Chapter 5

Women, autonomy and bodily integrity

Patricia Kennedy*

Introduction

While many women in Ireland have gained greater access to the labour market and by extension to welfare, new inequalities have arisen between groups of women. Many women in Ireland today have been able to enter the labour market because their less well-off sisters from around the globe have come to Ireland to replace them by doing both their cleaning and caring work in the domestic sphere. On the other hand, some women in low-paid jobs find themselves competing with women coming from Third World countries and Eastern Europe who are prepared to do this cleaning and caring work in the public sphere, working for longer hours and for less money. The number of 'language schools' in Ireland (viewed as fronts for illegal immigrants) has increased, and the number of 'wives' bought from China, Thailand and the Philippines has risen simultaneously, made easier by the World Wide Web. There have been official investigations into sexual slavery: Operation Quest was set up by the Gardaí in response to serious concerns and allegations in relation to trafficking of people, in particular of women and children. Serious questions have thus emerged in relation to rights: human, civil, political and social. This chapter theorises on the possibility of sustaining a socially acceptable standard of living outside the labour market and explores in the Irish context whether policies permit, encourage or discourage the de-commodification of labour. It explores the concept of personal autonomy, suggesting that the most basic aspect of autonomy is bodily integrity, which for women means control over one's own sexuality and reproductive capacities. De-commodification, citizenship, autonomy and bodily integrity are used to theorise Irish social policy in relation to women as workers, carers, cleaners and sex workers.

* I would like to thank Dr Kieran Allen and the MSocSc (Social Policy) class 2003–4 for their comments on this chapter.

Commodification/de-commodification

Since the publication of Esping-Andersen's *The Three Worlds of Welfare Capitalism* in 1990 there has been an eruption of writing on welfare regimes. Central to these writings is the concept of commodification/de-commodification. No one, however, has directly addressed the concept with the same attention as Esping-Andersen. In his seminal work, he devotes a 19-page chapter to the subject of de-commodification. He describes as 'the most conflictual issue in social policy' when 'labour power also became a commodity, peoples' rights to survive outside the labour market are at stake' (1990: 35). He reviews classical Marxist and liberal thought on the subject, concluding that 'Labor's commodity form has been a central concern of modern philosophy, ideology and social theory' (1990: 35). He notes that liberal thinkers and their contemporary followers opposed alternatives to cash as a variable that would interfere with market equilibrium. He accredits certain ambivalence to Marxists, with some arguing in favour of the abolition of wage labour and others looking to policies of social amelioration as the route to reform. Esping-Andersen refers to the Poor Laws as 'an active social policy designed to make wage employment and the cash nexus the linchpin of the person's very existence. Welfare, if not survival, came to depend on the willingness of someone to hire one's labor power' (1990: 36). The relevance of this argument for Ireland will become clear later in this chapter. He indicates that without state welfare or the assets of property the worker becomes imprisoned by the market and must behave as a commodity in order to survive (1990: 36). In looking at recent female immigrants to Ireland, this rings true. He notes that the commodification of wants and people, while strengthening capitalism, weakens the worker. Looking at freedom in the liberal sense of a worker's freedom to choose between jobs, employers, etc, Esping-Andersen agrees with Marx, Polanyi and Lindblom whom he suggests claim that 'it is a freedom behind prison walls, and hence fictitious' (1990: 37). He refers to labour's inability to withhold itself from the market 'without recourse to alternative means of subsistence' (1990: 37). This is often ignored in common discourse in Ireland today in relation to women working in the sex industry. It is often said that women work in lapdancing clubs and on the streets and in brothels because they choose to, but Ruhama (a project working with women in prostitution in Dublin) challenges the question of choice in the context of limited alternatives (personal communication, Febuary 2004).

Esping-Andersen reminds us of the vulnerability of the worker when commodified, who 'is easily destroyed by even minor social contingencies, such as illness, and by macro-events such as the business cycle . . . As commodities, workers are replaceable, easily redundant and atomized'. Esping-Andersen (1990) claims that de-commodification is a necessary prerequisite for workers' political mobilisation. Lewis (1992) argues that the worker he has in mind is the male worker whose mobilisation also relies on female support. Workers have differential opportunities for becoming politically mobilised. For example, how possible is it for the pregnant woman or new mother to become politically mobilised? Cousins refers to:

> The weakness of a transient category of persons with little organisational repre-
> sentation (pregnant women who are not in employment) in the formation of
> social policy and highlights the extent to which trade union priorities involve their
> own members rather than welfare recipients generally (and particularly women
> who are not in employment) (1995: 114–15).

Looking at changes in maternity entitlements for women in Ireland shows that not only have they become eroded since first introduced in 1911 but also that they have increasingly become payments to which only women employed in the regulated labour market are entitled (Kennedy, 2002).

Esping-Andersen indicates, in agreement with Polanyi, that de-commodifi-cation is a precondition for a tolerable level of individual welfare and security. It is also necessary to facilitate collective action and as Esping-Andersen concludes 'it is accordingly, the alpha and the omega of the unity and solidarity required for labor-movement development' (1990: 37). He points out that historically in relation to social policy, conflicts have mainly revolved around two issues: the degree of de-commodification which is acceptable and the quality of social rights. To liberate workers from market dependence would involve: 'The extension of rights beyond the terrain of absolute need; and second, the upgrading of benefits to match normal earnings and average living standards in the nation' (1990: 46). In the Irish context entitlement can be associated with need. This is the social-assistance tradition. Entitlement can also be on the basis of work history. This is the social-insurance tradition. Or, it can relate to universal rights of citizenship. As a result, access to the labour market and to welfare is stratified in Ireland. This is the crux of what this chapter explores in relation to women in Ireland.

Women's access to regulated employment

Employment is a general prerequisite for independence. Traditionally, the majority of women in Ireland have been denied access to paid employment. Ireland has been a society in which women, especially married women and mothers, were denied access to the paid labour market (Conroy Jackson, 1993; Smyth, 1993; Kennedy, 2002). This is now changing. Even though we have had employment equality legislation for almost thirty years, there still remains a gender pay gap with women earning 15 per cent less than men, according to the Department of Justice, Equality and Law Reform Consultative Group on Male/Female Wage Differentials (DJELR, 2003). However, the economic boom of the nineties, increasing house prices and smaller families has ensured that more mothers have entered the labour market. In 1971, married women accounted for only 14 per cent of the female workforce, whereas in 1996, 41.1 per cent of Irish women aged 15 or over were in the labour force (CSO, 1997). Almost 50 per cent of women living with a husband/partner in a family unit with children were in employment in June–August 2001 compared with 43.6 per cent three years earlier. The most notable increase in employment partici-pation was for mothers in family units where the youngest child was aged 5 to 14. In this category, the percentage in employment increased from 47.3 per cent to 56.2 per cent between mid-1998 and mid-2001 (CSO, 2001). The corresponding figure September–November 2003 was 61.3 per cent. For the same period, 53 per cent of all mothers were in the labour force (CSO, 2004).

Women working outside the home need a good standard of accessible, affordable childcare. This has never been available in Ireland where childcare facilities are underdeveloped and there is no tax relief on childcare. Few work-place nurseries are in existence (DJELR, 2003). An ideology which postulates that childcare provision is a private issue ensures that Ireland has one of the lowest levels of public childcare in the EU.

The Chambers of Commerce of Ireland in a 2001 study examines the issue of childcare in a labour market context from the employers' perspective. It highlights ongoing labour shortages, despite recent changes in the employment environment. It remarks on the impact that the lack of affordable childcare has on employers' ability to recruit staff:

> given that childcare still tends to be primarily the responsibility of women, the deficit of affordable childcare also raises the issue of equality of opportunity in terms of labour market participation (2001: 2).

It is argued in this study that the overall level of funding earmarked for the development of childcare in Ireland should be reviewed. While it acknowledges the allocation of €368 million under the National Development Plan and the anti-inflationary package introduced in 2000, it says there is a need for a much greater level of resourcing, arguing that an overall review of funding should be accompanied by a long-term strategy for the development and maintenance of the sector. It states that 'in order to attract and retain staff, employers need to continue to develop family-friendly arrangements for the workplace. This will pose challenges for small businesses in particular' (2001: 2). In half of the companies surveyed, women made up 50 per cent or more of employees. In 21 per cent of companies, staff with children aged 12 years or under comprised the majority of the workforce. Respondents in 57 per cent of the companies surveyed were aware of a query or complaint being made by an employee regarding childcare provision in the previous 12 months. Requests for flexible hours (38 per cent), or complaints about the cost of childcare services (33 per cent), were the most common. Thirteen per cent of the companies experienced a situation in the previous 12 months in which one or more of the employees resigned their post to care for children. Almost a third of companies (31 per cent) believed that the lack of affordable or available childcare had a negative impact on their ability to recruit or retain staff. Cost (72 per cent), unavailability (65 per cent) and poor quality (13 per cent) were the principal difficulties faced by employees when looking for childcare services (2001: 3).

Ehrenreich and Hochschild argue that in both rich and poor countries, fewer families can rely solely on a male breadwinner. In this context they ask 'who will take care of the children, the sick, the elderly? Who will make dinner and clean the house?'(2003: 3). In Ireland, who is fulfilling those tasks and what protection are such workers guaranteed? In the introduction to *Global Woman*, Ehrenreich and Hochschild argue that owing to globalisation, women are on the move around the world as never before in history. Images are presented in the media of women executives jet-setting, but what of the migration of women from poor countries where they work as nannies, maids and sex workers? (2003: 2). They argue that in the absence of help from male partners, many women have succeeded in tough 'male world' careers only by turning over the care of their children, elderly parents and homes to women from the Third World.

> This is the female underside of globalisation, whereby millions of Josephines from poor countries in the south migrate to do the 'women's work' of the north – work that affluent women are no longer able or willing to do. These migrant workers often leave their own children in the care of grandmothers, sisters and sisters-in-law. Sometimes a young daughter is drawn out of school to care for her younger siblings (2003: 2–3).

While there is a dearth of empirical research on this subject in Ireland, there is evidence to suggest that there is currently a booming industry in domestic nannies in Ireland (Reynolds, 2003). In the course of interviewing refugee and asylum-seeking women in relation to pregnancy and maternity in 1999–2000, I encountered many women who had left their own children in their countries of origin in the hope of sending them money and, at some stage, 'sending for them'. Many women had left partners also. However, this was generally not said to be for economic reasons but rather for political and civil rights violations. On another occasion I interviewed a Dublin mother, who is a regular user of a private leisure centre where, she claims, mothers swim while their children are in the care of the nannies they refer to, not by name, but as 'my Filipino'. Williams suggests that 'In many European countries migrants have limited access to social, civil and political rights yet they are part of a political economy which depends upon their labour' (1999: 682). She talks of the 'racialisation of welfare policies' (1999: 682). Daly and Standing (2001: 5) suggest that there is a tendency for migrants to be used to fulfil the role of carer: 'Many carers worldwide are migrant women and there is a chain of care stretching from the less developed nations to the industrialized countries'. Many leave their own care in the hands of others. Care work is the principal export of the Philippines. 'In all cases, those providing the care have to struggle with potential oppression and exploitation that is uncomfortable to contemplate, even for those of us far removed from the scene' (2001: 5). It is necessary at this stage to look more closely at what is involved in caring work.

Care work

Lynch and McLaughlin refer to 'love labour' as:

> not like materially productive labour as originally conceived. It is not about the moulding and manipulation of raw materials to create some desired end product . . . Love labour involves reciprocity in most cases . . . social relations are not one way (1995: 264).

They distinguish between caring for and caring about, and refer to the fact that 'caring for' can be commodified and that this is in fact a booming industry. However, caring about is more difficult to commodify arguing that 'one cannot provide love on a rational contractual basis like one provides other services' (1995: 261). As Lynch and McLaughlin explain, 'one cannot pay someone to love someone else . . . one cannot pay one to hug one's children and pretend that this is "one's own hug"' (1995: 263). The very nature of love labour is very much the type of work that is involved in caring for infants. When the care giver has her own demanding emotional, psychological, social and physical needs, both parties are vulnerable. Nic Ghiolla Phádraig (1994) refers to the vulnerability of the recipient of care, an issue which has become increasingly visible in feminist writing (Morris, 1991). Feminist writers, including Pateman (1988) and Delphy and Leonard (1992), have focused on the exploitative nature of caring work. Yet caring is something that very many women want to do and get the utmost enjoyment, satisfaction and fulfilment from this role (Benn, 1998). Daly and Standing argue that 'care is precious, and therefore suffers if it is treated as something close to forced labour' (2001: 1). They pose the question: 'How will carers obtain income security?' They suggest that in civilised democratic society, security will come only when recipients as well as care providers have economic security. This will only be achieved when caregivers and care recipients are represented by strong, democratic and accountable organisations ensuring that their interests are taken into account. They express optimism that 'in the next few years' great progress will be made in these respects (2001: 9).

Mary Daly (2001: 33) argues that care is part of the fabric of society and is integral to social development. Daly and Lewis (1998) define care as the activities and relations involved in meeting the physical and emotional needs of dependent adults and children, together with the normative economic and social frameworks within which these are assigned and carried out. Daly (2001: 48) refers to the quality of care work. This must guarantee optimal conditions of work for the carer. This would involve a choice in relation to doing the care work; conditions of work; job security; payment; hours and supports. It is necessary to question whether the carer can care for him/ herself also. Lewis argues that carers, whether paid or unpaid, share a dependent status as a result of their restricted access to the labour market and the implications this carries for earnings and pensions (2001: 64). She concludes that 'if care is not valued, it is degraded and exploitative' (2001: 72). Williams claims that 'care suggests duty, responsibility, obligation, power, control, oppression, conflict, altruism, love, solidarity and reciprocity' (1999: 678) and continues 'The values of care need to inform the values of citizenship: they involve concepts to do with responsibilities and relationships and they can gender practices of moral deliberation and dialogue grounded in everyday activities'.

Valuing caring work

In the decade following the publication of *The Three Worlds of Capitalism*, Esping-Andersen's work was the target of consistent and varied criticism in relation to his failure to address unpaid caring work, which is primarily undertaken by women (Taylor-Gooby, 1991), (Orloff, 1993), (Lewis, 1992), (O'Connor, 1993). Taylor-Gooby (1991: 96) criticises Esping-Andersen for his inadequate treatment of women and his concentration on formal employment to the neglect of unpaid informal caring. He suggests that divisions between formal and informal work exist where the public and the private meet and claims that in conservative/corporatist regimes care work falls on women in the informal sector and 'is outside the realm of welfare citizenship' (1991: 97). He criticises Esping-Andersen for ignoring the fact that participation in the paid labour market requires a 'support-system of unwaged work outside the labour market'. As Fiona Williams reminds us: 'a worker's independence is only achieved through hidden support systems: childcare, cleaning, shopping, cooking, etc' (1999: 676). This being an argument intrinsic to Marxist analysis and linked to accumulation, legitimisation and social reproduction, Taylor-Gooby acknowledges the value of women's work and the tremendous burden they have to bear. He concludes that 'welfare citizenship in capitalist societies is at least two dimensional'. It involves not only the political ideologies of liberal, social democratic and conservative regimes and their organisation of the relation between state welfare and social class conflicts but also 'the way in which government manages the unwaged work of social care and handles issues of equality' (1991: 103). In Ireland, it would appear that government policy is to ignore the issue of care work and also to ignore the unequal status it guarantees providers, both paid and unpaid of such care work.

Jane Lewis, joined in her critique of Esping-Andersen by other feminist theorists including Orloff (1993) and O'Connor (1993), also criticises him for ignoring unpaid labour and argues that the concept of welfare regimes must take into consideration the sphere of unpaid as well as paid work: 'work is defined as paid work and welfare as policies that permit, encourage or discourage the de-commodification of labour' (1992: 160). She acknowledges the value of such an analysis for women. Lewis and related theorists (Sainsbury, 1996) stress that the relationship between paid work, unpaid work and welfare is gendered. Furthermore, she claims that the concepts of de-commodification and dependency have 'a gendered meaning that is rarely acknowledged' (1992: 161). She criticises Esping-Andersen for his gender blind concept of de-commodification, saying '. . . de-commodification for women is likely to result in their carrying out unpaid caring work' (1992: 16). Williams writes of interdependence as 'the principle, which brings into play all those emotional, material, physical networks of unequal reciprocity, and creates the basis for autonomy'. She stresses that personal autonomy is only achieved through collective effort' (1999: 677).

Lewis argues that women have historically achieved welfare entitlements on the basis of their own dependency status, linked to the gendered division generally accepted as natural and linked to women's reproductive role. The position of women within the different states according to Lewis 'revolves around two related issues, the valuing of unpaid work and the sharing of it' (1992: 170). She concludes that 'political and institutional power is crucial not so much for securing material well-being, as for putting issues that are central to enlarging women's choices, like the division and valuing of unpaid work onto the agenda' (1992: 171). Orloff (1993), in dealing with Esping-Andersen's concept of de-commodification, writes of state, market and family relations in an attempt to introduce women's unpaid work as a variable. She refers to stratification, which occurs as a result of the gender dimension. She refers to gender differentiation in entitlements when rights to benefits are based on the traditional gendered division of labour. She refers to gender inequalities in relation to payments received by men and women usually associated with gender differentiation. Orloff introduces access to paid work and the capacity to form an autonomous household as aspects of de-commodification.

Esping-Andersen (1999: 44) in his later writings acknowledges that 'the concept of de-commodification is inoperable for women unless welfare states, to begin with, help them become de-commodified'. He suggests that:

> The concept of de-commodification has relevance only for individuals already fully and irreversibly inserted in the wage relationship. In practice, this means that it increasingly, does speak to women, too. Yet, it remains a fact that a large proportion of women, and some men are institutionally 'pre-commodified'; their welfare derives from being in a family. The functional equivalent for many women is family dependency. In other words, female independence necessitates 'de-familizing' welfare obligations (1999: 45).

This means policies that lessen individuals' reliance on the family; that maximise individuals' command of economic resources independently of familial or conjugal reciprocities. It is like the concept of de-commodification, more a matter of degree than of an 'either-or'.

Market participation and regulated employment are linked to citizenship status. Not everyone living in a society is permitted to partake in regulated employment. Only some people have a right to work. Participation in the labour market generally guarantees access not only to paid labour but also to welfare payments. Access to the labour market guarantees certain social rights. It is the gate to accessing welfare. There is another gate for those outside the labour market, which in Ireland has tended to be associated with residual welfare. T. H. Marshall (1950) refers to the extension of citizenship rights as an evolutionary process. He differentiates between civil, political and social rights. Civil rights are linked to the rights required for individual freedom, liberty of the person, speech, thought and faith, to own property, to make contracts and to justice. Political rights relate to one's right to participate in exercising political power and voting. Marshall defines social rights as encompassing 'from a modicum of economic welfare and security to the right to share to the full in the social heritage and to live the life of a civilised being according to the standards prevailing in society' (1950: 11).

Ruth Lister argues that without social citizenship, political and civil status will be undermined. She states that:

> Social citizenship rights also promote the 'de-commodification of labour' by decoupling the living standards of individual citizens from their 'market value' so that they are not totally dependent on selling their labour power on the market (1997: 17).

Lister stresses the importance of linking social citizenship rights with human need. She adopts Doyal and Gough's (1991: 54) model of human need, which stresses the importance of personal autonomy. O'Connor (1993) also values this concept.

Autonomy and bodily integrity

Sainsbury (1999:1) states that 'the bases of entitlement differ in their emancipatory or regulatory potential for women'. She refers to the extension of the concept of rights by feminist writers (Shaver, 1994) to include personal autonomy, going beyond the ability to form an autonomous household to incorporate personhood and bodily integrity. Friedman (1997), a feminist philosopher, reviews both mainstream and feminist writing on autonomy. Arguing that the concept was in the 1970s criticised by feminist philosophers as being too closely associated with individual liberalism, Friedman argues now that mainstream and feminist philosophers have come more into line with an emphasis on relational autonomy, recognising that personal autonomy for many women must incorporate the relationships which they value. However, I would argue that bodily integrity is the most basic human right. Feminist writers, particularly those often associated with radical feminism including Rich, Dworkin, O'Brien and Daly have long argued the centrality of bodily integrity: control over one's sexuality and reproductive capacities is central to women's liberation. This chapter seeks to link this feminist approach to writing by welfare theorists on personal autonomy and argues that this must become the crucial element of de-commodification. One is only truly de-commodified when one can exercise personal autonomy in relation to one's body, sexuality and reproductive capacity. In relation to welfare provision there are many areas where bodily integrity is crucial, for example in relation to the elderly and people with disabilities. However, the focus here is on non-national women in Ireland working as carers, domestic workers and in the sex industry.

In relation to bodily integrity, Williams refers to 'the right of the individual to protect his/her body against external or internal risk. The body is a site of control, resistance, and pleasure; it is inscribed in the social relations of power in which it exists' (1999: 680). She continues 'our bodies mark the physical boundaries of our sense of self, our own dignity and self-respect. Respect for the integrity of the body is fundamental to the maintenance of the autonomy of the welfare citizen' (1999: 680).

Sex work

In 1910, Emma Goldman, a feminist from a Russian Jewish family who emigrated to the USA while still in her teens, wrote:

> Our reformers have suddenly made a great discovery – the white slave traffic. The papers are full of these 'unheard-of-conditions' and lawmakers are already planning a new set of laws to check the horror (Schneir: 1994: 309).

These words could be stated in today's Ireland. While Irish women have always been involved in prostitution, the focus in public discourse nowadays tends to centre on non-national women. The media is full of tales of sex slaves in lapdancing clubs; at the beginning of 2004, a drama shown on national television, *Proof*, explored the issue of sexual enslavement in such 'entertainment' venues. O'Byrne (2003) discusses the complexity of defining slavery but he agrees that the features outlined by Bales and Robbins (2000: 16) are useful: 'That the slave is controlled by another person; the owner appropriates the labour power of the slave and that the slave's activities are controlled by the threat or use of violence'. The Universal Declaration of Human Rights guarantees certain rights in relation to: life, liberty and security of person (Article 3); not to be held in slavery or servitude; slavery and the slave trade shall be prohibited in all their forms (Article 4); no one shall be subjected to torture or to cruel, inhuman or degrading treatment or punishment (Article 5).

In Ireland in 2003, the Department of Justice, Equality and Law Reform launched *Operation Quest*, the Garda investigation into suspected links between lapdancing and criminal activity, and police raids, arrests and deportations have resulted. A focus group carried out by this writer with a group of university students in Dublin asserted that visiting a lapdancing club was an acceptable part of a night out for both young men and women. One woman I interviewed, who had visited a lapdancing club in Cork, had accompanied a male customer who had paid for 'a private dance' which involved sitting on his hands in a private room while the woman danced naked. The interviewee explained how she had talked to the dancer and praised her dancing to be told by the dancer that she was the first 'customer' to have spoken to her.

Donaghy, in the *Irish Independent*, 17 January 2004, wrote that women working in lapdancing clubs were coming to Ireland on 'student visas' on the pretext that they were attending classes full time. It was reported that one lapdancing club owner was so desperate to get foreign girls into the country that he set up a 'dance school' and so was able to bring dancers in to Ireland on student permits. The *Irish Independent* has also reported clubs applying for visas to bring in young women as 'cleaners' and 'nannies'. However, the newspaper claimed that the girls are working as exotic dancers and, in some cases, prostitutes. This has been verified by Ruhama, a Dublin-based project which works with women in prostitution. Gardaí have confirmed that women working in lapdancing clubs were paid by men for sex. The country's lapdancing clubs have consistently denied that clients are paid for anything more than a private dance with a girl. However, detectives investigating the clubs have been made aware that the dancers engaged in sex with clients after accompanying them home or to a hotel. The vast majority of young foreign women working in the clubs are coming here on student visas which allow them to work up to 20 hours a week during school time and 40 hours in holiday time. Gardaí believe club owners are exploiting a loophole in the legislation and while the women are registered as students, they are part-time students – attending courses one day a week – and full-time dancers (Donaghy, 2004).

Donaghy reported that since the Department of Enterprise, Trade and Employment suspended issuing work permits to lapdancers the previous year, club owners had been forced to find new ways to obtain girls. New legislation was being drafted by the Department of Justice at the time of writing that would bring Ireland into line with current EU trafficking legislation and which would significantly increase penalties for trafficking. So far, nobody has been charged here with trafficking in human beings but new legislation will make it easier for Gardaí to bring charges against those suspected of bringing people into this country for the purposes of sexual exploitation. Under existing legislation, trafficking does not apply if women are registered as students. Another difficulty for the Gardaí is that they must prove that the trafficker is making a financial gain.

The Ruhama Project reported in 2004 that as many as seventy women were trafficked in 2003 for use in the sex industry. Ruhama's objective is 'to offer a safe, non-judgemental, space to women involved in prostitution; to offer support tailored to each individual woman's circumstances and needs' (Annual Report 2001–2002: 3). It identifies the new challenges of lapdancing and sexual trafficking of girls and young women. The women are controlled and abused by traffickers and pimps. Violence and threats to their families back home usually result.

> From our own experience, anecdotal evidence and occasional encounters with foreign women on outreach we are aware of a very significant number of women trafficked into or through Ireland for the purpose of prostitution. Because of the level of fear in the women's lives and practical barriers such as the language barrier, it is quite difficult to make contact with women in this situation. (Ruhama, 2002: 12)

They refer to 'the presence and extent of violence, the trauma and psychological damage and the high level of anxiety raised by the threat of violence from their traffickers and the fear of being deported by immigration authorities' (Ruhama, 2002: 12). Involvement in prostitution is not confined to non-national women. It is indicated in the Ruhama Report that in 2002 there were notable peaks in April and August of women reporting that they were trying to make money for First Communions and back-to-school expenses (Ruhama, 2002: 7). As Connolly puts it, prostitution is 'a violence against women and as such a fundamental abuse of their human rights' (2002: 13). The Ruhama Report cites the 1949 *Convention for the Suppression of Traffic in Persons and the Exploitation of the Prostitution of Others*: 'prostitution and the accompanying evil of the traffic in persons for the purposes of prostitution are incompatible with the dignity and worth of the human person and endanger the welfare of the individual, the family and the community'.

In a statement of its philosophy and values, Ruhama declares: 'We understand sexual exploitation as a practice by which person(s) achieve sexual gratification or financial gain/advancement through the abuse of a person's sexuality by abrogating that person's human right to dignity, equality, autonomy and physical and mental well-being' (Ruhama Philosophy and Values, March 2003). In this context bodily integrity and personal autonomy are denied women in Ireland because they are allowed work in Ireland only outside the protection of the labour market. They are totally commodified. In order to survive they must sell not only their labour power but also their bodies.

Racialised citizenship

Coakley (1997: 181) defines social citizenship in terms of 'access to the average standard of living in a society, and to a sense of inclusiveness in the life of the community'. By this definition there is indeed differential social citizenship in Ireland. Between 1995 and 2002 the number of people seeking refugee status rose from 424 to 11,634 (Immigrant Council of Ireland, 2003: 50). Apart from a limited number granted permission to work in 2000, the majority are not allowed to work. Thus they are denied access to the labour market and associated welfare provision. Rathzel defines racism as 'all the ways in which equal rights are denied to groups because they are defined as not belonging to the nation-state in which they live' (1992: 25). Fanning et al. (2001: 5) indicate that asylum-seeking families in Ireland under direct provision experience extreme levels of income poverty and extreme deprivation including inadequate diet and inability to purchase sufficient and adequate food. Their study argues that extreme deprivation experienced by such families includes malnutrition amongst expectant mothers; ill-health related to diet amongst babies; weight loss amongst children; worries about the health of children, and hunger amongst adults. Kennedy and Murphy-Lawless (2002), in their qualitative study of refugee and asylum-seeking women in Ireland, report similar findings. Faughnan et al. refer to the system of direct provision as one of 'reduced welfare payments and stigmatising and institutionalising effects' (2002: 17). This study of the role of community welfare officers in relation to asylum seekers found that one fifth of CWOs questioned considered that the system of direct provision had no strengths at all. In relation to the weaknesses of the system, Faughnan et al. cite the CWOs as concluding that these included quality of life, with direct provision resulting in boredom and depression. Lister argues that the treatment of different groups of non-citizen residents 'operates as something of a litmus test for the degree of inclusiveness of substantive citizenship in any particular society' (1997: 43).

Yuval-Davis argues that there are contradictory citizenship processes between different groups of women. She raises questions in relation to citizenship and women:

> Their specific rights (and duties) as women – as wives, as mothers, and as reproducers of the next generation of citizens . . . women of different ethnicities and races (as well as women of different classes) have a differential access to the state, even as women. Any examination of women as citizens should include not only questions of sexual politics, but also questions of national and racist exclusions (1992: 15).

With reference to post-1993 Europe, Brah states: 'these structures of class, racism, gender, ethnicity and sexuality cannot be treated as "independent variables" but as interdependent' (1992: 19). Brah cogently explains this differential citizenship: 'Citizenship rights in Europe are currently underpinned by a racial division between *citizens, demizens* (people with established residential and civic rights in one of the member states but with 'Third Country' nationality) and *migrants* who essentially have extremely limited rights' (1992: 21–22). Daly and Standing suggest that 'Real de-commodification can only come from real freedom, which is precisely why some of us assert that the need for basic income security as an unconditional right of a 'Good Society' (Daly and Standing: 2001: 2).

Non-national workers

In recent decades there has been an increase in migration into Ireland from Eastern Europe and Asia and Africa. Much debate has raged in relation to the rights of non-nationals to obtain paid labour in Ireland. Debate has raged too in relation to citizenship status, which, once achieved, allows greater access to social rights. Different groups, stratified according to colour, race, nationality, gender and skill, have differential access to the regulated labour market. Like Irish mothers before the equality legislation of 1973, many are denied full access to welfare yet are also denied the opportunity to sell their labour legally. There has been some limited debate in relation to the employment of women, among them 'lapdancers' particularly from Eastern Europe. A trip through the public playgrounds of Dublin suburbs makes clear the important role as child-minders which immigrants from Eastern Europe, Africa and Asia are fulfilling in this grossly under-resourced area.

While the statistics are unreliable, the trends indicate that the number of non-EU migrant workers in Ireland is growing. 'In short, Ireland has moved from being one of the most homogeneous countries in the EU, to a country with a rate of change which is almost unparalleled in speed and scale' (Immigrant Council of Ireland, 2003: 11). The Immigrant Council of Ireland (2003) argues that migrant workers are involved in work in all sectors of the economy, but a large number are concentrated in low-skilled or unskilled employment in the service sector, catering, agriculture and fisheries and industry. Thirty-seven per cent are in the service industry. Twenty-five per cent are in catering, 16 per cent in agriculture and fisheries. Interestingly two per cent are recorded as being in 'entertainment'. The 2003 report cites an estimate by the UN that emigrants' remittances are second only to oil in the global generation of money and far ahead of foreign aid (2003: 21). The migrant worker is entitled to broadly similar rights as Irish nationals to employment, health and education at primary and secondary level for the children, housing and social welfare (2003: 35). There is no formal right of family reunification.

Ruhs (2003) shows that the overall number of work permits issued in Ireland to non-EU nationals increased from 5,750 in 1999 to 40,504 in 2002. This is an increase equivalent to 600 per cent (2003:14). He indicates that between 1999 and early March 2003, nationals of 152 different countries were issued with work permits. Five countries which topped the league accounted for 41.3 per cent of all work permit holders in 2002. These were Latvia (9.8 per cent); Lithuania (9.6 per cent); the Philippines (8 per cent); Poland (7.8 per cent) and Romania (6.1 per cent) (2003: 16). While the majority of permit holders were male, Ruhs indicates that there has been 'a feminisation of new work permit holders' (2003: 18) with a decrease in the share of males in total new work permit holders from 71.6 per cent in 1999 to 62.6 per cent in 2002. The majority of new work permit holders in 2002 were employed in Dublin: 40.38 per cent. Data presented by Ruhs (2003: 20) shows that 76.7 per cent of work permit holders were employed in the services sector in 2002. Using CSO data Ruhs shows that in 2002, 21.3 per cent of non-EU nationals were located in the service sector, hotels and restaurants; 16.3 per cent in financial and other business services; 14.5 per cent in the health sector and 10.8 per cent in the retail and wholesale trade. Interestingly, of those non-EU and non-OECD countries, 75.8 per cent of all work permit holders are in the domestic service sector (57.5 per cent are from the Philippines); 73.8 per cent in medical and nursing with 31.6 per cent from the Philippines) (2003: 23).

Ruhs indicates that the number of hours worked per week by non-EU workers were in excess of the average working hours for all those employed in Ireland (41.6 hours as opposed to 38.1 hours). The differential was greatest in relation to health (+ 15.66 hours); hotels and restaurants (+ 6.9 hours); wholesale, trade and retail (+ 5 hours) and personal and protective services (+ 4.8 hours). Informal interviews, which I conducted with Irish women working in contract cleaning firms in Dublin in February 2004, indicate that many workers feel threatened by the presence of non-nationals who are described as 'excellent workers who are willing to work for longer hours, for less money' than their Irish colleagues. Ruhs's study indicates that the lowest weekly pay offered to work permit holders was to personal and protective workers in the service sector of €253 per week, the equivalent of the minimum wage. Given that the majority of workers are in Dublin, high transport and housing costs guarantee a life in poverty for such workers. It also draws attention to the even more precarious situation of workers in the black economy without even minimal employment rights and minimum wage.

Conclusion

Historically, with high levels of emigration from Ireland, many hundreds of thousands of people who were outside the labour market had three options: 1) emigrate to access resources in another state; 2) survive, courtesy of the remittances sent home by family members who had chosen option one; 3) depend on what I loosely call here 'the mixed economy of welfare'. Despite popular discourse to the contrary, many emigrants were women who were denied – culturally and by legislation – access to the labour market and to welfare payments in Ireland. It would appear that there has been a reversal of this situation in recent years with what Ruhs (2002) describes as the 'feminisation of migration' into Ireland. There is ample evidence to show that Ireland is experiencing the globalisation of women's work and most apparently in the traditional work of women in caring, cleaning and prostitution (Ehrenreich and Hochschild, 2003).

It has been argued here that while more Irish women and in particular mothers have entered the paid labour market, they have been replaced in their traditional roles by non-national women, sometimes here illegally, in the most extreme cases as a result of trafficking. These women are commodified, forced into selling their labour and, in some cases, their bodies to survive. The luxury of autonomy, used by many writers in relation to the ability to form a household, is broadened here in line with radical feminist thinking to incorporate its most fundamental element: bodily integrity, control over one's sexuality and reproductive capacities.

Looking at the current situation in Ireland in relation to the de-commodification of women, the labour market and the welfare system could be described as apartheid. O'Byrne refers to apartheid as 'segregation, the legal and political endorsement and institutionalisation of discrimination . . . it involves the assigning of an individual at birth into one or another class of citizen' (2003: 241). Citizenship in Ireland is both gendered and racialised. In turn, access to the employment market and welfare is stratified according to gender and nationality. Women's autonomy and bodily integrity are not guaranteed. This, in the most extreme cases, results in sexual slavery. In other cases, women are denied access to regulated employment. When in such employment they are imprisoned owing to the linking of work permits to the employer rather than the employee.

A central issue is in relation to whether income security should be guaranteed only for those linked to the labour market. This would be through an insurance scheme. Daly and Standing (2001) question whether there should there be a basic income for all and if so 'who are all?' They question whether income security should be attached to all forms of labour, paid and unpaid or to all forms of existence. Standing outlines the social insurance/social assistance and the citizenship models (2001: 27) and calls for the 'extension of universal human rights' (2001: 28). This necessitates further exploration of rights, be they human, civil, political or social.

Chapter 6

Fathers, identity and well-being

Michael Rush

Introduction

Fatherhood is becoming increasingly central to debates about Irish family policy. This chapter argues that social policy perspectives on fatherhood in Ireland bear similarities to the debate on fatherhood in the USA where it is framed within a neo-conservative and neo-liberal preoccupation with rising social pathology and the perceived welfare dependency of lone mothers. It contrasts the new politics of fatherhood in Ireland and the USA with fatherhood discourses from Sweden, where the debate is framed around an axis of the sharing of unpaid labour in the home through parental leave regimes and public responsibility for childcare. Emerging policy debates in Ireland are mapped out here by examining the discussion on fatherhood contained in the *Final Report of the Commission on The Family: Strengthening Families for Life* (Commission on the Family, 1998) and in the research and publications from the Springboard Family Support Initiative, a community-based early intervention programme to support vulnerable families.

A major development in welfare theory has been the introduction of a male-breadwinner analysis approach to comparative social policy, which argues that political feminism has had little impact on welfare state development in Sweden (Lewis, 1992: 162). Male breadwinning analysis is here contrasted with Swedish gender equality discourses to demonstrate the continued importance of social democracy and feminism to welfare outcomes in Sweden. The chapter contrasts economic liberal attitudes to biological fatherhood with compulsory biological fatherhood in Sweden. It examines relatively new research into the importance of a genealogical identity to children that is beginning to have wider impacts on legislation in relation to children's right to information about their biological father.

The politics of fatherhood can be analysed by use of a continuum of fatherhood. One end of this continuum represents approaches to the politics of fatherhood based on a new politics of conservative masculinity and an adherence to traditional male breadwinning. Family diversity and especially one-parent families are crowded out with this approach and it has negative welfare outcomes for poor families. Typical of this approach is the politics of fatherhood in the United States. On the other end of the continuum we find the politics of social democracy and feminism, which is characterised by parental leave regimes, public childcare and support for family diversity. The approach has positive welfare outcomes for poor families. Sweden typifies the approach. The debate on fatherhood in Ireland is analysed here by use of this continuum.

Fatherhood and family policy in Ireland

Non-resident fathers are receiving increasing attention in Irish social policy. At Christmas 2003, the Unmarried and Separated Fathers of Ireland (USFI) held a march under the banner 'give us our rights to love and care for our children'. The group also rallied media coverage in February 2004 for a father-of-two on hunger strike after receiving a 60-day gaol sentence for failing to pay maintenance. Their overall demand is for joint custody and equality of access to children for unmarried and absent fathers. The campaign release from the USFI in support of the father on hunger-strike protest read as follows:

> If your relationship breaks down in this country, and you are a man, your children are taken away from you. Now, it seems that you get thrown in Jail, too . . . we now urge the Judiciary to take a hard look at this family law system, which, as others before me have said, is depriving children of their Fathers on a wholesale and industrial basis. We would also ask them to take heed of the statement made by Supreme Court Justice Keane that, 'Fatherless homes are to blame for crime'.

Family diversity, fatherless families and the well-being of children are all emerging as central themes to popular views of social breakdown and social pathology as shown in the following quotation:

> One impact of divorce is the growing number of absent fathers, which Professor Casey feels is contributing to juvenile crime. She believes Chief Justice Ronan Keane was right when he said recently that absent fathers are contributing to the rise of juvenile crime and lawlessness (*The Examiner*, 9 February 2004).

By blaming fatherless homes for social pathology while expressing benign concern about children's welfare, the demands of the USFI in Ireland are similar to the demands of the Fathers Responsibility Movement (FRM) in the United States. The FRM works to put fatherhood at the centre of US national policies. The FRM can be located within a US neo-conservative paradigm of reducing the entitlement to welfare to children in only the poorest of lone-parent families. Within this paradigm, biological fathers are portrayed as excluded from fatherhood (that is, the practice of fathering), either as poor and vulnerable young fathers excluded from lone-mother families, or secondly as 'absent fathers' following divorce or separation. The contribution of fatherhood to childhood and child socialisation is seen as critical both to the individual well-being of children and to maintaining social order. Gavanas (2004) breaks down the FRM into two wings: the pro-marriage wing, that sees marriage as the key to solving social problems; and the 'fragile family' wing, that is more concerned with unemployment, racism and discrimination. The two wings are competing voices in American fatherhood politics where fatherhood, marriage, work and sexuality are all central themes in the new politics of masculinity.

In Ireland, the *Final Report of the Commission on the Family: Strengthening Families for Life* (Commission on the Family, 1998) depicted a societal preference for maternal childcare in the home, as opposed to non-maternal childcare outside the home, that was not incompatible with the social policy provisions of the 1937 Constitution (Fanning, 2003: 14; Commission on the Family, 1998: 62). As well as expressing concern about mothers in paid employment, *Strengthening Families for Life* depicted social concern about the changing status of fatherhood. The report raised particular concern about public images of fatherhood in the media and television and in situation comedies where 'wives are shown to be more practical and connected, children to be more with it and savvy', while 'Dad is a little dumb'. (Commission on the Family, 1998: 405; Hillman, 1996: 80). *Strengthening Families for Life* endorses perceptions of a crisis of masculinity. It argues that joint parenting should be encouraged irrespective of family type, except where fathers are known to be abusive. It further argues that the ideal of greater involvement of fathers in the care and upbringing of their children is not supported in the sphere of birthing practices, in work, in the legal sphere and the sphere of statutory services (1998: 406). The Commission on the Family provided a tabulated guide entitled *Six Ways to be a Better Dad* derived from the South Australian Office for Families and Children. Public investment in men's groups and a public and private debate on 'good fathering' and 'good enough fathering' are key recommendations (1998: 418). The agenda for change includes the demand for a Constitutional declaration enshrining 'the equal rights of the father and mother to the guardianship of their child where the child is conceived through consent, irrespective of whether both parents live together' (1998: 434). Young 'vulnerable' fathers are recommended for targeted programmes that address their labour market situation through a New Opportunities Programme for Men. Perceptions of the 'feminised' nature of child rearing and the gender bias in State services to families are also depicted (1998: 439).

Strengthening Families for Life (Commission on the Family, 1998) led directly to the implementation of the Family Support Agency Act (2001), and the subsequent establishment of a national Family Support Agency in May 2003 which offers a national Family Mediation Service and develops community-based Family Resources Centres. Irish family policy and family support services are in a period of exponential growth and are spread over a number of government departments. In 1998, the Department of Health and Children launched the Springboard Family Support Initiative, an early intervention programme to support families with children at risk of going into care, dropping out of school or getting into trouble with the law. The success of the initiative has led to the permanent employment of 66 family support workers based in 17 projects throughout the country. The Springboard Initiative resulted in a substantive increase in research and publications on family support and fatherhood. Key reports include *Fathers and Families: Research and Reflection on Key Questions* (McKeown, 2001) and a *Guide to What Works in Family Support Services for Vulnerable Families* (McKeown, 2000). The Springboard Initiative reports are written by researchers and published as key government research findings by the Department of Health and Children. The policy strategy, articulated in the introductions to these reports, is to keep fathers in the picture alongside mothers. The rationale is that an 'inclusive society requires an inclusive family' as 'the importance of family life cannot be underestimated'. It is the state mobilisation of fathers to help counteract negative child well-being on the basis that 'fathers' involvement in quality parenting is important for the development and well-being of their children, and their participation in this parenting can contribute to increased parental equality, both within the home and outside the home' (McKeown, 2001: i).

Family well-being has emerged as a central goal of Irish social policy. In a report called *Family Well-being: What makes a Difference?* physical well-being is measured using the Symptom Check List or SCL and psychological well-being is measured using the Ryff Scales of psychological well-being (McKeown et al., 2003: 29). Key findings of this research are that mothers in one-parent families have poorer psychological well-being and the aggression of mothers may be having a detectable effect on the physical well-being of fathers in Irish families (McKeown et al., 2003: 70–5). Such findings are being introduced to the discourse of Irish social policy with no evident controversy. In the report *Family Well-being and Family Policy, Review of Research on Benefits and Costs,* published as part of an overall evaluation of the Springboard Family Support Initiative, four priorities for public action are identified: (1) child poverty; (2) quality services; (3) reducing family instability and conflict; and (4) supporting marriage (McKeown and Sweeney, 2001: 68). Although child poverty in Ireland emerges as a priority issue in the Springboard Initiative research, the relevance of poverty to well-being is obscured by the use of psychological and physiological measurements.

For example, the risks to family well-being from poverty are discounted by the Springboard Initiative with the argument that 'family structure is more important than poverty in determining behavioural and psychological problems' (McKeown 2001: 17; McLanahan, 1997). Fatherhood and the inclusive family are seen as more important than addressing economic inequality in the fight against social problems. The message is that children need fatherhood and unless the trend towards divorce is halted the inter-generational instability on the well-being of children will be powerful and result in high levels of personal disorganisation for years to come (McKeown, 2001: 17; Booth, 1999). Springboard argues that the family law system is a woman's resource. This is because of the fact that 85 per cent of cases are initiated by women, in relation to two main functions: issuing barring orders and maintenance orders (McKeown, 2001: 23; Fahey and Lyons, 1995). The Springboard Initiative utilises secondary research to argue that marriage produces 'substantial benefits for men and women in the form of better health, longer life, more and better sex, greater earnings (at least for men), greater wealth and better outcomes for children' (McKeown, 2000: 6; Waite, 1995: 499). The Springboard Initiative supports the institutions of marriage and highlights the potential dangers of divorce. It establishes active fatherhood and family well-being as policy goals that are partially detached from policy goals to address economic inequalities.

The Irish reports and studies and the claims of fathers' groups in Ireland have some normative assumptions in common: that fathers are excluded and systematically discriminated against; that children need fathers; that fathers are excluded from lone-parent families; that they are excluded from families after divorce and separation; that physical violence and aggression between partners are more commonplace from women; that state services and the legal system are biased against fathers; and, crucially, that men's groups are a positive development for gender politics.

O'Toole (2002) argues that the evaluation of the Springboard Family Support Initiative (McKeown et al., 2003) mythologises the Irish family of the past and relies on statistical reports that can only fail to capture the dynamics of different family types in Ireland. She challenges the reports' questioning of the statistics from the Task Force on Violence Against Women (1997), based on women presenting for services, through use of gender neutral prevalence studies that purport to show that domestic violence is just as likely to be inflicted on men by their partners as vice versa. O'Toole claims that 'nowhere to be seen is the considerable amount of research that challenges the assumptions, methodologies and findings of these gender neutral studies' (O'Toole, 2002: 128).

Fatherhood and welfare outcomes for children in the USA

The trend towards neo-conservative hegemony in welfare debates on father-hood and human reproduction is challenged by Ackerlof (1998), who concludes that it is men without children who are mainly responsible for rising crime in the USA. The postponement of marriage as a rite of passage means men get married later and, until they do, they contribute less to economic growth and social stability and are in greater danger of placing themselves and others at risk. Ackerlof is attempting to shift the blame for rising social pathology away from welfare and 'welfare mothers' and their children and on to men. However, such arguments have yet to stem the influence of conservatives such as Murray (1984) on welfare outcomes in the United States. Conservatives blame the availability of welfare to one-parent families for rising crime despite there being no correlation between the availability of welfare and out of marriage births over time and across states. One response to rising crime in the USA has been to blame welfare for causing poverty and therefore the response has been to take welfare away from the poorest children who need it most (Ackerlof, 1998: 287).

The fatherhood debate in the USA is epitomised by Blankenhorn (1995) in *Fatherless Families: Confronting Our Most Urgent Social Problem.* The con-servative paradigm does not blame fatherless families for social breakdown. Within this paradigm the one-parent family is in itself deemed to be social breakdown. Conservative welfare politics have led to the introduction of Time Limits and the Temporary Aid to Needy Families (TANF) programme, that have been called 'the single greatest break from past policy' (Grogger, 2003: 394). Under the old programme of Aid to Families with Dependent Children (AFDC), single parents with a child under 18 were entitled to receive cash assistance. The TANF which was introduced in 1998 made eligibility to cash assistance for families time limited to 60 months during their lifetimes. The aim of the time limits is to introduce welfare insecurity to mothers with children under 13 years of age, and in particular mothers with young babies. The policy goal is to make mothers postpone their claim for welfare until they really need it and to replace welfare dependency with labour market or informal welfare dependency (Grogger, 2003). The implication for biological non-resident fathers is obligatory financial support for their children, rather than emotional support, whether or not they are in a position to pay.

These welfare reform measures are part of a Republican Party vision of 'cultural war' aimed at appealing to working-class men by 'valorising tradi-tional masculine virtues' (Orloff and Monson, 2002: 84). The paradox is that US social policy does little actually to support male breadwinning and offers little to men who are not successful in the market. The other major shift in US social policy initiatives has been forcing 'deadbeat dads' to pay child support. Fathers who do not pay maintenance are named and shamed on local television (Blankenhorn, 1995: 144). In the USA, child support policy is framed in terms of public enforcement of private, individual responsibility. Paternity establishment attempts to 'make men accountable' for non-marital sexual activity, the policies attempt to 'discipline fathers into bread-winning' (Orloff and Monson, 2002: 85). Monson's study in Wisconsin portrays child support staff interrogating mothers of non-marital children about the father's identity and whereabouts. Women are questioned about their sexual partners, sexual practices, and a father, issued with a paternity order, is in effect required by the summons to state whether he is convinced of the mother's sexual fidelity. Once fathers are successfully identified they can be forced into job training to pay child support. If fathers continually fail to pay, refuse to pay or miss court appearances they are subject to a 'shirking order'. Bench warrants are issued but only acted on if a man is charged with another offence. Black and Hispanic men are the disproportionately high recipients of 'shirking orders'. There have been tentative moves to allow younger men to care rather than pay by engaging in special projects but the overall thrust of US paternity policy has been to turn the crisis of fatherhood or fatherless families in the US into a crisis of reproduction for marginalised groups thereby reinforcing inequalities based on race and class. It is a 'clear example of the impact of policy liberalism on gender relations.' (Orloff and Monson, 2002: 85).

In the USA economic liberalism and religious conservatism have combined to force a moral withdrawal from welfare (Stoesz, 2002). By contrast Van Kersbergen (1995) highlights the role of social Catholicism and Christian democracy in generating welfare state development and welfare state legitimacy in Europe. Van Kersbergen compares the German, Italian and Dutch welfare states and argues that social Catholicism rather than a reformation-based Protestantism influenced welfare state development in those countries. Van Kersbergen makes the bold claim that in essence there are two routes to welfare, the Protestant secularisation route and the social capitalist route. In the latter, social Catholicism and Christian democracy are the major influences (Van Kersbergen, 1995: 232). The present paternity regime in the US bears similar ideological hallmarks to the Dutch Protestant politics of anti-interventionism and welfare state opposition and exhibits the lasting influence of the seventeenth-century American colonial tradition where the Protestant Reformation augmented patriarchal authority inside and outside the home (Mintz, 1998).

A legacy of such patriarchal traditions was that until the recent past young school-going couples were forced to marry and spend their whole lives together when a teenage girl found herself pregnant. Now, in the new world of sexual freedom, boyfriends feel a reduced responsibility to marry their pregnant girlfriends (Ackerlof, 1998: 288). However, while the 'shotgun wedding' may be a thing of the past, it is arguable that in relation to the social relations of sex and reproduction that 'shotgun responsibility' remains part and parcel of US paternity policies. In contrast to the growth of conservative attitudes towards the social relations of human reproduction and sex in the USA, in the EU the post-postponement of marital responsibilities and the liberalisation of sexual attitudes are seen as a major contributor to the life satisfaction and well-being of the under-20s (Micklewright and Stewart, 1999: 711).

One main outcome of the fatherhood debate in the USA is the creation of a sizeable conservative men's movement. Another outcome is the removal of welfare entitlements to children in poor families and lone-mother families, thereby increasing child poverty and public neglect through the efficient use of targeting strategies that introduce welfare insecurity. These developments serve to sustain a religious conservative vision of coupling sexual relations to reproductive relations and confine them within the institution of marriage.

In contrast to the US case, the welfare of children born outside marriage in Sweden has traditionally been a social policy concern. For example biological fathers who did not support their children were deemed 'negligent providers' at the Social Democratic Conference in 1905, and compared with strike-breakers (Ohlander, 1991: 64). Legal and economic fatherhood was part of an overall social democratic project and from 1927 child welfare officers were assigned to oversee the economic support for the child (Bergman and Hobson, 2002: 94). Where a woman had sexual relations with more than one man it did not result in a dismissal of a paternity claim. It was considered reason enough for a man to have committed an act that could have caused a child to establish possible paternity, rather than leave a child without a father. From 1933, Sweden moved towards establishing biological paternity on the basis that it was in the best interests of the child to establish their true biological father. This was part of wider trend towards social engineering motivated in part by eugenic concerns of social fitness rather than child well-being per se (Bergman and Hobson, 2002: 96). Although the State would usually end up footing the bill, in Sweden de-familisation had to be preceded by family formation based on biological parenthood and acceptance of biological fatherhood.

Male breadwinners

In a highly influential article, Jane Lewis (1992) distinguishes welfare regimes by the extent to which they can be described as 'male-breadwinner', 'modified male-breadwinner' or 'weak male-breadwinner' systems. Lewis suggests that the feminist movement had paradoxically been historically stronger in Britain, which is a male-breadwinner welfare regime, than in either France (a modified male-breadwinner regime), or Sweden (a weak male-breadwinner regime). She argues that although welfare states in France and Sweden offer women more than in Britain, women's own demands in these countries played no significant role in their better treatment (Lewis, 1992: 159). Lewis claims the issues of valuing unpaid work and the sharing of it were never addressed directly by welfare regimes and that while Sweden, ostensibly a dual breadwinner regime, had gone some way to addressing the first, it had never touched upon the second (Lewis, 1992: 170).

Bergman and Hobson, in a contrasting analysis, describe how participatory fatherhood in Sweden has been promoted since the 1970s through a series of publicity campaigns of men with babies in their arms. These images broadcast two messages: firstly, that fatherhood is masculine, not feminine, with the image of a weightlifter wearing a T-shirt bearing the Swedish flag designed to appeal to working-class men and, secondly, that participatory fatherhood is Swedish and patriotic – to care for children is beneficial to Swedish society (Bergman and Hobson, 2002: 107). In 1994, a year of financial crisis in Sweden, the Liberal Party with the support of the Christian Democrats introduced the 'Daddy month'. This was couched in gender-neutral terms. Two months of the one-year parental leave available to Swedes had to be taken by each parent and the rest could be decided according to family preference. Each partner had to take one month of parental leave in the year following the birth of a child leading to the inception of the 'Daddy month'.

The passage of this parental leave regime to support fatherhood in Sweden had the support of women's groups and of a Working Group on Fathers established by the government in 1993. However, the Daddy month was passed as part of a deal with the Christian Democrats that included a care allowance for mothers. Feminists placed opposition to legislation granting a paid care allowance to mothers at the top of the Social Democratic agenda and it was repealed the following year when the Social Democrats returned to power (Bergman and Hobson, 2002: 109). The allowance was seen as undermining gender equality goals of social democracy. The importance of sharing unpaid care and domestic labour to Swedish society is demonstrated by the reform of the parental leave regime. However, the power of Swedish feminism to shape welfare outcomes, as demonstrated by the reversal of the care allowance legislation, is perhaps more significant to theoretical welfare debates. It also demonstrates that Swedish feminism and Swedish gender equality strategies crowd out payment for care labour and love labour in the home, because primary loyalty is to the labour market.

Bergman and Hobson (2002: 123) argue that 'compulsory fatherhood' in Sweden, in contrast to the USA, brings an obligation to care rather than an obligation to be the main source of economic support. Antecedents of such societal attitudes to fatherhood can be found in the institution of the 'Stockholm Marriage', in which men and women published marriage banns but never married. This arrangement allowed men to cohabit and have children without accepting the formal responsibilities of fatherhood (Hobson and Morgan, 2002: 14). Swedish feminists argue that moral invective about the 'lone-parent family' is increasingly less influenced by traditional religious concerns but perhaps more tenaciously influenced by our 'persistent adherence to the early industrial reproductive strategies of male bread-winning' (Sommestad, 1997). It is arguable that negative attitudes towards lone-motherhood, family diversity and welfare in the USA are now being bolstered by a combination of economic liberalism, racism, religious morality and an abiding adherence to the reproductive strategy of male-bread-winning. Olah et al. (2002) have argued that the private costs of families has escalated to such an extent in the US that men, particularly educated men, have been turning away from household fatherhood, while state support for families in Sweden has strengthened men's roles as carers and paradoxically helped maintain their traditional roles as providers (Olah et al., 2002: 57).

Socio-genealogical identity and biological fatherhood

Owusu-Bempah and Howitt (1997) developed the concept of socio-genealogical connectedness (SGC). SGC refers to the extent to which children identify with their natural parents' biological and social backgrounds. This in turn depends upon the amount of 'quality information' about their parents that children possess. SGC theory suggests that the more information, the deeper the sense of connection but if the information is damaging, the child is less inclined to want to be associated with it. The better the connectedness the better adjusted is the child. In Britain, the Children's Act (1989) establishes that parental information is an essential factor in children's development. In Ireland, however, a child born outside marriage has no automatic right to have their paternity established and there is no requirement to have a father's name on a birth certificate (Richardson, 2001: 26). Adopted children have no right to see their original birth certificate.

The United Kingdom, in a recent review of fertility legislation, ruled children's rights to know their genetic inheritance outweighed sperm donor's rights to privacy, a move supported by the Human Fertilisation and Embryology Authority (HFEA) the fertility watchdog. Both Austria and Sweden have made similar moves with no reported loss of donors, although the age of donors increases when anonymity is removed. Switzerland and The Netherlands have also extended children's rights to access information about their donors (*The Times*, 17 January 2004).

In Ireland in 1998, the Department of Social, Community and Family Affairs surveyed a sample of 1,000 unmarried applicants for the One-Parent

Family Allowance Payment and found that 79 per cent of them had both parents' names on the child's birth certificate. A similar survey in 1999 on 1,000 separated applicants for One-Parent Family Allowance found that 83 per cent of these had both parents' names on the children's birth certificates (NESF, 2001: 104). The surveys suggest that in the absence of any enforced requirement to register a father on the birth certificate, about 80 per cent of applicants for lone-parent allowance do so yet that still leaves 20 per cent of children in one-parent families with no father's name on their birth certificate.

Non-resident fathers in Ireland are mobilising support under the banner of 'children need fathers not welfare'. Conservative fatherhood is emerging in Ireland as a social force critical of diversity in relation to family structure and fatherless homes. The impact of the emergence of similar movements in the USA would suggest this is a worrying development for the many children already living in poverty in Ireland. On the other hand, there is growing evidence that positive identification with a biological father is a factor in children's well-being. Recognition of the father on the birth certificate has been demanded in Ireland from the Children's Rights Alliance and the Constitutional Review Group. Both have recommended a child's right to identity requires constitutional recognition (Richardson, 2001: 26). However, the courts in Ireland are traditionally sceptical and remain 'unwilling to recognise that any significant weight should be given to paternal bonding' (Conroy, 1998: 93).

Empirical research, anthropology and social capital

Seltzer (1998) challenges the American neo-conservative paradigm by asking whether non-marital childbearing and divorce reduce family size thus increasing its capacity for care and the capacity of parents' education to benefit children. Seltzer calls for theorists to document associations between socio-demographic change and develop child well-being indicators that sustain the claim that men's roles matter for children. The empirical evidence still suggests that men's roles are peripheral. The only major study carried out in Ireland into the division of housework and childcare found that mothers not only do the majority of the housework but are also the primary carers for children (Kiely, 1995). Norwegian studies on home alone fathers, i.e. fathers taking parental leave while their female partners are at work, are providing new insights into fatherhood. The studies show how children influence their fathers' care practices in the absence of the mother translating the child's needs for the father. The Norwegian research involves seeing children as active agents who contribute to the production of the adult world and their place within it (Brandth and Kvande, 2003: 25). The Nordic studies mirror research carried out in Northern Ireland that sought to show how important it is to bring 'sociological, philosophical and psychological analysis to bear on the problem of how informal welfare was shaped, and how it might relate to that provided by statutory social and health services, as well as voluntary organisations' (St Leger and Gillespie, 1991: viii; see also Moore, 2004).

While there is widespread evidence (Ackerlof, 1998) to suggest that becoming a father impacts positively on a man's own well-being, the evidence of the positive impact of fatherhood on children remains modest. Yet the myth of beneficial fatherhood in a context of androgynous caring (Mintz, 1998) crowds out diversity of family structure and public responsibility for childcare without the support of any widespread empirical evidence. However, social capital theorists and anthropologists are beginning to reveal the nature of the social relationships that underpin the engendered habitus of human reproduction and child rearing in different national and social settings. Anthropological studies are providing the critical insights required for theoretical development, for example Bourdieu consistently refers to his own study of the Kabylia (Bourdieu, 2001). Social policy theory also requires the clarification of key concepts and measurement instruments to examine the relationship between fathers, fatherhood and well-being in children especially on an intra-national basis. First and foremost the concept of well-being itself requires clarification. As an inequality measurement instrument, well-being was crystallised into a scientific artefact by Amartya Sen (1985) in *Commodities and Capabilities*. Sen acknowledges the influence of Albert O. Hirschman and George Ackerlof, amongst others. All are theorists who work within a para-digm of social choice to counter classical liberal economy based on the 'bemusing' concept of utility. Sen argues that the concept of utility is 'disposed to regard human beings as rational fools' (1985: 4). Sen's measurement of well-being has been adopted by the United Nations Human Development Reports (HDR). Measurements and conceptualisations of well-being based on US psychology and physiology currently being used by the Springboard Family Support Initiative in Ireland, however useful they are to clinical interven-tion and social services, fall within a paradigm of pathology rather than of social choice.

Public responsibility for child well-being in Ireland

The welfare state in the nineteenth century gained legitimacy at least in part from the mobilisation of women (Bock and Thane, 1991) to protect children from having to work and from having to make a financial contribution to private patriarchal household arrangements. Since then, welfare states in Europe have maintained children outside the labour market in the first instance through the family wage which has since been gradually replaced by a combination of marriage taxation subsidies, universal child benefit and increasingly through public childcare services (Montanari, 2000). More recent pragmatic social policy responses in Sweden and Norway have seen cohabitants with joint children treated as married couples for the purposes of social security (Hatland, 2001: 135). The continued maintenance of children by the welfare state requires a social choice rather than a rational economic choice since the value of the product of reproductive labour, the child, in modern dual earner economically liberal societies, is becoming invisible or meaningless except as a potential source of future labour (Jensen, 1994: 63). In contrast, the Brazilian Institute of Geography and Statistics reports that the number of children between the ages of 10 and 14 who must work in the great metropolises increased by 50 per cent between January and September 2003, and by 76 per cent between September 2002 and September 2003 (Udry, 2004: 3). In the nineteenth century the feminisation of childhood resulted in the labour market protection of children across the western world because the labour market participation of children was radically perceived as the social exclusion of children.

In the Irish case, the demand for more women in the workplace as a result of economic growth led to demands within successive Social Partnership agreements for childcare to be addressed as a labour market gender equality issue. Subsequently an Expert Working Group on Childcare culminated its work with the publication of a National Childcare Strategy (1999), which led to the establishment of County Childcare Committees to assist in the development of the mixed economy of childcare services. However, while EU Guidelines recommend that by 2010 90 per cent of children over three and 33 per cent of children under three should be provided with childcare, research in Ireland (Rush, 2003c, Rush, 2003a) shows that only about 30 per cent of children are accessing centre-based childcare in urban areas and in rural areas informal childminding is the only type of childcare accessed by over 90 per cent of children. This childcare profile has resulted in the nascent pursuit of a policy strategy of 'combination care' involving a mix of paid child-minding and centre-based sessional care in rural areas (Rush, 2003a). Two distinct perspectives have informed the childcare issue in Ireland. They are 'the child protection and development perspective' and the 'gender and labour market perspective' (Brudell, 1998: McKeown and Fitzgerald, 1997). In relation to childcare services and gender equality in the labour market, Irish feminists and trade unionists have influenced the shaping of the National Childcare Strategy (Rush, 2003c, Rush, 2003a).

Welfare provision in relation to financial support for families to access childcare services is weak. For example, a 'creche supplement' was previously available under the old Supplementary Welfare Allowance scheme to families in emergency accommodation or where it was deemed necessary for the child's social or cognitive development. Refugees and asylum seekers including families waiting to have their cases processed were also eligible for the payment. As a welfare payment the childcare supplement recognised both the social health benefits of non-maternal centre-based childcare settings and the principle of public responsibility for the well-being of all children in Ireland (Rush, 2003b: 16). However, the Minister for Social and Family Affairs in the Budget 2004 speech while voicing reassurances in relation to developing appropriate alternative measures to the crèche supplement emphasised that it was a short-term social support, available in specific circumstances, rather than a long-term childcare support. The Union of Students in Ireland (USI) was one of the organisations which criticised the Government for introducing 37 per cent cuts to the childcare allowances for adults in second chance education programmes. Support for the childcare costs of low-income families remains a contested issue in Irish social policy and one which was identified as a priority in a nationwide public consultation for the National Anti-Poverty Strategy (Cousins, 2003: 20).

In relation to family diversity and one-parent families, international comparative research by Eardley (1996) found that Ireland had the fewest time limits in all OECD countries for one-parent family allowance, i.e. lone parents have an entitlement to welfare until the youngest child is over 18 or after if the child is in full-time education. The research mapped the international shift to neo-liberal workfare arrangements and found that Ireland more than any other country had resisted such policy shifts. However, Conroy (1998) has argued that maintaining women and children on welfare is part and parcel of the general subordination of women as secondary earners and beneficiaries within the Irish welfare regime (Conroy, 1998: 94). It is in such a context that child poverty in Ireland has increased to the extent that the poverty rates of Irish children contribute to a negative correlation between GDP growth and child well-being in the European Union (Micklewright and Stewart, 1999: 698).

The National Anti-Poverty Strategy aimed at reducing deprivation and has been successful to some degree. Eardley (1996) coined the term 'From Safety Nets to Springboards' to illustrate the dominance of an economic liberal discourse in relation to the reforms of social assistance programmes in OECD countries. It is a discourse which also appears to be evident in the name of the Springboard Family Support Initiative. Without a safe place to land, springboards might well spell welfare insecurity for targeted welfare subjects, and particularly for children. The new politics of fatherhood in Ireland claims children need fathers, not welfare; however, research in Ireland has shown that the social implications of being born outside marriage are transient for the majority of pre-school children, particularly those who live with their mother in the home of their maternal grandmother or in a house-hold subsequently established by the mother with a partner (Flanagan 2001: 40). Locating children as individual welfare subjects requires recognising the welfare entitlements of children and their mothers, whilst acknowledging research (Owusu-Bempah and Howitt, 1997) on the potential benefits of positive paternal identification.

Since 1987 and the introduction of Social Partnership, Irish social policy has managed to avoid economic liberal paths to workfare and neo-conservative moral retreats from the welfare state. Instead Ireland has maintained a moderated neo-liberal package of reduced welfare effort, i.e. the percentage of GDP spent on welfare (Peillon, 2001), with guarantees of continued welfare security for beneficiaries of social welfare, including the long-term unemployed and lone-parent families. In the case of lone parents, support for such a package has paradoxically depended on the absence of an adequate childcare infrastructure to facilitate lone-parent entry into the labour force. Currently Ireland's social welfare package accommodates family diversity by main-taining families in relative poverty without time limits. Any downturn in the Irish economy would require increased welfare effort to maintain a commit-ment to EU social policy goals of social protection for families outside the labour market. This would mean a return to the levels of welfare effort that marked the era prior to the period of sustained economic growth. However, there are barriers to such a strategy. Firstly, since the passing of divorce legislation and the publication of *Strengthening Families for Life* (Commission on the Family, 1998) the strength and influence of what Van Kersbergen terms social Catholicism has waned in Ireland. Subsequently, the language of Irish social policy and family policy seems to have taken an ideological shift in the direction of economic liberalism and neo-conservatism, so much so that the National Women's Council of Ireland and the Community Platform, two of the social partners in the Community and Voluntary Pillar, rejected the sixth consecutive Irish Social Partnership Agreement since 1987 on the basis that it 'proposes a paradigm shift' and sustains poverty and inequality (www.cwc.ie). Secondly, fatherless families and welfare are increasingly coming under attack from conservative and patriarchal forces.

The Council of the Religious in Ireland–Justice Commission (CORI) have remained social partners, and as the voice of social Catholicism in Ireland, they champion the rights of the poor against neo-liberal encroach-ment and emphasise the importance and usefulness of unpaid care labour to the State (Taylor, 1995). Future welfare debates and outcomes will partly depend on whether social Catholicism in Ireland remains a widespread social phenomenon and whether it can resist aligning itself with the broad church of the new right, that is presenting the world with a politics of scarcity, moral Puritanism and promoting a crisis of the welfare state (Powell, 1998: 271) within which the new politics of fatherhood in Ireland is deeply entrenched.

Conclusion

The persistent adherence of Ireland and the US to the reproductive strategy of male breadwinning has been contrasted to the Swedish reproductive strategy of state welfare combined with gender equality in the labour market. Ireland has made a modest ideological shift towards gender equality in the labour market and public responsibility for children through the establishment of County Childcare Committees. The ongoing relevance and critical importance of social democratic and feminist politics to Swedish welfare outcomes provide a contrast to male-breadwinning analysis, and to the influence of the new politics of masculinity on negative welfare outcomes for children in the USA. Equally significantly, the feminisation of childhood brought on by nineteenth-century industrialisation has been seen to have had a lasting influence on the well-being of children through the subsequent influence of feminism in protecting children from the labour market through the development of the welfare state.

However, there is a paradox between the introduction of social rights and children's rights in the context of increasing economic inequality and child poverty. Social choice and rational choice are contesting paradigms in relation to the concept of well-being. The former is concerned with a public response to poverty and well-being through the provision of welfare, while the latter is concerned to develop pathological explanations of negative individual well-being within families in an overall context of combating social pathology. Increasing international recognition of the significance of biological fatherhood to children's genealogical identity contrasts with the dearth of evidence to support the argument that household fatherhood is making a positive difference to children's well-being.

The new conservative politics of fatherhood in Ireland bears similarities to the conservative politics of fatherhood and masculinity in the USA where religious Puritanism thrives on an economic liberal politics of scarcity to crowd out diversity of family form. This new politics of masculinity contrasts with State feminist approaches in Sweden where diversity of family structure is recognised through compulsory biological fatherhood and public responsibility for children is facilitated through parental leave regimes and public childcare services within an overall context of gender equality in the labour market and family income subsidies.

Within an international continuum Ireland has moved towards the goal of social control in relation to fatherhood debates and family policy but without the active pursuit of maintenance from non-resident fathers except in cases where maintenance has been agreed and defaulted on. Internationally, Ireland has the fewest time limits in relation to welfare for lone-parent families. In contrast to the US case, the goal of Irish social policy is to eradicate deprivation through targeted welfare provision and maintain security rather than foster insecurity for welfare subjects. Gender equality in the labour market, public childcare and parental leave regimes remain underdeveloped social policy goals. Ireland combines a modified conservative morality with a modified economic liberalism and reflects an ideological distance from both Boston and Stockholm. The case of fathers highlights the differing as opposed to the converging trajectories of Irish, US and Swedish welfare regimes and illustrates the continuing relevance of social choice to social policy.

Ireland does not fall on one side only of the continuum of fatherhood. With regard to the politics of masculinity and fatherhood it is on the United States side. To some extent the Springboard Family Support Initiative and *Strengthening Families for Life* (1998) both demonstrate aspects of this. It is more on the Swedish side of the continuum regarding its National Childcare Strategy (1999). This is reflected in its emphasis on an Equal Opportunities Childcare Programme (2000–6) within an overall framework of gender equality in the labour market and to a lesser degree with its weak parental leave regime. Of the two influences, the Swedish influence of gender equality in the labour market and public responsibility for childcare seems more contested within the Irish welfare system.

Chapter 7

Poverty and insecurity

Anne Coakley

This chapter examines the way in which poverty and its variant social exclusion are being reproduced in Irish society as we move into the twenty-first century. The essence of poverty is determined by social living standards (Combat Poverty Agency, 2002a). Irish society is displaying growing levels of income inequality and glaring gaps in the levels of security and insecurity for different social groups. This has crucial outcomes for an ontological sense of well-being. By this I mean a deep sense of well-being which includes health and social and economic security both at the individual, household and group level. The chapter begins by outlining the growing levels of inequality in Irish society despite the official reduction in consistent poverty. It argues that poverty has not been eliminated but reconstructed in official discourse, which is contested by research evidence and by government-funded bodies. The chapter goes on to explore the outcome of government policy in the areas of housing and property, health and well-being, workfare and the spatialisation of poverty into zones of social exclusion.

In a global society, poverty is a contested and dynamic concept and its prevalence and persistence reflect the kind of society in which we live, the nature of political decision making and the groups in society that benefit most from such decisions. Social exclusion and social inclusion are particularly associated with EU social initiatives. The Lisbon Summit in March 2000 committed member states to the promotion of social inclusion through a range of social initiatives. The term social exclusion is somewhat ambiguous. Some social policy analysts argue that it is just another word for poverty, but one that is preferred in a political context in which governments are unwilling to be explicit about the existence of poor people: 'The concept of exclusion becomes part of a new hegemonic discourse, undermining the poverty discourse with its focus on material inequality' (Born and Jensen, 2002: 263). In official discourse poverty is connected with and often replaced by a discourse focusing on social exclusion.

Social rights

The emerging social democratic consensus in Europe in the post-Second World War period was that the expansion of the welfare state was based not upon establishing a minimum level of welfare but upon an extension of social as well as civil and political rights. In the Fordist period, the Beveridge-type welfare state influenced developments in Irish welfare provision. Developments during this period gave responsibility to the welfare state for the provision of key services for workers including social housing, free education, social welfare for groups outside the labour market and the development of personal social services. While the alleviation of poverty was an important consideration in the expansion of social rights for any democratic state, formal equality remained an aspiration and not an explicit policy objective (Taylor, 2003). For example, Ireland's membership of the European Union promoted gender equality in welfare rights, yet the Irish government conceded these rights only when women actively fought for their recognition.

With the development of neo-liberal policies, there has been a paring down of many services that had come to be regarded as basic citizenship rights.

> The central trust of many developments in the welfare state during the 1980s was to tighten the grip on entitlement policing. Social rights, as an attribute of citizenship, have been gradually eroded as governments sought to reduce public expenditure, privatise public industry and to reassert the primacy of individual self-help (Taylor, 2003: 313).

The concept of citizenship in neo-liberal discourse replaces the citizen with the consumer. The post-industrial society of today is a society of consumers and has created the need for new kinds of rights which have little to do with inequality; 'Citizenship in neo-liberal discourse loses its equalizing function and becomes a highly-privatised matter requiring often only regulating bodies to secure its effectiveness' (Delanty, 2000: 21). From the neo-liberal perspective the welfare state's role is a residual one acting only as a safety net for those unable to secure employment. The European perspective of social inclusion and exclusion which emanates from the EU is one in which paid work is seen as the key to social inclusion.

Under the old welfare order, citizenship emphasised social rights and connectedness. In contrast, consumer rights define us as private individuals. The consumer society is the society of the individual and so expressions of poverty are individualised and social exclusion localised and internalised in particular spatial zones. In this new welfare order social needs become transformed into individual responsibility and blame; the dominant message is that as consumers not as citizens we are free to choose 'the good life'. There are a number of different discourses that mediate and find expression in this domain. On the one hand, there is a dominant discourse of normality presented by the media of high earners consuming property as a capital investment. On the other hand, is a discourse of the 'abnormal', of the excluded, of those who cannot afford to buy their own home, of those who cannot obtain or hold on to a job, and who cannot afford to pay for private health insurance. These become the 'other', the dependant, and a burden on the rest of society.

Discourses on poverty

In order to place the Irish government's social policies on poverty into context, social policy has to be seen as contradictory and complex in a world that is fluid, changing and inherently complex and fragmented. We need to examine the ways in which social policy is constructed and reconstructed through shifts in dominant ideas about the nature of social problems and of social membership (Fanning, 2003). Watson (2000) draws on the work of Foucault to understand developments in social policy in favour of meta-narratives, which attempt to explain the social/political/economic world within one totalising framework. Watson argues that Foucault's thesis on power and knowledge as intimately connected and intertwined is important for social policy. One consequence of the new forms of power, according to Foucault (1977, 1979), was an increasing focus on decisions based on statistical measures of what is normal as opposed to decisions based on notions of right and wrong or justice. Classifying and ordering became standard techniques of normalisation:

> This kind of normative ordering of the population in the nineteenth century continued apace throughout the twentieth century with a plethora of government surveys, reports, censuses and commissions establishing notions of average and expected forms of individual behaviour and social life (Watson, 2000: 69–70).

The new means of governance was constituted in the new forms of knowledge available through the statistical monitoring of the population. Isin and Wood (1999) outline the shifts with the rise of neo-liberal technologies of government. One of the most important is the new relationship between expertise and politics. The legitimacy and authority of new knowledges derive not from their truth and validity but from their ability to assess performance (Isin and Wood, 1999). Among the new modes of circulation of knowledges are enumeration, calculation, monitoring and evaluation. Watson suggests that Foucault's notion of discourse as a framework of meanings, which are historically produced in a particular culture at a particular time, help us to think critically about social policy. What is important are the ways in which people and institutions have the power to define the terms of the debate or the way a problem is to be understood. The place of the expert is key. So, for example, it is not just a question of how the poor are actually treated but also how different discourses act to produce certain outcomes – marginalising some groups or creating others as victims. If the social is understood as the site where needs become politicised, contested and interpreted, then what is crucial are the processes by which certain needs are politicised and others are not (Watson, 2000). In the most recent historical period the government's response to poverty has been fragmented, diluted and increasingly spatialised. An official discourse defines the parameters of poverty as 'consistent' poverty supported by research that shows its decline during the Celtic Tiger period and reinforces the purported success of government policy. In contrast a view focusing on relative poverty and growing inequality would bring to the fore ideas of redistribution of wealth and resources and of social justice.

A question of inequality

The shift from earlier discourses to Ireland's semi-peripheral integration into global capitalism has produced a corporate culture and a perspective that emphasises individualism, entrepreneurship, competitiveness and flexibility. These are attributes to be cultivated by the individual, and which educational institutions are expected to adopt and use as dominant societal values (Kirby et al., 2002). Behind this political rhetoric there are quite distinct processes in society, serving to make distinctions economically and socially between different groups. Globalisation means that we cannot examine poverty and social exclusion without examining the interconnections between the way capitalist society is evolving globally and the ways it is being reproduced at the local level:

> Wealth and poverty are distributed across space as the result of societal and increasingly global processes of investment, disinvestments, restructuring and economic reorganisation which takes advantage of existing spatial differences in order to maximise profitability and security (Tovey, 1999: 98).

Other writers confirm that poverty and its variant social exclusion are part of the structural changes in global capitalism. Contemporary social exclusion is a product of the phased shift in the character of contemporary capitalism. 'It is an inherent property of polarized post-industrial capitalism' (Byrne, 1999: 78). This post-Fordist phase of economic growth is marked by the replacement of jobs with 'flexible labour' and of job security by 'rolling contracts' and fixed-term appointments (Bauman, 1998b).

Two important structural changes in this period, fundamental at the level of individuals and household, are the possibility of mobility and growing income inequality. These factors contribute to a growing insecurity and a lack of well-being for social groups who bear the brunt of such changes. Byrne (1999) notes that there is evidence to suggest that the shift from industrial to post-industrial social structures involves a closure of mobility opportunities. In the Fordist era a considerable degree of upward social mobility was often but not always mediated through educational attainment. Turner (1994) is more pessimistic about such possibilities. He argues that while governments attempt to reform the education system to provide equality of educational opportunity, there will always be inequality in social outcomes. This is owing to the fact that different social classes possess different types and amounts of cultural capital (intellectual and educational qualifications), which they transfer to their children (Bourdieu, 1984). Tovey and Share (2003), in reviewing social mobility research in Ireland, note that despite an appearance of openness in terms of the types of people that become professionals and managers there is an extremely low level of upward mobility from the working class to the managerial classes. This is consistent with the very substantial inequalities of opportunities that are evidence of the persistence of patterns of relative advantages. It seems that the distribution of class resources or cultural capital shows little change over time. The introduction of free second-level education in Ireland in the 1960s was seen as a very positive expansion of social rights. Schools gradually introduced fees because grants from the government are not sufficient to cover the costs of books and many other activities. The government's intention on 'educational disadvantage' is not to improve universal provision but to spatialise it. The outcome is limited efficiency, and distortions that arise from the geographical unit used to delineate disadvantage, the urban-rural divide and the emphasis on quantity rather than quality in the allocation of additional resources (Walsh, 1999).

Ireland's historically low levels of unemployment since the advent of the Celtic Tiger must be scrutinised in the context of international developments. The American model of developing a highly profitable new sphere of low-waged services, while maintaining overall employment levels, could well be applied to the Irish case. What is significant is the combination of low wages, insecure employment, and dependence on means-tested benefit as supplements to low income. In Britain and the US public policy has actively promoted a flexible labour market. Figures for the UK show that the real incomes (after housing costs have been taken into account) of the lowest decile have declined by 25 per cent (Byrne, 1999: 81–2). In Ireland, the bottom five deciles received just over 18 per cent of total income in 1973; by 1994 this had declined to 11.5 per cent. At the other end of the distribution, the top two deciles have increased their share of income, from 46.7 per cent in 1973 to almost 52.5 per cent in 1994 (Collins and Kavanagh, 1998). The authors conclude that disposable income remains highly concentrated at the top of the income distribution. An analysis by the CORI Justice Commission on the implications of budget decisions and national agreements for income distribution found a dramatic widening of the gap between the poor and the better off in the period 1994–9 (CORI, 1999).

A comparative analysis of income inequality across the EU indicates that Ireland's income distribution is among the most unequal in Europe. Ireland along with Greece has the second highest proportion of its population under the low-income threshold, set at 60 per cent of the median equivalised income per person in each member state. This is surpassed only by Portugal (Eurostat, 1999). The move in the second half of the 1990s to low tax rates was intended to give the impression that the reductions in tax were of benefit to most people. However, closer analysis shows that the tax packages were heavily weighted towards high-income earners and had marginal effects on the incomes of lower earners (O'Hearn, 2003: 50). Insecurity and low wages are the basis for a reconstruction of the relationship between labour and capital on a global scale (Byrne, 1999). Social exclusion is an active part of this process and is produced when incomes are excessively unequal. The poor must live in the same society as that created for the rich. Their poverty is aggravated by economic growth, just as it is intensified by recession (Bauman, 1998b: 38).

Consistent poverty discourse

Data on poverty confirm the growing inequality between different social groups. However, there has been a shift in the dominant government discourse on poverty, which centres on consistent rather than relative poverty. Consistent poverty is defined as being below 50–60 per cent of average household disposable income and at the same time experiencing enforced basic deprivation on at least one item on a set of deprivation indicators. Recent research shows that consistent poverty, a measure of low income and basic deprivation, affects 5.5 per cent of the population and represents a continuing decline from the 1990s (Nolan et al., 2002). However, relative income poverty shows a contrasting trend. In 2000, 22 per cent of the population had incomes below 60 per cent of the median. The comparable figures for 1998 and 1994 were 20 per cent and 15.6 per cent (Combat Poverty Agency, 2002b).

In the 1990s policy on poverty in Ireland was formalised by the National Anti-Poverty Strategy (NAPS, 1997) and the revised NAPS document (2002) following the United Nations social summit in Copenhagen in 1995. The Strategy Framework describes itself as an ambitious plan to address the most serious issues that requires putting poverty among the issues at the top of the national agenda. Townsend's (1979) classic definition of relative poverty is adapted by the NAPS:

> People are living in poverty if their income and resources (material, cultural and social) are so inadequate as to preclude them from having a standard of living which is regarded as acceptable by Irish society generally (NAPS, 1997: 3).

It identifies vulnerable groups including women, children and young people, older people, people with disabilities and ethnic minorities. The policies required to meet the challenges contained in this definition would have to focus on redistribution and social justice. The NAPS report states that its global target over the period 1997–2007 aims at considerably reducing the numbers who are consistently poor. The reduction in this statistical figure is part of the 'success' discourse of government. This discourse draws on a particular aspect of poverty research to interpret and construct notions of average and expected forms of individual behaviour and social life (Watson, 2000). The strategic aims of NAPS favour a targeted and spatialised response rather than a universal framework. The key areas identified include: educational disadvantage, unemployment, income adequacy, disadvantaged urban areas and rural poverty. The revised NAPS document (2002) includes health and housing as new themes.

What Charlie McCreevy, when Minister for Finance, referred to as the 'poverty industry' is a site where the NAPS targets have become politicised, interpreted and contested. Government-funded agencies including the Combat Poverty Agency (CPA) and the National Economic and Social Forum (NESF) have been expressing disquiet about the failure of the government to reduce relative poverty (Combat Poverty Agency, 2000; NESF, 2000, 2003). These agencies are contesting the dominant discourse influenced by their work and communication with community groups.

A review by the Combat Poverty Agency (2000a) acknowledges the important role played by NAPS in raising awareness of the need for anti-poverty polices within the political system. However it argues that a rising economic tide does not lift all boats. Further, a review by the National Economic and Social Forum (NESF, 2000a) focuses on the growing inequality in Irish society. While the process of target setting contained in the NAPS report is applied to explicit measurable targets such as the reduction in consistent poverty, such targets have not been developed for all the identified themes, and performance indicators are needed against which these targets can be assessed. The report acknowledges that recent developments in the Irish economy have resulted in lower unemployment:

This has not, however, eliminated poverty. Indeed the new environment is one in which the issue of poverty has become more complex, with the addition of new marginalized groups, such as ethnic minorities, while the relative position of those at the bottom of the income ladder has deteriorated still further (NESF, 2000a: 27).

The Forum recommends that the NAPS global target should encompass relative poverty indicators and that these should be subject to regular review in the light of changing socio-economic circumstances.

The proceedings of the consultative meeting of the NAPS Social Inclusion Forum (NESF, 2003a) give further voice to a contested discourse on poverty highlighting the lack of progress and the frustrations felt by those working in local community organisations:

> Many of the participants expressed their frustration at what they saw as the very obvious contradictions that arise between strategies and stated commitments and actions, the dichotomy between theory and practice (NESF, 2003a: 23).

This was raised in relation to both the EU and national policies. In particular the criticisms focused on the gap between policy, political commitments and actions. For example, the stated commitment to anti-poverty strategies, and the actions, particularly in budgetary decisions, which contradict this. The NAPS has a commitment in relation to unemployment yet the government implements cutbacks in unemployment programmes and community development programmes. The report articulates the lack of participation and sense of disengagement from the policy process among people experiencing poverty and the need for their active participation in research on poverty.

Property insecurity

Property is a favourite investment for Irish people according to a newspaper report (*Sunday Tribune*, 1 February 2004), which estimates that there has been a major increase in the number of Irish people who own more than one home. According to the report, average Dublin prices are now 50 per cent higher than those in the rest of the country. Cork is also doing well; it is reported that this is partly because of the huge number of equity-rich Dubliners buying holiday homes in the area. The use of the term 'property' has become much more dominant in the media and official circles, meaning a capital investment, whereas 'housing' is associated with the basic social need for shelter. In previous periods home was associated with family life and children growing up, now homes have been reconstructed and commodified as properties with equity and value, with an emphasis on privatised spaces.

There is a media-driven obsession with property acquisition underwritten by property agents. This is linked to the increase in the value of property in the past decade. Consumers with capital can purchase and increase their wealth from investments in property. Headlines in newspapers give a flavour of a way of consuming property in our society that exudes an air of frivolity and fun: 'A Step in the Right Direction', 'Brewing up a Storm in Foxrock', 'Dancing up the Property Ladder' (*Sunday Tribune*, 19 October 2003). The possession of property has become associated with personal identities and dreams: 'Hideaway has "hushed isolation" near city'; 'young and cool first time buyers'; 'Stunners to excite Market'; and for high earners with spare cash 'A Unique Property Investment and tax saving opportunity'; 'tax relief available against all income and all rental income' (*The Irish Times*, 23 October 2003).

Alternatively, the most basic measure of inequality in our society is that between the property rich and the property poor, those who are struggling to pay inflated mortgages and those dependent on the partly subsidised private rented sector. In the post Second World War period the right to housing and shelter was part of a social rights package and countries such as Britain and Ireland engaged in a strong social housing programme. Behind the contemporary images of consuming property is the breakdown of this social house-building programme: 'a populist social housing regime that had provided affordable and reasonable accommodation for successive generations of low-income households' (O'Hearn, 2003: 49). While the Irish government's social housing provision has been reduced, the traditional policy of subsidising home ownership has been relatively overtaken by capital grants and tax incentives for capital investment in property. This has led to insecurity at the lower end of the market. In the period from 1971 to 1999/2000, the social rented sector declined from 13.3 per cent to 8 per cent. Yet the assessment of local authority housing needs carried out in March 2002 showed an increase of 23.5 per cent from 1999 in the numbers requiring local authority housing (National Action Plan against Poverty and Social Exclusion 2003–5). It is also of interest to examine the two most common categories of housing needs in the local authority assessments. Figures for 1999 show these to be those unable to afford their own accommodation and overcrowding (NESF, 2000b: 18). In this era of neo-liberalism the government favours the subsidising of the private rented sector rather than a programme of public housing. One may ask who benefits most from a poorly regulated, variable quality and insecure private rented sector. Over 54,200 persons were in receipt of a rent supplement at the end of 2002 with the overall cost of rent supplements increasing by 41 per cent from 2001 to 2002 (National Action Plan against Poverty and Social Exclusion 2003–5). The government's response to the homeless and the new social strata of refugees and asylum-seekers who are in direct provision hostel-type accommodation is a further dilution and paring down of the right to shelter. The reconstructed meaning of social housing in government discourse is mainly a subsidised private rented sector. Property poverty is now part of the changing complexity of poverty. The vast speculative profits made by a small number of individuals from the rezoning of land in urban areas are now the subject of a number of government tribunals including the Flood Tribunal. In reality, the rezoning of land and the building of private housing estates with no ancillary services or schools continue unabated in the counties surrounding Dublin.

In the dominant media discussions we are bombarded with images of consuming properties and lifestyle as if this is the norm. In contrast the abnormal is to be found in 'flawed consumers' (Bauman, 1998b), the homeless, those on local authority housing lists, those who cannot afford to buy a home or those who live indefinitely in the poorly regulated private rented sector. Many young people in secure state jobs, who in previous periods could have afforded to purchase their own homes, now cannot afford to gain entry into the property market in Dublin. As a result, they have to relocate to commuter towns such as Mullingar and Kinnegad.

Unequal health and well-being

One of the most fundamental outcomes of poverty and unequal access to economic and other resources is the disabling effect on security and well-being. That is, on economic security and health and well-being. Poverty undermines an individual's sense of well-being and sense of belonging, how 'persons' are signified and made relevant in a given society (Born and Jensen, 2002). The social self develops and is mediated by the dynamics of 'choice and constraint'. This dynamic is crucially dependent on the social distribution of material resources (Twine, 1994).

Poverty is not just about having an inadequate income but it is also a social and psychological condition, 'as the propriety of human existence is measured by the standards of decent life practised by any given society, inability to abide by such standards is itself a cause of distress, agony and self-mortification' (Bauman, 1998b: 37). The growing level of income inequality in Irish society has far-reaching effects above and beyond material deprivation The poor in a consumer society are socially defined, and self-defined, as defective and deficient in some way, i.e. as flawed consumers (Bauman, 1998b: 38)

Marmot and Wilkinson (2001), in writing on socio-economic determinants of health and their prevalence, found that within a country life satisfaction levels register virtually no change when average income increases substantially. What is important is not the absolute level of material prosperity but how it compares or places a person in relation to others in society. Correlations between income and health should be interpreted primarily as correlations between health and relative, rather than absolute, income or material standards. Many of the socio-economic determinants of health have their effects through psychosocial pathways: 'More egalitarian societies, that is societies with smaller differences in income between rich and poor, tend to have better health and increased longevity' (Wilkinson, 1999: 259). Wilkinson cites evidence of the social environment becoming less supportive and more conflictual when income differences are bigger.

The quality of people's social relations seems to have a powerful influence on their health. Low social status and poor social relations are probably two of the most powerful risk factors influencing population health, 'that a crucial source of chronic anxiety, related both to social hierarchy and inversely to friendship, is likely to centre on feelings aroused by social comparison to do with confidence, insecurity, and fears of inadequacy' (Wilkinson, 1999: 262).

Irish research highlights some of the negative health outcomes of low income for families (Daly and Leonard, 2002). Poor health was common and one in three households registered health problems in relation to children. Nolan and Whelan's study of cumulative disadvantage (1999) shows that urban local authority tenants display relatively high levels of psychological distress and comparatively low levels of life satisfaction. However, this is entirely attributable to the impact of living standards and socio-demographic composition pointing to unemployment, household, income and lifestyle deprivation as powerful predictors of distress. My own research (Coakley, 1999) highlights how mothers in low-income households engage strategies to manage poverty and to hide it from their children and from the community. Decisions made, for example, not to go into debt to refurbish rooms in the house produced feelings of guilt and shame and had psychological and social repercussions. Some mothers noted that their teenage children did not want to bring friends home as they were embarrassed about the 'state' of the place. Mothers sometimes had to choose between paying a household bill or replacing a necessary item of childrens' clothes. They were conscious of the public acceptability of their children's clothes and school lunches in order to ensure that their children would not be labelled negatively in school.

Research on older people shows that a significant number sought increased opportunities for social participation but suffered risks of poverty, of spending time alone and security risks (Garavan et al., 2001). Twenty-eight per cent of the people in the study lived alone and most of these were women. Almost half of those living alone spent 10–14 hours in the 'waking' day alone and another two thirds were alone for 5–9 hours daily. Women rated their quality of life as significantly lower than men. Older people and in particular older women have been officially identified as a group vulnerable to poverty yet it is those that the Government decided to target in its social spending cutbacks in the past year. The Home Help scheme, intended to assist mostly older people to live in their own homes, was cut back by an hour here and a few hours there. Apart from the initial outcry from these people and their relatives in radio talk shows, the matter received little further public attention and the cuts were implemented nationwide with huge implications for the well-being of the those affected and the women workers who were engaged in this low-paid community type work.

Social employment and workfare

The European perspective is a discourse of 'active' welfare states, with a goal of reconnecting the workless with the labour market in contrast to the old 'dependency' – promoting welfare states (Lister, 2002). Women's labour force participation has been important to the growth of the Celtic Tiger. The government has promoted dual earner households as the route out of poverty for families through the individualisation of the tax system. An analysis of data for the period 1991–6 shows a very strong growth in women's employment at both ends of the occupational hierarchy (Breathnach, 2002). However, despite the rapid increases in women's participation rates, women's earnings accounted for only 15 per cent of total household income in 1994. Significantly, increases in women's employment rates in the period 1987–94 were greatest among wives married to low-earning husbands. However, these women have experienced only modest wage gains compared with the wives of husbands with earnings above the average (Nolan et al., 2000a). Part-time work continues to be dominated by women. The absence of universal public childcare in Ireland and the over-reliance on subsidised private provision places further financial constraints on working parents.

The Irish state has actively funded programmes for the reintegration of the long-term unemployed and other social welfare recipients into the labour market. Expenditure on employment supports increased from less than a quarter of a million in 1990 to just under £200 million in 1999 (Department of Social, Community and Family Affairs, 1999). From 1998 the state began to reduce funding for such training programmes, and funding for passport benefits attached to such programmes including rent and mortgage supplements. Underpinning this neo-liberal discourse is the notion that poverty can only be addressed by employment (Fanning, 2003: 15). In 1999 the government decided to restructure the Community Employment (CE) programme and to reduce the number of participants by approximately 2,000 per year to a target of 28,000 by 2003 (Department of Social, Community and Family Affairs, 2001). Other schemes for unemployed people including the jobs initiative scheme have also been reduced. Many of these schemes are based in low-income communities working with children, the elderly and teenagers. Many services provided through these projects are an essential part of the social economy. However, the state is adamant that in a high employment economy the main objective is to promote 'workfare' not welfare and to move people on from welfare dependency.

Indeed, the government links the significant decrease in consistent poverty with the reduction in welfare dependency and the expansion of labour market opportunities since the mid-1990s. Social employment schemes provide an opportunity of developing the social economy at local community level with the provision of much-needed services for groups outside the labour market. It provides training for the participants, part-time working hours (which allow households to cope with childcare) and participants are freed to take on additional employment. A particularly positive aspect of the various social employment schemes is their universal nature for those outside the paid labour market and not subject to spatial zoning. In one study all participants on social employment schemes reported very positive outcomes, including the opportunity to earn occasional additional income (Coakley, 1999).

Spatial zoning and re-zoning

Irish welfare policy has a strong history of targeting and means-testing those outside the labour market. A focus on spatiality is part of the discourse on the reconstruction of poverty. This, according to the government, requires targeted intervention and funding despite research evidence and NAPS policy statements that contradict this. 'The spatial aspects of poverty, deprivation and disadvantage are spatially pervasive phenomena which affect virtually every part of the country and every type of area within the country' (NAPS, 1997: 53). Nolan and Whelan were unable to find any evidence of substantial neighbourhood effects and this is consistent with international research. They conclude that there is: '[a] failure to acknowledge the limits of what can be achieved by area-based initiatives' (1999: 120). Other research is critical of the latest development in the plethora of area-based programmes in the last 15 years (Pringle, 1999; Walsh, 2002). The major expansion of territorial strategies in both Britain and the United States came with the 'rediscovery' of poverty in the 1960s. Pringle (1999) notes that the British programme echoes the political ideology of such schemes in Ireland. By identifying small areas of 'multiple deprivation' the problem of poverty could be confined to black spots and could then be depicted as abnormal. The teams engaged in the projects in Britain described it as an exercise in cosmetic planning and they were closed down in 1976. Positive territorial discrimination took off in Ireland in the mid-1980s and was followed by a range of area-based schemes in the 1990s, the most well known being the local partnerships and LEADER programmes funded by the EU. More recently the Irish government launched the RAPID programme as a high profile programme that would 'fast-track' resources to 'black spot' areas. However, it is a low-cost programme and resources from projects have to be drawn from existing budgets of the organisations involved and no substantial additional finance is available.

The concern by some analysts centres on the cosmetic nature of these spatial interventions which neglects the structural causes of poverty that operate within society to create social inequalities (Pringle, 1999). Research has failed to identify a specific location for poverty so 'the search for a local solution for what is essentially a structural problem is doomed to failure' (Walsh, 2002: 30). The nature of cumulative disadvantage for groups can be understood only when it is located in the context of wider social and economic change:

> The emergence of marginalized groups detached from the labour market has to be understood in the context of competition between social classes for secure positions, and in the means of access to such positions (Nolan and Whelan 1999: 119).

The dominant perspective fails to acknowledge research that shows the limits of local initiatives, which cannot provide solutions to problems whose causes are national or international. Community-based projects have the potential for innovation only if the communities can be empowered and resourced. If the emphasis is on social inclusion then social services must be aimed at the community as a whole and so are seen as benefiting everybody. It is only then that they can foster social integration and a sense of community (Bauman, 1998b). The zoning of areas of social exclusion is in contrast to the spread of private commodified leisure services. For example, it is reported that the private health club industry may have reached saturation point in some places and there is evidence of a price war in certain areas of Dublin (Slattery, 2003). Instead of policies that create spaces of exclusion it would seem more appropriate to provide the public services and infrastructure to create community spaces such as community centres, public swimming pools and playgrounds which in many areas are haphazard or non-existent.

Conclusions

In the most recent historical period there is fragmentation, dilution and increasing spatialisation in the Irish government's response to poverty. The official perspective defines the parameters of poverty as 'consistent' poverty supported by research that shows its decline during the Celtic Tiger. The

government applies new thinking to measure, validate, evaluate and cate-
gorise groups of people who may be vulnerable to poverty. Monitoring progress
is assigned to various inter-departmental groups with little or no financial
backup. The issue of child poverty, for example, has become part of a way of
measuring the reduction in consistent poverty. State policy has facilitated
growing inequalities as more and more people are forced to exit out of welfare
dependency and into the low-paid job sector. The movement of immigrant
workers across Europe gives this sector a new dynamic. The opportunity to
address the social provision deficit in Ireland remains available with per capita
income well above the European average. 'The windfall of revenue that came
to the state in the second half of the 1990s represented a fund that would have
enabled it to ease the inequalities that resulted from the Celtic Tiger, while
beginning a transformation towards the high service and higher-welfare
models of continental Europe' (O'Hearn, 2003: 52).

The lack of ontological security and lack of well-being arising from the
differential accumulation of exposures and experiences that have their sources
in the material world has critical implications for family life, for children grow-
ing up, for a sense of belonging to a community and for inter-generational
happiness. Greater income inequality has a major influence on denying some
groups a sense of dignity, respect and personal worth.

> the effect of income inequality on health reflect a combination of negative
> exposures and lack of resources held by individuals, along with systematic under-
> investment across a wide range of human, physical, health and social infrastructure
> (Lynch et al., 2000).

The policy of targeting and zoning identifiable spaces of exclusion, despite
research evidence to the contrary, may have the effect of positioning people
with ascribed characteristics so that they become the 'other'. Much of the
Irish research on poverty contests the official discourse and places an emphasis
on the structural causes of poverty. Strategies for spatial and community
intervention must have an emphasis on empowerment (Nolan and Whelan,
1999). The definition of poverty needs to include quality of life indicators and
measures of social capital that might more accurately reflect the lived
experience of poverty (NESF, 2003a).

The changing complexity of a global society produces new social risks,
which impact differently according to social class, gender and race. The
interconnections between risks and opportunities generated by attachment to
the labour market and other forms of inter-generational and life insecurities
must be acknowledged (Room, 2000). The transitions in migration, for
example, impact on systems of intergenerational supports and resources.
However, the individual and family continue to be organised through and

embedded in local networks of care and support and the differentiated nature of these supports produce very diverse responses to the processes of global-isation (Fink, 2001). While paid work is elevated to a citizenship obligation, unpaid work including community, voluntary and caring work is devalued (Lister, 2002). How can a discourse measuring consistent poverty, targeting and spatialising exclusion, and the increased commodification of public services address the complexity of poverty risks including property poverty, inequality of resources, powerlessness and unequal health and well-being? Does it address issues such as the increase in indirect taxes, the rising cost to families of 'free education'? The success story of the Nordic countries in having the lowest poverty rates in the OECD is due particularly to the much greater emphasis on the provision of services than on benefits (Pearson, 2003).

It endorses a vision of society based on principles of sustainability and increases in social capital. As put by Tovey: 'The displacement and inequality fostered by capitalism is neither temporary nor accidental, therefore what poor people need is not greater integration into it, but greater insulation and protection from it. Policies should support and strengthen institutions and movements which help to disengage local disadvantaged groups and economies from domination by capitalism' (1999: 114).

Chapter 8

Equity, efficiency and healthcare

Jo Murphy-Lawless and Suzanne Quin

Introduction

The work of caring in the form of services to maintain, improve and regain well-being is at the heart of the public service professions of health care. In line with international trends, the Irish health care system operates in a climate of increasing uncertainty about current and projected costs. Spending on health services is characterised as a 'black hole' and these services are pressured to become more efficient to help stem spiralling costs. Yet there is considerable uncertainty about what constitutes efficiency and how this can be balanced with the need for equity as the principle of fairness, especially with the increasing strength of private medicine as a market commodity. The very meaning of efficiency may be increasingly contested in the near future, affected by radical free-market perspectives that sit uneasily alongside the established tradition of twentieth-century national public health care systems with the concomitant public service ethos. Health services also face demands for greater professionalism, accountability and excellence in practical and clinical work and yet it is unclear how to achieve these outcomes when, in many areas of provision, skilled staff is the most necessary resource, the cost of which rises inexorably (Wren, 2003: 234–5).

This chapter seeks to explore these complexities in the context of the Irish health care services, where we can see the features of the kind of bureaucratic capitalism Sjoberg describes. We also want to relate our examination of these issues to similar developments elsewhere. The chapter begins with a section discussing the concepts of equity and caring and the links between them. It continues with a discussion of Richard Titmuss's classic argument on the importance of building health for society as a whole and how this is more important than ever in a period of rapid economic and social changes related to globalisation. We then raise questions about citizen involvement and decision making with regard to health services. Increasingly, in moves to reinvigorate democratic decision making on issues about core human needs that affect well-being, citizens across many countries and societies are seeking to open up new fora for participatory democracy (Wainwright, 2003). Using Bauman's argument about the need for such opportunities for exploring our worries and anxieties, we consider the importance of challenging governments to raise their stakes and make the development of health and well-being with services to support them a fundamental good for society.

At family and community level, many are aware of the inadequacies of health services as they encounter the grievous difficulties of swelling waiting lists and sub-optimal care. This is especially marked for more marginalised sections in Irish society. These unhappy personal experiences reduce the quality of people's lives and generate anxiety and a sense of helplessness. There is a distance between them and the state that has been charged with responding to their needs for welfare and well-being and which often now appears to be retreating from this undertaking.

This negative dynamic has been noted in relation to the status of the welfare state in other advanced economies (Mishra, 1999). Indeed the nature of the contract between the state and its citizens may be changing and doing so in deeply inegalitarian ways. That is a key contention of Bauman (1998b: 56–7), who argues that we now live in a period in which the balance of favour is turning against the welfare state and its public services: with the perception that standards of care are falling, and as public services tend more towards selectivity and away from universality, those who have less need of these services are less inclined to support them. Also the primacy of the notion of 'consumer choice' creates a scenario where people who have means wish to make choices and thus reject the 'one size fits all' nature of public services (1998b: 58).

Such developments have a particular resonance in Ireland where the unequal nature of Irish society has been remarked upon in relation to health outcomes. Wren (2003: 15) points to international research indicating that the greater the levels of inequality in a society, the worse its overall health becomes. O'Toole (2003: 75–6) cites the disparities in health profiles between the better-off Irish citizens and those in the lowest socio-economic groups, commenting that the poor who have greatest need of health services find it hardest to gain access. He terms the two-tier system in Ireland that places those who cannot pay on long waiting lists an 'apartheid system'.

This apartheid is being challenged by groups and communities in Ireland, albeit in a largely unco-ordinated movement. Single-issue groups, such as people with disabilities, or local communities concerned about proposed hospital closures, are attempting to ask searching questions about decision making on the allocation of health resources.

At the same time as communities and the health services themselves are both struggling with these political and economic realities, theories about health and its maintenance are also changing. These are moving towards a more holistic focus in which health gain and wellness are seen as the objectives towards which health services should be striving (WHO, 2000). Such aspirations seem very difficult to translate into effective care systems, given the realities of the increasingly individualised and fragmented society that these services are trying to support. There are multiple strains on the public service professions as they try to reconcile core values of caring with the everyday contexts in which they carry out their work.

In 2003, the Economic and Social Research Institute published research on equity and health services in Ireland, presenting amongst others the following data:

- 22 per cent of outpatient visits for care by specialists are made by the richest one fifth of the population, yet their level of chronic illness is 14.5 per cent;

- The poorest fifth of the population, experiencing 38 per cent of all chronic illness, can garner just 20 per cent of outpatient visits to specialists;

- The poorest fifth of the population is most reliant on prescription drugs – 37 per cent, compared with 11 per cent of the richest one fifth of the population

(O'Regan, 2003).

The issue of a lack of equity in respect of the Irish health services stands out clearly, if, as this research concludes, the richest have greatest access to outpatient health services while having the least illness.

Sjoberg (1999: 54) speaks of this kind of increasing gap between the privileged and the disadvantaged sectors in the developed and developing world as a locus of critical investigation. His concern is related to the way in which bureaucratic structures as an integral part of capitalism 'have come to support and sustain privilege, as well as the processes by which social triage is produced'. Of course part of the postmodern project is a proliferation of specialisation, difference and diversity. Yet the hierarchical power relationships and routinisation that sustained the growth of modernity have also cultivated anew the growth of gross inequalities in a period when consumerism and cheap labour have a global meaning.

Bureaucratic capitalism, Sjoberg argues, produces and relies on centralised power and decision making and on hierarchical power relationships, all lessons learned within the period of modernity and carried forward to the state-corporate partnerships of postmodernity. The rapid proliferation of new markets for new goods and services that has enabled the global corporate sector to flourish has not taken place within an 'organisational vacuum' but within this same context of bureaucratic capitalism. In respect of specialisation of knowledge, for example, although it has been dramatic in its growth, it continues to be embedded and to operate within tried and tested forms of 'hierarchical coordination and control' (1999: 49). There are huge impacts here for the production of social triage, especially if, as Sjoberg concludes, organisational forms are more intent than ever on preserving their reality over and above the disparate realities and agency of individuals. Thus, although we continue to require the 'standardised' delivery of 'work' from hospitals and schools, we do so in a frame of reference that distances control over decision making from the individual, that increasingly downgrades Keynesian welfare economics, and that very effectively ignores those who are marginalised.

From patient to consumer and from bureaucrat to manager

The traditional medical model institutionalised inequality between service providers and service users. The 'benevolent despot' approach characterised the relationship between the professional giver and the lay recipient. Just as the former was expected to play a dynamic role while acting 'in the best interests of the patient', the latter was expected to be a grateful and passive receiver of professional care. However, the advent of 'what has become known as the "new public health" and the associated practice of health promotion have effectively redefined "the patient" as the entire population and in the process have transformed the relationship between patient and doctor that lay at the heart of the traditional health care system' (Langan, 1998: 100). Health care users are no longer limited to those who are ill but encompass the whole population.

A significant feature of the 1980s and 1990s was the shift from the Keynesian model of welfare, grounded in egalitarian and collectivist values, to the dominance of economic models of welfare which emphasised the values of pluralism, individualism and self-reliance. Critiques of the traditional welfare state approach characterised it as paternalistic, inducing dependency and wasteful of scarce resources. The dominance of economic discourse turned patients into consumers while service providers were encouraged to adopt principles and practices of management. In this process, '[the] consumer came to be represented as the most normal and desirable role through which people's wants and needs could be met' (Clarke, 1998: 20).

However, the language of consumerism conceals some fundamental differences between commercial markets and public services. As Clarke (1998) points out, in the commercial market a rise in demand for a good is seen as positive and the appropriate response to increase supply. A rise in demand in the public market is not necessarily interpreted or responded to in a similar manner. Taking health care as an example, a rise in demand for acute hospital care is more likely to result in efforts to curtail demand through the process of rationing rather than automatically leading to increased provision.

O'Sullivan (2003) considers the appropriateness of the consumer model for health care since it is based on two questionable assumptions. The first is that health is a consumer good that can be bought and sold and secondly that the doctor/patient relationship is primarily economic rather than based on trust and commitment. He questions whether the market-based contractual model is an adequate framework for vulnerable people (e.g. users of health care) who often do not have access to all relevant information and cannot act in a wholly independent manner.

The principles of access, choice, information, redress and representation are seen as key to the empowerment of the consumer in public welfare (Clarke, 1998: 23), while managerialism has become the new discourse of service providers. This discourse has 'offered a set of prescriptions for producing economies . . . highly compatible with the idea of a more self-reliant welfare consumer' (Newman, 1998: 336). Hence, Newman (1998: 337) argues, managerialism 'can be understood as an ideology, not as a set of neutral techniques' as it is often presented. Managerialism offers a set of discourses which may encompass different knowledge bases, goals and ways of relating. Common to all is the language of the discourse in which terms such as 'innovation', 'dynamism', 'customer' and 'performance-centred' appear in implicit contrast to the paternalistic, rule-bound and controlling characterisation of traditional bureaucracy.

Changing aspects of health in an era of globalisation

Illich (1996) discusses the medicalisation of health that has stretched the brief of health care to encompass not just those who are sick but also those who are well. People who are healthy now access health services to be reassured that they are. Physicians, he states (1996: 17), have become 'the socially responsible professional manager not of a patient, but of a *life* from sperm to worm'. Hence the clientele of health care now encompasses all and the boundaries of what is possible are constantly stretched. However, the hazards of health care are now entering the public domain more explicitly. Research on iatrogenic disease indicates that a substantial percentage of health service users may find their health status has worsened as a direct outcome of their encounter with health care.

According to Blank (1997), limitless appetite for medical technology, more than any other factor, explains the growth in health spending. This, he argues, is intensified by three factors:

- The deification of doctors

- The medicalisation of social problems

- Exaggeration of minor symptoms – we expect physicians to confer immortality and freedom from pain.

There are no easy solutions to health care issues. Some of these problems – such as access – arise from our system of provision in Ireland; others stem from changes in demography, medical knowledge and technology that transcend our national boundaries. For health is also a global issue, as pandemics like HIV and SARS highlight, and no country can readily find the answers to the very complex entity that health and its absence have become. At the same time, the working concept of health has changed from the strict lack of disease to an all-encompassing sense of well-being defined by the World Health Organisation as 'not merely the absence of disease or infirmity' but 'a state of complete physical, mental and social well-being'. Yet this state is one that remains at best aspirational. As Skrabanek (1994) cynically commented, ordinary people may only experience such well-being at fleeting moments in the course of their lifetime. The WHO definition of health strives for a utopia which, in current conditions, is unobtainable; the WHO itself has been unable to deliver its promise on its Millennium Development Goals to contain and reduce AIDS, tuberculosis and malaria, three treatable disease entities that account for the overwhelming excess mortality in Poor World countries and amongst the poorest classes in Rich World countries (Farmer, 2003; Horton, 2003). Weak political strategies are thought to account for its failure to respond to Poor World countries, who, in 2002, requested $1.2 billion from the Global Fund to Fight AIDS, Tuberculosis and Malaria, receiving instead 700 million dollars (Horton, 2003: 337–8).

Medical science is also implicated in visions of a health utopia to which we can never aspire, especially while scientific research (most usually carried out in a corporate pharmaceutical complex) and its benefits are selectively targeted, with the wealthy gaining the substantial benefits of new therapies. The myriad press releases about the latest potential medical 'cure' deflect from the real dilemmas of how to provide best possible care and how to pursue a preventative model of building good health in the context of a challenging political climate that seeks to 'hollow out' the welfare state, in Mishra's (1999) inimitable phrase. He argues that this hollowing-out un-anchors health care as a social responsibility and in so doing devalues universality and social citizenship.

There is yet another troubling dimension to the globalised context of healthcare and healthcare provision. Ireland, like all other advanced economies, contributes to the reproduction of inequalities because of increasing reliance on trained medical personnel from countries of the South. Irish personnel (both doctors and nurses) to staff the health services are in short supply, with a significant reliance on non-EU doctors to fill the majority of the 1,193 generic registrar posts (Wren, 2003: 158). Irish-born and trained doctors in their thirties are largely absent from the system, having emigrated for better career possibilities. In 2000 alone, Ireland gave contracts to 55 anaesthetists from India and Pakistan. The problem here is the 'brain drain' from countries that can ill afford the loss of skilled medical personnel. Having invested the funds to train their medical personnel, poor countries from the south then lose this resource to rich countries without any financial compensation. In the WHO Declaration, Health for All by the Year 2000, adopted in 1977, the organisation set out the target of a doctor for every 5,000 people and a qualified nurse for every 1,000 people in 'developing' countries. Those targets cannot now possibly be met, as a global medical market has increasingly attracted doctors and nurses to advanced countries. It is thought that for the poorest 25 countries of the world, the current ratio is one doctor for every 25,000 people (Frommel, 2002).

Nursing provides an even more telling example of this growing dilemma of staff shortages. Caring and the work of nursing in giving care have long been seen as central to the ability of a patient to recover from illness and disease. However, there is now an extensive debate within nursing as to what constitutes care and about the distinct selflessness that the traditional nursing role implies (Clarke, 2001: 30–4). Cited as 'one of the cornerstones of the modern Irish health service' (Commission on Nursing, 1998: 3), the nursing profession in recent years has begun to demand radical changes in training, pay and professional issues. When these issues were not addressed by the government, despite the recommendations of the Commission on Nursing in 1998, non-response led to the first ever nurses' strike in Ireland in 1999.

There is, at present, an acute nursing shortage, with recruitment and retention beginning to dominate discussions on the future of nursing. The most recent figures on nursing vacancies indicate that in the first quarter of 2003 there were 946 nursing posts vacant in the Irish health service (Donnellan, 2003). It is estimated that 4,800 Filipina nurses are currently employed to fill gaps in the service; a major gap opens up in 2005, when there will be no graduates that year because of the moves to relocate all nurse training within the third-level sector, with a shortfall of 1,500 posts expected as a result. This is a typical pattern in relation to nursing across many advanced economies and has resulted in what Parreñas (2003) terms a 'care deficit' which has been filled by migrant workers, such as the several thousand Filipina nurses in the Irish system. But this movement of health workers from Poor World countries, although it temporarily 'solves' staffing problems in Ireland, creates individual deficits for migrants' families left at home as well as contributing to the deficits in extremely poorly resourced health care systems in

Poor World countries. Recent calls have been made for the WHO as part of the UN system to develop a convention on the recruitment of health care workers from poor countries (Frommel, 2002; Pang et al., 2002). Solutions must be found so that the improvement of staffing levels in advanced economies is not at the expense of the poorest.

Equity, caring and well-being

In the seventeenth century, Izaak Walton (1593–1683) wrote 'Look to your health; and if you have it, praise God, and value it next to a good conscience; for health is the second blessing that we mortals are capable of; a blessing that money cannot buy'. Good health is as valued in the twenty-first century as it was 500 years ago, the essential difference being that it is now recognised that the likelihood of having good health as well as having access to health services is positively related to wealth and status in society.

The National Economic and Social Forum (1996) conceptualised equality as having four stages, each with different objectives and outcomes. The first involves a minimalist approach which defines equality in terms of equal rights to participate in the economic, social, political and cultural life. Attention is focused on institutional barriers to access based on grounds other than those directly related to need. In terms of health policy, this is the level that is operating at present in that overall policy is directed to ensuring that no one is unable to access health care on account of lack of means (Curry, 2003). The basic problem with this approach is that removal of formal barriers to access will not in itself guarantee equality of participation.

Having the abilities and resources to access such rights is the next level – that of equality of participation. What is required at this level is the active encouragement and facilitation through proactive means. Policies to pursue this objective are, by their nature, enabling rather than mandatory. Good will on the part of providers could be regarded as an underlying assumption of this approach. However, equality of participation may not lead to greater equality in effect. Barriers such as the contextual situation of individuals and communities as well as the depth and range of disadvantages experienced may act as obstacles to greater equality. There is evidence of this approach to service provision in health care in Ireland. Enabling legislation and policies are directed by meeting need 'as resources permit' – a recognisable feature of Irish health care.

The third level of equality is that based on outcome for those with different means and opportunities. Policies targeted to meet this objective must address differentials in terms of both aims and results. An obvious example in relation to health care is policies to promote equalisation of health status across different socio-economic groups. Achievement is measured by the extent to which differentials are reduced or eliminated in relation to morbidity and/or pre-mature mortality, an area in which there is scope for much improvement in Ireland (Balanda, 2001, Barry et al., 2001, European Commission, 2003)

The fourth level of equality objective is that of equality of condition. At this level, equality is about equal status in society by virtue of citizenship. Equality is central to all policy formulation which incorporates heterogeneity of the population in relation to variables such as ethnicity, race, gender, age and impairment. The importance of equality of condition is well illustrated in relation to people with disabilities. Oliver (1996) applies Marshall's concep-tualisation of citizenship incorporating civil, political and social rights to the situation of people with disabilities. He argues that in relation to each of the three aspects of citizenship those with disability are prevented from full participation in social, economic and cultural life. In regard to health care, for example, people with disability, because of their low participation in the workforce, are less likely than the population in general of being able to access private health care. Public sector health care may not have sufficient resources and/or be prepared to use such resources for the benefit of those with disability as opposed to spending on curative or preventative health measures. Even simple physical access to doctors' surgeries and health centres may prevent them from accessing basic health care programmes theoretically provided for all such as routine screening or family planning (Kallianes and Rubenfeld, 1997; Tighe, 2001).

Can quality professional caring occur when health professionals act as unwilling gatekeepers of scarce resources and as arbitrators of conflicting needs as well as having to achieve and maintain high levels of technical expertise in their field of practice? Quality care is not just about technical competence. Ludmerer and Fox (2001: 127) suggest that the effective health professional must be capable of 'competent caring'. This involves more than just technical competence but also the capacity to relate on a human level to those who are at the receiving end of technical care. This latter element, which involves concern for the patient, has been eroded by a preoccupation with the tech-nicalities of caring. Cassell (2001: 108) comments that 'for ages, the centrality of the patient has been much spoken about, although in recent times the words have been empty'.

Professional caring is different in essence from altruistic care provided by family and friends. However, it is of central importance to the concept of holistic health. It is the combination of personal commitment, interpersonal skills and contextual circumstances that allows this level of relatedness to occur. Overcrowded and/or poor quality facilities, time pressures and lack of resources are not conducive to providing quality care. In relation to the situation of service providers, the Commission on Financial Management and Control Systems in the Health Service (2003: 24) commented that 'one of the strengths of the health service are the very many dedicated and committed people working in all areas of the sector. . . . They deserve no less than the opportunity to work in a system which will support them in doing what they wish to do: offer the highest quality service to the public'.

Challenges to securing health and extending health services

Richard Titmuss, in *Birth, Poverty, and Wealth*, his seminal work on the linkages between personal health and well-being and the health of the community as a whole, quotes René Sand, who said in 1935 that 'health is purchasable . . . Each country within certain limits, decides its own death rates' (Sand, quoted in Titmuss, 1943). For Titmuss, this notion conveyed complex, interlocking decisions and circumstances as diverse as a government's international policy making, an individual employer's decision to close his business and lay people off work, which would have an impact on their health and the health of their families. With singular prescience, Titmuss argued 'we have yet to formulate a standard of positive health as an absolute good in itself unrelated to industrial or military considerations' (Alcock et al., 2001: 26). This perspective from 60 years ago has importance for us as we try to come to terms with national constraints on maintaining and developing social standards in an era of globalisation.

Mishra (1999) argues that the movement towards globalisation indicated by the growth of multinational corporations and the increased international production of goods and services has been accompanied by a shrinking tax base in many national arenas, which itself has resulted in reductions in social spending. Yet while other social benefits are being cut back, the commitment to health spending continues to receive 'strong support from the vast majority of the population' (1999: 47) in many advanced economies. To deal with this popular electoral support for health, Mishra identifies a general trend by governments to avoid wholesale cutbacks in health provision thus incurring voter wrath, and instead to use 'incremental' cutbacks, where user charges and fees are raised. The range of services is reduced, the quality of services declines, and moves towards privatised health care provision are encouraged.

Ireland is not immune to such developments. In a country striving to retain its recent patterns of economic growth in a globalised market, overall spending on health currently absorbs €8.3 billion or just one quarter of current government expenditure (Wren, 2003: 227). However, this spending, which in 2001 exceeded EU average spending on health, also represents a very belated investment in a health care infrastructure which had been badly depleted by the late 1980s, when total expenditure was only 57 per cent of average EU spending. At the same time, 'stealth cutbacks' are also a feature of current government policy. These are exemplified in two recent Budgets by substantial rises in accident and emergency charges, hospital bed charges for those who are non-insured, non-medical card holders, and the ceiling charge for the drugs refund scheme for those requiring medication and without a medical card. At the same time, the Department of Health and Children is one of the principal beneficiaries of the Budget for 2004.

The conundrum of health spending in Ireland appears to centre on what Wren (2003: 225), quoting the then Minister for Health and Children, has referred to as a 'black hole' of unlimited demands for more spending. At the same time, there are genuine problems of access to services in a society that experiences marked health inequalities, compared with other EU countries. For example, men and women in Ireland have significantly higher rates of death from cardiovascular disease and other circulatory diseases, compared with the average figures for the EU as a whole (Eurostat, 2000). Ireland has the highest premature death rate of any EU country. There are gender differences as well, with the overall rates of cancer for women in Ireland higher than the EU average. Irish women contract more cancer types at relatively high rates compared with the EU averages for women. They experience the highest rate of oesophageal cancer amongst women in the EU (Cancer Consortium, 2001). Issues of lifestyle, and the challenges these present to government health prevention and promotion strategies, appropriate and timely interventions and treatments, are all implicated in such figures.

Ireland has successfully undertaken a huge drive to encourage multinational diagnostic, biotechnology and pharmaceutical companies to locate themselves in the country, with now 120 such companies, a workforce of 20,000 and outputs standing at over 29 per cent of the country's total exports. Ironically, despite the strength of the sector, our health care system cannot afford to make full use of what is produced here. There is a shortage, for example, of an important range of drugs to treat rheumatoid arthritis (RTÉ Television News Bulletin, 16 October 2003).

These findings suggest that a debate on the values that should underpin the Irish health system is vital. We will next explore the history and recent and current dilemmas of health care provision in Ireland, before discussing how future health provision might begin to meet the challenge that Titmuss threw down six decades ago.

Evolution of the Irish health system

The Irish health system has evolved in a piecemeal way. Historically, religious and philanthropic effort developed services to meet perceived needs of certain groups over time which resulted in a fragmented system on which a structure was superimposed. Thus the development of health care in Ireland can best be characterised by the term 'incrementalist'. This can be defined as creating a system by simply adding on to what currently exists. Subsequent developments are not necessarily interconnected, can be added to or taken away, and missing is a basic plan of what is to be created in the first place. It is remarkable that it was not until the 1990s that there was a serious attempt to create an overall plan for the development of health care (Curry, 2003). Prior to that, while plans and discussion documents were produced for different elements in the system, there was no overriding statement of intent about what health services should comprise and the principles underlying them. A notable feature of the strategy document of 1994 (Department of Health, 1994) was the acceptance of the public/private mix of health services as an acceptable and even desirable feature of Irish health care. This approach was continued in the subsequent strategy document of 2001 (Department of Health and Children, 2001a) while the importance of addressing inequities in access to public health care was acknowledged.

The historical forces that have created these inequities have been well documented by Barrington (1987). The strength of these forces is still evident in Irish health care (Wren, 2003). Traditionally, the Catholic Church has played a major role in ensuring a residualist approach to public provision in health care. Not only has it intervened on a policy level (at its most evident in the Mother and Child Scheme proposed by Dr Noel Browne), but, through direct provision, has created and reinforced a two-tier system of public/private provision in both health and education services. Witness the fact that some of the major providers of private hospital care (such as St Vincent's, the Mater private hospitals in Dublin and the Bon Secour Hospital in Cork) are run by religious orders. These are hospitals which, by virtue of being adjacent to parallel public facilities, can benefit from them at the opportunity cost to public patients.

However, all of the deficits of the health care system cannot be laid at the door of the Catholic Church. Those in political power have not shown the inclination or the ability to effectively challenge the deeply unequal system that has been created through the acceptance of what is a socially divided and divisive model of state provision. Vested interests in health care, in particular hospital consultants, have also played a key role in the development and maintenance of the system. But the most telling problem has been the absence of political will that is prepared to grasp the stinging nettles of fundamental health care issues.

The legal system too has to be included in the framework. It has played a developmental role, in which potential service users have had recourse to legal processes to establish rights to services or as users to redress issues of neglect or malpractice. But another way of putting this is that the legal system comes into play when individuals, specific groups and even communities have lost trust in the formal health care services and in health policy making. There have been major examples of this in recent years, with both court actions and government tribunals involved. Two tribunals on the scandals of contaminated blood products emanating from the national Blood Transfusion Service Board that affected over a thousand people dominated public attention over a period of years in the 1990s, without, however, any prosecutions following in their train (Wren, 2003: 109–10). The possibility of going to law is thought to contribute substantially to a climate of defensive practice on the part of service providers and an adversarial context for resolving patient grievances is by no means ideal. On the other hand, high profile civil cases seeking to prove medical negligence will continue to take place, not least because the country lacks effective national systems for independently and rigorously auditing practice, and because the issue of the failure to provide genuine self-regulation of doctors by the Irish Medical Council has not been resolved.

The growth of private health care

Public attitudes and perceptions have also played their part in sustaining the system of health care currently in existence. The size of the private insurance market in Ireland is an expression of lack of trust in the public system as well as guarding self-interest. Overall lack of confidence in the system is fuelled by media reports. For example, in 2003 alone, *The Irish Times* carried 165 articles on hospital waiting lists. This media coverage is reinforced by first-hand experiences of insufficient resources and personnel. A website, Waiting List Watch, is now maintained by irishhealth.com.

The growth in private health care may also represent a response to a growing sense that health is increasingly a personal responsibility. Social theorists like Ulrich Beck (1992) and Zygmunt Bauman (1998b, 1999) have explored how in this recent era of post-industrial capitalism what Beck terms the 'risk' society is a far more fragmented one. Without the security of the older forms of family and work, buttressed by the Keynesian welfare state, the individual citizen has to shoulder life's burdens largely alone. The peculiar contradiction this creates in relation to health is that although health in these more uncertain times is a major focus of attention in our society, the maintenance of health has become an obligation for the individual rather than society as a whole (Beck-Gernsheim, 2000). Bauman (1998b) argues that the reluctance of governments to raise taxation to cover rising health care costs for the population as a whole is a message that the middle classes have heard and hence there has been a corresponding increase in private health care insurance.

Private health care has been facilitated by subsidy through the taxation system. Those who can afford it have responded by being prepared to pay not inconsiderable proportions of their income to cover themselves ('each way' to use betting terminology), so that they will have faster access to hospital and consultant care. From the policy makers' viewpoint, the fact that 45 per cent (Deloitte & Touche, 2001: 15) of the population is covered by private insurance is a mixed blessing. On the one hand, it has resulted in those who can afford it paying more than they might be prepared to pay via taxation, thus freeing more resources to the public system for those on lower incomes. On the other hand, it can be regarded as a massive vote of 'no confidence' in the public health care system as well as a statement that, as a society, we have chosen to live with the thinking that ability to pay is an acceptable determinant of access to health care.

Without a significant change of direction, the increase in private medicine in Ireland will continue to grow. It is time to challenge the issue of health care being more attainable for some on the basis of ability to pay. Eliminating differences in access to public health care is important, but as long as there is a parallel system of private health care then inequity is inbuilt. Furthermore, developments in medical knowledge and technology have to be considered in relation to this existing inequity. Rose (2000: 67–8) has argued that although the new genetics promise cures for diseases such as cancer and heart disease, these potential developments and the huge funding programmes that underpin them expose a political problem of deepening inequalities that are already firmly embedded in our societies. The existence of private medicine offering such potential developments or additional or different interventions to more privileged groups could permanently exacerbate inequalities, while raising the threat of eugenics and biological determinism. As Paul Farmer (2003: 226) has stated, we need to debate as a matter of urgency who benefits from such scientific developments.

Decision making on health priorities

Extending the concept of health from the absence of disease has increased the breadth and scope of what health care entails. Potentially the demand for health care is insatiable. The problem is that, depending on which vantage point used, each element of health care provision can be regarded as a priority. Reconciling conflicting demands in the context of finite resources presents major challenges to policy makers and service providers.

Mustard (1999: 331) points out that providers of health care may promote the belief that medicine is the 'primary determinant of health and well-being'. This concept has been a useful device in both publicly and privately financed systems to create political climates to help providers to capture more resources. Ironically, to address effectively some of the major causes of health inequalities would require deflecting resources outside the health care system into housing, education and, perhaps most importantly, social security. The Health of Our Children Report 2001 states that 'poverty is the most important social factor associated with ill health in children' (Department of Health and Children, 2001b: 30). As Barrington (1998) has pointed out, the response of the health services to health problems arising from poverty has been to treat the symptoms rather than seeking to address the underlying causes. Doorley (1998) argued that the health sector should be more vocal in promoting greater spending on social security as a means of reducing health inequalities. This is in the context of pressure to increase health spending on all aspects of health care, preventative and curative.

The fundamental question is how much and what proportion of our resources we are prepared to spend on health and what we can expect in return. That rationing of health care occurs is evident, for waiting lists are but a form of rationing. Over the past decade or so there has been a gradual shift globally towards what the World Health Organisation has termed the 'New Universalism' (WHO: 2000). Rather than all possible care for everyone, it implies delivery to all of a quality service based on principles of access, effectiveness and cost of essential care as it is defined. This implies explicit choice of priorities among all possible interventions and raises further the need for informed public debate about resources and real goals.

The Health Strategy (Department of Health and Children, 2001a) listed equity, people-centredness, quality and accountability as the four principles underlying the delivery of health care in Ireland. However, the questions arise as to whether or not they are mutually compatible, whether they can be of equal import or whether in practice one becomes *prima inter pares*. If rationing is an ongoing feature of health care, who determines what will have priority? The Swedish Parliamentary Priorities Commission in 1995 set out ground rules about the use of scarce health resources. The Commission selected three principles in establishing priorities, giving precedence to their ranking order. These principles were:

- Human Dignity: all human beings have equal dignity and the same rights regardless of their personal characteristics and their socio-economic status.

- Need and Solidarity: resources should be focused on greatest need, especially taking into account those at particular disadvantage from being unable to articulate their needs for themselves.

- Cost Efficiency: when choosing between different options, aim for a reasonable relationship between cost and effect in relation to treating the same condition.

Focusing only on preventative activities with documented benefit poses particular challenges to health promotion/disease prevention activities. It is notoriously difficult to claim that a health promotion strategy is a success or failure because of the number of controlled and uncontrollable variables involved. The consistent trend with much health information literature and related government media campaigns has been to emphasise individuals' decision making and to speak of health in individual terms. Divorcing and de-contextualising health from social, economic, gender, age and other core factors means that the complexity of people's lives are not addressed, therefore rendering much health promotion material irrelevant. Practitioners and researchers have urged governments and agencies to recognise that for this reason, campaigns that exhort people to modify their behaviour are counter-productive (Daykin and Naidoo, 1995). As knowledge about the cause of diseases grows, particularly in relation to genetic predisposition to different illnesses, it is likely that prevention strategies will become a more central focus of health care, but these strategies must honestly address the problems of how health inequalities arise in the first instance.

The implications for health care are enormous in terms of both cost and delivery. Sheinfeld and Arnold (1998) provide the following example in relation to the mutant gene common in families at high risk of breast cancer based on US figures and costs. If just one per cent of the total female population were tested the cost would be several billion dollars. It is possible that 0.1 per cent would test positive predicting a lifetime risk of breast cancer. For that 0.1 per cent health care options might include counselling, chemoprevention, more frequent screening, prophylatic treatment or gene therapy. Potential costs for surgery alone they estimate could cost in the region of $11 million.

Different values to guide the decision-making processes

Debate about the fundamentals of the health care system in Ireland is essential. But debate must be all-inclusive and given the inequities within the Irish system, this implies that meaningful political participation of those most affected by the current inequalities must be developed. There are a number of related points to be made about developing such a public debate. The first relates to the term 'consumer'. As part of the government's health strategy, *Quality and Fairness: A Health System For You* (Department of Health and Children, 2001a), an increase was called for in consumer representation and formal representation structures. Great caution must be exercised in relation to this term 'consumer'. For, if Zygmunt Bauman (1998b: 26) has flagged the issue accurately, the road to self-identity in these postmodern times entails 'daily visits to the market place' as a consumer; those who are poor participate in the most limited manner possible, defining what social exclusion now means. This is why we need to replace this word 'consumer' representation with the far more potent and accurate term of 'citizen'. And it is as citizens that we need to consider the use of, and our participation in, the 'agora', that space which merges the public and private and where 'private worries' from everyday life can become 'public issues' in order to debate the meaning of the 'common good' (Bauman, 1999). Government-led consultation exercises on major issues must ensure that strategies are set in place to ensure that people are actually included in and part of decision making. We need to be creative in making this space for debate in a very different way, even though it is one that may arguably prove more challenging for government departments. Activism from below may prove disquieting for policy makers, but may in fact make the democratic system far healthier.

The closure of the maternity units in Monaghan and Dundalk in March 2001 is a case in point. At first, faced with those closures, many people in these local communities reacted in protest and argued that they wanted exactly what they had once had restored, namely consultant-led units. As time lengthened, and people felt government and the policy makers growing more remote and unresponsive to their demands, new fora opened up for debate. The establishment of the Kinder Review Group, although it was an appointed process from within bureaucracy of the health authority in question, the North Eastern Health Board, did include people from the community in the form of the activist group, Patient Focus. The cross-border public seminar on different options for childbirth management held in Monaghan in June 2001 was a major contributor to helping establish a debate based on evidence of what systems of maternity care flourish. Gradually, the notion of a different option, that of midwifery-led care, has become understood as a better alternative to what the communities had in the first place. For numbers of complex reasons relating to professional boundaries and perceived expertise within the fields of healthcare and medicine, midwifery-led care may not necessarily be a favoured option by many professionals. But that does not alter the fact that these communities through a process of activism and debate have gradually come to a different understanding of what best serves their maternity needs at local level. The public debates regarding the recommendations of the 2003 government-commissioned Hanly Report on medical staffing and its recommendations on closures of smaller accident and emergency facilities, if supported, may well produce a similar depth of activism and debate and new understandings about what is really needed to secure first-class health care. The types of fora used in other countries, such as consensus conferences, may help to produce what Iredale (1999: 183) terms 'a decision-making culture that is both evidence based and inclusive'.

Our health care system has come to accommodate and to live with a lack of equity owing to the lack of political will mentioned earlier. The pretence that all goals can be achieved hinders engagement in real debate about resource distribution and rationing based on principles that promote the common good. This raises again the question of the acceptability of having alternative access for those who can afford to pay. An open process of debate on these issues would undoubtedly produce great tensions, but ones that might ultimately be 'healthier' for the decision-making process.

Conclusion: the need to debate the value of caring and equity in health care

The proliferation of the number and range of professionals engaged in providing services is a feature of modern health systems. In Ireland, the costs of paying such personnel form the largest element of current expenditure (Commission on Financial Management and Control Systems in the Health Service, 2003). A common feature of those entering the health care professions is the desire to provide care for others in some way. This altruistic motive can be challenged by their subsequent experiences as service providers. Insufficient resources, poor working environments, inadequate recognition and recompense, lack of support and being the targets of public frustration and expressions of anomie are cited as reasons why groups such as junior doctors, nurses, physiotherapists, social workers are experiencing significant levels of occupational stress. The danger is that altruism can change to cynicism or can result in professionals leaving the system altogether. This is an established pattern in relation to nurses, as we have already seen. In effect, the altruistic motivation of caring is undermined by a version of Sjoberg's 'bureaucratic capitalism' that is focused on constraining social action that will gain genuine equity and access.

Sophisticated technology has added a further dimension to the human gap between the cared for and the professional health carer. Crowther (1993: 115) argues that as medicine advances and becomes 'rather more a science than an art', this progress has tended to 'leave behind the necessary skills of communication, kindness and understanding for a sick fellow human being'.

Increasingly, the importance of a holistic approach to health care is gaining recognition. The concept of caring is an essential feature of this approach. Quality health care requires professionals who develop the capacity to treat with care and sensitivity those that are sick. This is a challenge in the face of the multiple demands of modern medicine in what is most frequently less than optimal conditions that reflect the increasing tensions between medicine as a global market entity and health and its maintenance as a social good.

During their training and subsequent career, doctors, nurses, physio-therapists and other paramedical staff are required on a routine basis to inflict pain and discomfort on others in the course of carrying out procedures deemed to be in the best interests of the patient. Such experiences, in themselves, carry with them a high risk of stress and burnout. Without adequate preparation and ongoing support for staff, there is a danger that their sensibilities will become blunted, at a high cost for themselves and, more importantly, for their patients. The ability to maintain the capacity to empathise and, at the same time, to be objective in professional judgement is a balancing act that is not easy to achieve. If this capacity is not developed and fostered, patients will not receive good quality care. The growing trend to see health care staff as a site for patient advocacy – with, for example, occupational therapists having this built into their training – means it is more critical still to protect profes-sionals who are doing caring work and advocacy work in tandem.

It is an opportune time to consider the creation of a new term for those on the receiving end of health care. The traditional term of 'patient' implies passivity, 'one who is long-suffering and forbearing' (Viney, 1983: 51). Yet, as discussed earlier in this chapter, the use of the term 'consumer' in relation to health care is equally unsatisfactory since those who are sick cannot operate under assumed market conditions of having sufficient knowledge and choice. 'Consumer' in the context of health care implies a level of power that is not a reflection of reality of those at the receiving end of health services in Ireland. There is an argument for substituting the term 'client' as currently used by social workers and a number of non-medical professional groups such as lawyers and architects. However, this term does not incorporate the ideals of cherishing and care that are central to holistic health care.

Article 25 of the Universal Declaration of Human Rights states that 'Everyone has the right to a standard of living adequate for the health and well-being of himself and of his family, including food, clothing, housing and medical care and necessary social services, and the right to social security in the event of unemployment, sickness, disability widowhood, old age or other lack of livelihood in circumstance beyond his control.' Through this 'moral standard' (Sjoberg, 1999: 58), we have the benchmarking tool to measure equity in the creation of good health and the responses to ill-health in our society. The compatibility of equity of condition with existing public provision and the two-tier system of health care in Ireland are core questions to be resolved. We argue that full citizen engagement is vital to that resolution and that only through such a process of engagement can we hope to begin to challenge and abolish the current range of inequities embedded in our health services. The establishment of a genuine and robust participatory democracy built on a distinctive public space where strategies can be developed and then channelled through the conventions of current representative democracy (Wainwright, 2003) is vital to achieving such a process of reform.

Chapter 9

Difference

Alastair Christie

Introduction

The phrase 'celebrating difference' has become a catch phrase in political parlance, but is rarely accompanied by debate about the nature of difference, or how difference might be valued. Celebrating difference suggests a consensus that difference exists, that we all know and recognise when we see it, and that we can celebrate this difference without being implicated in it. Questions arise, therefore, as to how differences are produced; whether we should welcome all forms of difference; how some differences come to be more important than others; and why. Indeed, the absence of clarity about what is meant by difference has resulted in it becoming one of the most debated and contested terms of our time (Brah, 1996). In Ireland, an interest in difference has been stimulated by public claims for recognition from diverse groups including disabled people, gays and lesbians, and as a result of increased in-migration to Ireland, which has resulted in the establishment of new ethnic communities in Dublin and around the country. The growing awareness of social diversity in Ireland has put claims to being 'Irish' into question in new ways, opening up differences within this category, which has, until recent years, been constructed largely in homogeneous terms.

In this chapter I focus primarily on theoretical discussions of difference and their relevance for social policy. I illustrate how social policy both implicitly and explicitly constructs and reconstructs difference. Social policy, as a set of discourses and practices, constructs differences and similarities *between* and *within* particular groups. But it is important to ask why some differences gain particular social significance, often achieving the status of 'common sense' in political and social policy debates. My aim, then, is to explore the ways in which social policy actually constructs difference, or brings certain differences into being. In order to locate this construction and reconstruction of difference within a specific Irish social policy context, I consider policy approaches to Travellers and to the promotion of equality.

First, I examine three reports from Commissions/Task Force on Travellers in Ireland. I argue that these reports, which represent developments in social policy approaches to Travellers as a category marked as 'different', reveal the workings of difference in an *implicit* way within social policy itself. Second, I discuss how social policy has started to use difference *explicitly* as a basis for policy making by examining Equality Authority reports, which demonstrate that, in debates about equality, differences have to be named. While analysis of the reports on Travellers suggests that the basis for articulating difference through social policy is sometimes *implicit* and much contested when explicit, the Equality Authority reports *explicitly* identify difference as the ground (albeit still contested) on which social policy is to be developed.

A new consciousness of difference, evident in social policy as well as other spheres of life, has led to an increased awareness of culture as an important site in which inclusion and citizenship are negotiated. This is linked to the development of a 'politics of recognition' based on calls for the recognition of *cultural* differences. These cultural differences are mapped onto difference of class, gender, and sexuality, as well as ethnicity. However, social policy has not traditionally been concerned with culture. Its focus instead has been primarily on the relationship between welfare and citizenship, and how social, economic and political rights are supported within various forms of the welfare state. Although we could argue that culture is now another '"sphere" to add to society, economy and polity', Bottero and Irwin (2003) suggest that culture has to be engaged with as 'a method through which material relations acquire shape and meaning' (2003: 463). In other words, the very meaning of differences and relations across differences are constructed through culture, not least via the discourses or language we use to identify social categories. The concept of cultural citizenship, then, may be a useful way forward in developing more inclusive forms of welfare that respond to claims for recognition. In the concluding section of this chapter, I consider how cultural citizenship might provide conceptual and political spaces for rethinking social policy in ways that engage reflexively with 'difference'. In other words, I suggest that the concept of cultural citizenship may offer grounds for social policy practice that recognises its own implicatedness in reproducing difference in certain ways and that is constantly open to examining how social policy practice may be exclusionary.

'Difference' in social policy

Social policy is largely developed in response to social 'problems' and these 'problems' are often associated with people who are represented as 'different'. Moreover, our 'common-sense' understandings of the social world are based on the differences we construct between groups and individuals. It is important to note that differences tend to be understood in terms of dualisms, for example, settled/Traveller, white/black, and able-bodied/disabled. Poststructuralist theorists argue that the terms on each side of these dualisms are not valued equally. One term acts as the dominant term against which the other term is defined, or marked out as different. So this mode of constructing difference through dualisms is imbued with power, as for example in the dualism 'white/black', where 'white' operates as the norm against which 'black' is identified as different. Differences tend to be constructed on the basis of what is assumed to be 'normal'/'natural' and what is thereby constructed as 'abnormal'/'unnatural'. Those defined as different are often made inferior and such groups may be defined as *having* problems or *being* problems so that a social policy response is required. Social policy both reflects and potentially challenges 'common-sense' notions of difference depending on how it formulates the social 'problem' and a policy response to it. The processes of differentiation that are part of social policy practice highlight the needs and abilities of groups, but often in ways that continue to privilege the needs of the dominant group. This is most evident in social policy initiatives relating to Travellers, which are discussed in more detail below. Because dominant groups tend to be represented as the 'norm' by which other groups are judged, social policy makers can either accept these cultural assumptions or move towards unsettling them. Difference, as a term then, tends to apply only to minority groups, while majority group cultures remain invisible, unquestioned and free of surveillance.

All social policies carry the constructions of difference, and the reworkings of difference in order to promote social inclusion. However, in the following section I consider the specific context of social policy reports relating to Travellers in Ireland and how policy has reworked constructions of Travellers as 'different' over time. The intention in this chapter is not to offer a detailed examination of wider social policy on Travellers (see Fanning, 2002a), but to use the three reports on Travellers to examine how constructions of 'difference' operate to produce particular subject positions for both the settled and Traveller communities. The discussion in this chapter, in part, assumes a constructivist approach which identifies the ways in which particular identities appear 'natural', but are, in fact, historically and socially constructed. However, the main concern here, in line with what is often identified as the 'cultural turn', is to examine how difference is produced through discourse and language, and the dualistic structures of meaning that tend to structure these. While Fanning (2002a) adopts a constructivist approach to examine the impact of racism and social exclusion on Travellers, this chapter considers how social policy discourses and language attempt to define the meanings of Traveller and settled identities. Official reports and government legislation are important sites in which groups are constructed as 'different' in certain ways and provide evidence for how differences are constructed differently over time. I want to suggest that the ways in which 'difference' is constructed in these reports has a profound impact on the formation and implementation of social policies directed towards the Traveller community.

Ever since the seventeenth century, and especially since the nation-building nineteenth century, being settled or 'sedentarism' has been represented as progressive, whereas nomadism has been viewed as 'backward'. Jim Mac Laughlin argues that there was growing intolerance towards those variously described as 'gypsies', 'tinkers' and 'itinerants' in post-independence Ireland (1999). However, it was not until the 1960s that major social and structural changes resulted in Travellers becoming increasingly defined as a social problem for settled communities. Road 'improvements', housing and shopping developments, new farming practices and changing patterns of consumption and production resulted in traditional halting sites disappearing and Travellers becoming more dependent on state benefits. Increasingly, Travellers were represented as 'different from' the settled community in such a way that they were identified as a social problem for the settled community that needed to be solved. Indeed, government-commissioned reports on Travellers since the 1960s track the changing language and terminology by which Travellers were identified as 'different'. The following three sections of this chapter examine the workings of difference in these reports and how these workings impact on policy initiatives in this area.

Report of the Commission on Itinerancy (1963)

In the 1960s, local dissatisfaction about the presence of Travellers, as well as the implementation of the new economic and political programme for modernisation, led to the government establishing the *Commission on Itinerancy* (Helleiner, 1995). The official term to identify Travellers at the time was 'itinerants'. The Commission's report was the first attempt by central government to identify the needs of Travellers and to consider how they might be included within the settled community. This process of inclusion was linked to the new phase in Irish modernisation that was initiated with the government's *Programme for Economic Expansion* in 1958. A central goal of this programme was to increase employment in an emerging industrial sector, provide employment for rural poor, including Travellers, and to reduce emigration. Identifying the 'needs' of Travellers was seen as a first step in the process of their inclusion in this national project. The policy aim was, therefore, the inclusion of Travellers in the settled community by encouraging them to adopt the norms of settlement and waged employment.

While the Commission identified Travellers as having specific needs and a different lifestyle from the settled community, Travellers were not considered a distinct group as such.

> Itinerants do not constitute a single homogeneous group, tribe or community within the nation, although the settled population are inclined to see them as such. Neither do they constitute a separate ethnic group (Commission on Itinerancy, 1963: 37).

Although identified as having different needs and lifestyle from those of settled Irish people, Travellers were, unlike gypsies and travellers in other European countries, considered to be Irish. They were not seen as having a separate collective identity but were represented in the report as descendants of peasants who were forced into landlessness and mobility during years of British colonial rule. This account of Travellers' origins based on 'hegemonic post-colonial nationalist ideology of "monoculturalism"', defined Travellers as victims of colonialism who should be given the 'opportunity to return to being part of the settled community' (Helleiner, 1995: 533). Irish nationalism placed particular importance on land ownership, so it seemed 'natural' and patriotic for Travellers to give up their nomadic lifestyle and to refrain from infringing the rights of landowners (Mac Laughlin, 1999). Although a stated aim was to identify the needs of Travellers, this policy initiative was driven by the land ownership and sedentary values of the dominant group.

Travellers' and the settled community's lifestyles were represented as being in opposition rather than holding the potential for a complementary relationship (Mac Laughlin, 1999). This construction of difference as oppositional reduced the potential for the development of common interests between Travellers and the settled community. Yet, paradoxically, the underlying policy aim was to undo the difference by creating incentives for Travellers to assimilate within the settled community. The 'natural' state of Travellers was represented in the report as being part of the settled community, and this was to be achieved mainly through the provision of housing.

> The immediate objective should be to provide dwellings as soon as possible for all itinerant families who desire to settle. Eventually the example given by those who successfully settle should encourage the remainder to leave the road (Commission on Itinerancy, 1963: 661).

The provision of education was seen as the other main route towards the assimilation of Travellers. Education was considered an 'urgent necessary, both as a means of providing opportunities for a better way of life and of promoting their absorption into the settled community' (1963: 67). Traveller children were not to be taught about their own culture, but rather to be taught in ways that would facilitate their inclusion within the settled community.

Although the rhetoric of the report is dominated by constructions of difference between Travellers and settled people, it also constructs gender differences within the Traveller community (Helleiner, 1997). Nomadism was associated in the report with physical, social and economic deprivation, which was represented as having a particularly harmful impact on women and children. Through the association of women with domesticity and the family, they were identified as having more to gain than men Travellers from adopting a settled lifestyle and were, therefore, expected to be particularly motivated to move away from nomadism. Women were constructed as having a crucial role to play in socialising the next generation into a settled lifestyle, so their roles as mothers needed to be protected. The report downplayed the economic activities of women and represented them as economically dependent on men Travellers. While, in general, the report failed to recognise the economic contribution of women, begging was identified as 'a vitally necessary part of the real income of the majority of itinerant families' (1963: 90). As begging was done mainly by women, Helleiner (1997) points to the report's inconsistency with regard to how women's economic activities are represented.

Helleiner (1997) argues that the Commission advocated a particularly gendered form of assimilation into the settled community. Indeed, the report can be read as strategically emphasising gender differences in order to bring about consent within the Traveller community for assimilation policies. The adoption of female homemaker/male breadwinner model was to be encouraged within the Traveller community by the recommendation that men be given 'elementary knowledge of skills such as carpentry, welding, plumbing, elementary repair and servicing of machinery' (1963: 71), whereas women were to be offered 'tuition in housekeeping, cooking, washing, child hygiene and other domestic knowledge'. It was recommended that local voluntary groups should make 'arrangements for lessons in cookery, housekeeping, hygiene' (1963: 108). A similar gendered pattern of education was to apply to male and female children with 'woodwork and elementary metal work for boys, and knitting, needle work, simple cookery and domestic training for girls' (1963: 68).

The report demonstrates how, in particular circumstances and contexts, the Traveller community is constructed as both different from and similar to the settled community. Travellers were defined as Irish citizens rendered nomadic by colonial oppression and now needing reintegration with their fellow citizens in the settled community. Resistance to integration was represented as a rejection of citizenship and unwillingness to move out of a subculture of poverty. In this way, the report promises assimilation by suggesting that Travellers are not really different from settled people while at the same time constructing Travellers as different mainly because of the social problems they are seen as presenting. Ultimately, the social exclusion and poverty experienced by Travellers are identified as their own fault because they want to hold on to their 'difference'.

Report of the Travelling People Review Body (1983)

By the 1970s, academics and Travellers themselves were describing the Travellers' way of life in terms of 'ethnicity', and the term 'itinerant' was losing its currency (Helleiner, 1995). Slowly, the government's policies of assimilation were seen to be failing, and Travellers were increasingly being represented as a distinct ethnic group, which experienced racial discrimination (Kenny, 1997). In 1983, the *Report of the Travelling People Review Body* (1983) constructed Travellers 'as people with their own distinctive lifestyle, traditionally of a nomadic nature but now not habitual wanderers. They have needs, wants and values which are *different in some ways* from those of the settled community' (Travelling People Review Body, 1983: 6 [emphasis supplied]). The Travelling People Review Body was established to examine 'the needs of Travellers who wish to continue a nomadic way of life' (1983: 3) and to consider in particular the educational, employment and housing needs of the Traveller community. The report moved away from the goal of assimilation, in which difference could be eradicated, to the goal of integration in which support would be given to Travellers choosing to adopt a settled way of life. While Travellers were seen to have 'different needs, wants and values' (1983: 6), integration was still based on Travellers adopting settled lifestyles. The report betrayed an unwillingness to accept nomadism as a sustainable way of life. Travellers who wanted to maintain their nomadic lifestyle, the report stated, 'cannot hope to receive adequate education. Nor can they avail of services such as health and welfare which are significant in the life of all people' (1983: 16). Travellers who maintained nomadic lifestyles were still identified as 'problems' and located within a subculture of poverty. To help Travellers move out of this subculture, the Review Body argued that it was necessary to employ 'the most able and experienced social workers' (1983: 100). This work was expected to be 'challenging' for these professionals, reinforcing the view of Travellers as presenting intractable social problems. To further encourage Travellers to relinquish their nomadic lifestyle, the Review Body also suggested that newly-weds should be given priority in the allocation of housing to 'lessen the risks of regression to a Travelling way of life' (Travelling People Review Body, 1983: 45). The nomadic lifestyle was therefore represented as backward and a problem requiring professional attention, but also as a 'bad habit' that needed to be broken.

There is less discussion in the 1983 report of the similarities between Travellers and settled people apart from the statement that Travellers 'should be treated as individuals of Irish origin with the same rights as all other citizens' (Travelling People Review Body, 1983: 31). As in the 1963 report, Traveller difference could be put to one side within a discourse of Irish citizenship that represented Travellers and the settled community as having equal rights. The project of assimilation, although less explicit in the text, is most evident in the photographs included in the report. For example, the photograph in the chapter on accommodation shows a group-housing scheme with a line of large boulders in the foreground. This representation implies that a group of Travellers had permanently swapped their nomadic lifestyle for a settled existence and did not welcome Travellers' trailers on the common space in front of their houses. Two other photographs construct gender difference as similar to settled gender norms with a woman learning to use an industrial sewing machine and young men developing their skills at welding. These photographs, in some ways, sum up the report's approach to Travellers by representing Travellers as individuals who have similar needs to any other Irish citizen that are most effectively met through integration in the settled community. Difference is largely represented as a product of disadvantage and poverty that can be left behind only by adopting settled ways of life. While the report supports the view that 'Travellers' traditions and way of life . . . must be catered for and protected as much as possible' (1983: 15), as Crowley (1999) points out, no particular resources were allocated to promote Travellers' nomadic culture.

Report of the Task Force on the Travelling Community (1995)

A Task Force on the Travelling Community was appointed in 1993 to, amongst other things, 'advise and report on the needs of travellers and on Government policy generally in relation to travellers, with specific reference to the co-ordination of policy approaches by Government Departments and local authorities' (Task Force on the Travelling Community, 1995: 10). The Task Force included five Traveller members and its report in 1995 acknowledged that Travellers had a distinct ethnic identity and culture that should be valued. However, in trying to identify with a distinct Traveller culture, the Task Force argues that '[i]t is difficult, given its intangible nature, to define a particular culture. We can only describe Travellers' culture in terms of what we see as different from "Settled" society' (1995: 71). It is not clear from this statement whether the 'we' included the Traveller members of the Task Force who would have had a lived experience of Traveller culture. The culture of Travellers is defined again as those activities that are different from, as opposed to similar to, the settled community. Traveller culture and settled culture are homogenised and emptied of the many differences *within* and *across* these cultures. Traveller culture is reduced to those aspects of the Traveller ways of life that are pushed outside the dominant settled culture. This marginalisation of Traveller culture limits the possibility of alliances between settled and Traveller communities based on any common interests. As in the previous reports, the focus on how the Traveller community is 'different from' the settled community leaves sedentarism unquestioned and homogenises both groups.

Divisions of opinion existed between members of the Task Force resulting in an addendum to the main report, signed by four dissenting voices. The authors of the addendum argue that alternatives to the Travellers' nomadic way of life should be encouraged. As in the two previous reports, the addendum predicted that integration with the settled community was inevitable and part of a 'natural' evolutionary process. Travellers were represented as 'a skilful and colourful group of people travelling the roads of Ireland admired for their skills, services and trades' (1995: 289–90); an 'exotic' group that was 'out of synch' with modern Ireland. Not only is the nomadic lifestyle seen as unsustainable, but is identified as 'inordinately expensive on the taxpaying community to maintain for the questionable benefit of a small section of population' (1995: 289). The addendum thereby represents Travellers as dependent on the settled community and as making little contribution to Irish society. The potential policy response to the needs of Travellers is constructed in relation to the perceived interests of the taxpaying settled community. So, in a report that for the most part identifies Traveller difference in terms of ethnic difference that should be recognised and respected, the dissenting addendum reinstates the settled 'we' as those who define 'the' difference and thereby the 'entitlements' of Travellers.

Difference is constructed in multiple and sometimes crosscutting ways in these reports and the above discussion draws attention to some of these. Even the language by which Travellers are identified as a social category changes from 'Itinerants' to 'Travelling People' to 'Travellers'. But difference is also at the centre of each of these policy reports in other ways. First, 'difference' is represented in terms of dualisms as, for example, between settled and Traveller communities, and men and women. These dualisms operate in such a way that power is invested in the dominant term or norm, thus dis-empowering the term or category identified as different. Second, all differences are established in relation to an assumed norm. While in the 1983 and 1995 reports respect for Traveller lifestyle is called for, this respect is to come from those in the settled community whose way of life never comes into question. Representations of Traveller culture only have meaning when contrasted with assumed culture of the settled community. When difference works in this way, the norm remains largely unchallenged. It is assumed to be 'natural' and gains the status of 'common sense' within political and policy debates. Few questions are posed with regard to how settled communities might have to change to facilitate nomadic lifestyles or how settled cultures might also be represented as nomadic. For example, in a time of mass travel and globalisation, a nomadic lifestyle is often represented as one to which we should all aspire. Third, the recognition of difference, i.e. the recognition of Travellers as having a distinct culture, or as an ethnic group, while placing value on that culture, also tends to fix that culture and assume homogeneity within it. Representations of Traveller culture become locked into a set of values that tend to define the ethnic group as homogeneous. In the following section of the chapter which focuses on social policy and the promotion of equality, I argue that differences are more explicitly embraced as multiple and crosscutting.

Difference as a basis for social policy

In this section of the chapter I examine two policy reports published by the Equality Authority: *Towards a Vision for a Gender Equal Society* (2003a) and *Building an Intercultural Society* (2003b). Both reports are concerned with the promotion of equality by explicitly addressing difference and both reports use a framework for achieving greater equality based on redistribution, recognition, representation and respect. They reflect, therefore, a shift in the theoretical literature that increasingly addresses questions of difference in relation to recognition and redistribution in particular. I use this framework here to discuss the two reports and to introduce specific theories of difference.

The Equality Authority is an independent body established by the Irish government in October 1999 under the Employment Equality Act 1998 (see Doyle, 1999 for a discussion of the introduction of the Employment Equality Act 1998 and previous equality legislation). It replaced the Employment Equality Agency and has a specific role in implementing the Employment Equality Act 1998 and the Equal Status Act 2000, as well as a more general role in promoting equality. The Equality Authority is also required to provide leadership in 'celebrating diversity in Irish society'. This liberal call for the 'celebration of diversity' obscures the hierarchical and discriminatory ways in which difference operates and collapses all differences into equivalent markers of diversity. To return to the legislation, the Employment Equality Act 1998 prohibits certain types of discrimination in private and public sector employment, whereas the Equal Status Act 2000 moves the prohibition against discrimination beyond the workplace and into the public arena where people buy goods, use services, obtain accommodation and participate in educational establishments. Both Acts outlaw discrimination on nine distinct grounds:

gender, marital status, family status, disability, sexual orientation, age, religion, race and membership of the Traveller community. Difference is, therefore, located at the heart of the legislation.

In 2002, the Equality Authority recommended the inclusion of the new grounds for equality claims in the legislation. These were the grounds of socio-economic status, criminal conviction, political opinion and Trade Union membership. As yet, these grounds have not been incorporated within the equality legislation. The existing nine grounds are more inclusive than similar legislation in Northern Ireland, which specifies discrimination on the grounds of disability, race, religious belief, political opinion, sex or married status. Indeed, the variety of grounds for discrimination in the North and the Republic reveal the significance of the context in which the differences are defined. The use of such defined categories in legislation and policy is pragmatic but does not reflect the complexity of 'lived' difference. Further, defined categories of difference feed into an 'add on' approach to difference, demonstrated by the Equality Authority's recommendation to extend the grounds of discrimination to new areas. Although the Equality Authority recognises the possibility of multiple forms of discrimination (Pierce, 2003; Zappone, 2001), the grounds for discrimination are named as distinct within the legislation. The interrelationship between multiple differences and the complex formation of group identities is difficult to provide for within legislation. To incorporate multiple and crosscutting differences within a recognisable legal discourse is virtually impossible because legal argument and the grounds for equality claims are usually based on the notion of 'difference between'.

The Equality Authority plays an important role in furthering the debate about difference and equality via the publication of a wide variety of reports on these themes. The first report considered here, *Towards a Vision for a Gender Equal Society* (2003a), was prepared as part of the development of the National Action Plan for Women. This plan arose as a result of the UN Fourth Conference on Women (Beijing) 1995 Platform for Action which required commitment from national governments to 'take priority action for the empowerment and advancement of women'. *Towards a Vision for a Gender Equal Society* argues for gender equality legislation in which 'the diversity of women is acknowledged, valued and accommodated in policy and institutional practice' (2003a: 5). The second report, entitled *Building an Intercultural Society* (2003b), was published as part of the consultative process that is described in *Towards a National Action Plan Against Racism* (Department of Justice, 2002). The government was prompted into developing this national plan following the World Conference against Racism, Racial Discrimination, Xenophobia and Related Intolerance held in Durban, South Africa in September 2001. The Equality Authority's report, *Building an Intercultural Society*, draws on the report from the World Conference to develop equality goals for an anti-racist and intercultural society i.e. a society that is already accepted as constructed through difference. In the following sections I discuss theories of difference that inform these reports under the headings of *recognition* and *representation.*

Recognition

Social policy has always been concerned with issues of redistribution and equality. However, Fraser (1995) argues that since the 1980s there has been a growing shift in thinking from a politics of redistribution to a politics of recognition in which difference provides a valid basis for the allocation of resources and the promotion of cultural change. By the 1980s, feminists and black activists had started to highlight the limitations of gaining greater equality through existing systems of welfare redistribution. Feminists had moved from seeking to eliminate inequalities based on biologically deterministic theories of sexual difference to exploring difference *between* women (Brah, 1996). In particular, feminists examined how the category 'woman' was produced differently in relation to 'race', sexuality and class. Fraser (1997) uses the term 'multiple intersecting differences' to describe the interconnections between gender and other 'axes of subordination' (1997: 180). In a similar way, the Equality Authority report, *Towards a Vision for a Gender Equal Society,* explicitly takes up these questions of recognition and intersecting differences.

> Recognition is a key issue when the diversity of women is considered . . . There can be a failure to give value to this difference and to tease out the practical implications of this difference for policies, procedures and practices. This failure can be the causal factor for exclusion. (2003a: 14).

Explorations of differences between women in feminism led to the identities of women not being 'so much rooted in women's shared oppression by men but in women's shared identity as different from men' which resulted in 'a shift towards political identity rooted in difference' (Williams, 1996: 67). Increasingly, activist groups started to link struggles for 'redistribution' with demands for 'recognition' of difference. Policy makers also began to identify difference and how it works to disadvantage groups as a legitimate concern. Questions were raised not just about who receives and who pays for welfare services, but also how these services were to be delivered and received (Williams, 2002). For example, even when health care services were made considerably more accessible, cultural stereotyping continued to impact on the way services were delivered and was identified as affecting who gained access to particular services. Recognition of difference has, therefore, become a central concern for contemporary policy makers who have moved beyond assuming that universal services and rights alone will lead to greater justice and equality.

The report *Towards a Vision for a Gender Equal Society* (2003a) provides an agenda for the redistribution of resources to women by highlighting the need for gender sensitive anti-poverty strategies; access to training to meet the specific needs of women; and changes in taxation and welfare policies so that they promote women's economic independence. In relation to the *recognition* of gender difference, the report seeks to promote cultural equality through such measures as promoting media representations that reflect the 'reality of women's lives and aspirations' (2003a: 14) and developing educational systems that counter gender stereotyping and promote gender equality. Although the report, *Building an Intercultural Society* (2003b), prioritises economic opportunity, education and accommodation as part of its agenda for intercultural redistribution of resources and opportunities drawing on relevant sections of the National Anti-Poverty Plan to build the case for redistribution, it also argues for *recognition* of cultural difference. This recognition is to be achieved through the promotion of cultural equality in open debates about multiple identities, challenges to stereotyping, and positive recognition of different identities in the spheres of education and the media in particular.

Both of these reports describe the 'multiple intersecting differences' (Fraser, 1997: 180) that exist within the social categories of women and Black and minority ethnic. Yet, *Towards a Vision for A Gender Equal Society* focuses almost exclusively on the changing position of women and includes no discussion about the implications a gender equal society would have for gender relations. Like the reports on Travellers, which failed to question sedentarism and the lifestyle of the settled community, this report leaves the position of men and dominant constructions of masculinity unquestioned. However, here there is a more *implicit* problematisation of men's positions in society than there is of the settled community in the reports on Travellers.

These Equality Authority reports demonstrate the great difficulties encountered by those concerned with the politics of recognition in attempting to find inclusive descriptive terms. *Building an Intercultural Society* states that the term 'Black and minority ethnic group' is used to include the Traveller community. However, at least four times during the report the phrase 'Black and minority ethnic community including Travellers' is used. The 'adding on' of Travellers suggests that this group is not always comfortably included as Black or indeed as an ethnic minority. If Travellers' identity is dominantly constructed as different from the settled community, we might ask in what ways, apart from their experience of racism, can Travellers be included with Black and minority ethnic groups who follow settled lifestyles? Fraser (1997) strongly argues that recognition of difference needs to be linked to a politics of redistribution. For policy makers this would involve the assessing of disadvantage in terms of material resources as well as how differences (e.g. cultural, gender and sexual differences) produce disadvantage through disrespect and discrimination. Fraser (1997) suggests that there is no neat theoretical move that can resolve the redistribution–recognition dilemma, but if we are planning to develop more radical forms of democracy, she posits 'No recognition without redistribution'(1997: 187) as a promising rallying cry for this project.

Representation

Iris Marion Young (1990) argues for new forms of representation based on difference. For Young, strategies for equality based on universal citizenship have failed because universal provision privileges dominant or hegemonic cultures and lifestyles and further excludes disadvantaged groups. Definitions of universal humanity are never 'neutral', but reflect the standards and values of dominant groups. In seeking a more inclusive notion of universal citizenship, Young (1990) argues for the recognition of diverse social groups with distinct cultures, histories and experiences. She argues strongly for the inclusion of voices that have been traditionally excluded by presumptions of a common humanity. Failure to recognise different groups, she suggests, results in processes of assimilation that allow privileged groups to ignore their own privilege. If different groups are to be respected they need to be *represented* as different.

Young also argues for a radical democratic pluralism that 'acknowledges and affirms the public and political significance of social group differences as a means of ensuring the *participation and inclusion* of everybody in social political institutions' (1990: 168 [emphasis supplied]). These institutions would enable oppressed and excluded groups to develop their collective identities, generate and debate policies, as well as have the power of veto regarding polices that affect them. Privileged groups would hear the voices of groups that are usually excluded and all citizens would have their differences affirmed. In this way, the voice of the 'other' would be represented and institutionalised within policy and decision making. For Young (1990), all groups benefit from the representation of disadvantaged groups in decision-making processes because a better sense of the 'common good' is achieved.

The representation of difference between and across groups, according to Young (1990), provides a basic criterion by which policies and processes can be judged. Fundamental questions can be asked in evaluating policy initiatives such as: Who is speaking for whom? And, who is determining the criteria to be used to make these judgements? Young's (1990) arguments for group representation that values difference have been critiqued for inadequately defining what constitutes a group, essentialising differences between groups, not recognising differences within groups, and turning politics into a process that principally focuses on affirming or recognising group difference (Phillips, 1991). Her approach may place too much faith in social justice being achieved through the representation of different groups in the policy-making process. The overcoming of cultural domination is, after all, unlikely to be achieved through representation and recognition alone (Phillips, 1997). Yet, recognition, and the respect that it is seen as conferring, is increasingly central to debates about policy making that addresses difference.

The report *Towards a Vision for a Gender Equal Society* can be seen as taking up Young's call for representation when it identifies how women are underrepresented in political institutions, the judiciary and other private and public organisations. The report, quoting from the Platform for Action, reiterates the view that:

> Women's equal participation in decision making is not only a demand for simple justice or democracy but can also be seen as a necessary condition for women's interests to be taken into account (Equality Authority, 2003a: 10).

The report calls for the equal participation of women and men in these organisations and institutions. It points to the underfunding of groups where women are represented and recommends that these groups increase their involvement at all levels of participatory democracy. Representation is seen as *respecting* undervalued aspects of women's lives. Such respect would be 'concerned with the caring and emotional sphere and with generating the opportunities for all to develop their full potential' (2003a: 7). The goals identified largely focus on the equal participation of men and women in caring for children and other adults. In this section of the report it argues for additional 'resources for women who experience violence, to challenge and change men's behaviour' (2003a: 13). In a similar way, the report *Building an Intercultural Society* identifies the underrepresentation of Black and minority ethnic groups in all areas of public governance and calls for their increased participation at all levels of participatory democracy and a strengthening of those groups that represent Black and minority ethnic groups. The report states that an intercultural society 'requires visibility and representation by Black and minority ethnic communities in all areas of public life. At present there is little such representation' (2003a: 21).

Bhikhu Parekh (2000) argues that in multicultural societies public spaces need to be provided that promote intercultural dialogue in which new forms of difference and solidarity can emerge. Parekh's (2000) vision of a multicultural society is one in which a common culture is created out of difference. This requires the development of an approach to multicultural education that questions monocultural and Eurocentric assumptions within dominant groups. This form of education would explore the diversity of cultures and experiences that are produced in any community. Such an education would explore differences between cultural groups, with the goal of transforming *both* minority and majority communities. Parekh's vision of a multicultural society has been critiqued as failing to address the question of the imbalances of power between 'minority' and 'majority' groups. It is these imbalances in power that lead to particular cultures being stereotyped and identified as 'other' (Yuval-Davis, 1991). However, Parekh's vision of multiculturalism points to possibilities of recognising and working with difference by deconstructing 'whiteness' and promoting 'other' voices. For such a transformational dialogue around difference to occur, particular preconditions need to be established and power differences need to be openly addressed. One precondition of dialogue across difference should be the establishment of equal respect between the groups in dialogue (Benhabib, 1996). In my concluding comments, I ask whether the concept of cultural citizenship might provide some pointers for the development of transformational dialogue across differences within social policy.

Conclusion

In this chapter I have argued that social policy both *implicitly* constructs difference and *explicitly* engages with the concept of difference. I have also suggested that there is a growing acknowledgement that both *redistribution* and the *recognition* of difference are central to the development of social policy, and that recognition requires the development of new forms of *representation* which foster and require *respect* for different groups and differences within groups. The concept of citizenship has provided an important theoretical link in social policy between the individual and the modern nation state. A characteristic of modern democratic governments is that they seek, to a greater and lesser extent, to protect the civil, political and social rights of citizens. However, given the above discussion, we might ask how well these rights have addressed discrimination and exclusion based on mis-recognitions and negative constructions of some groups. The centrality of language and dialogue to the recognition of difference emerges in the above discussion of the reports on Travellers and the promotion of equality. The cultural construction of difference is central to experiences of exclusion and disrespect. Moreover, cultural constructions of difference have material effects because it is through culture that our lives and identities gain meaning. These negotiations of culture and cultural constructions of difference have become more complex in what is increasingly characterised as the 'age of migration' (Castles and Miller, 2003). Cultural, as opposed to national, citizenship has been advocated as a way of promoting new forms of social solidarity that transcend national boundaries and incorporate difference (Stevenson, 2003). Social policy has been developed to promote social solidarity. However, the emergence of new social movements around, for example, gender, 'race', sexuality and disability, disrupts the notion of 'normal' citizens that benefit equally from universal social policies. If culture is not fixed, but fluid and hybrid, then there is no automatic connection between culture, social policy and the nation state. Therefore, the conceptualising of difference is an urgent task for social policy makers.

As argued in this chapter, theories that emphasise *difference between* groups, to a greater or lesser extent, essentialise the status of 'different' groups. Their cultures become at least temporally fixed so that they can be compared to other groups. Specific aspects of the groups are highlighted and other features are marginalised, or ignored. For example, if groups are defined by gender, features such as 'race', colonialism and class tend to become secondary. Approaches that emphasise difference *between* groups can result in ahistorical and static definitions of groups that underplay processes of group formation and how factors such as racism and nationalism may influence group definitions (Anthias, 1999). The Equality Authority reports tend to focus on representation based on the need for increased participation of women and Black and minority ethnic groups in existing democratic systems. Perhaps wider questions could be asked, as suggested by Young (1990) and Parekh (2000), about the nature of democracy and the potential to create spaces which facilitate dialogues and debates across difference in ways that keep power dynamics in question. These theorists of difference have demonstrated that universality is often claimed in the names of structures of power that represent only certain sections of the community. Although theorists of difference challenge universal notions of the person or citizen, there is an underlying 'assumption of the universal right of all not to be treated unjustly or oppressively' (Connor, 2001: 276). The problem, as Fraser (1997) and Young (1990) argue, is not just about distribution and recognition, but the unequal power relations that affect opportunity and contribute to restrictive definitions of who counts as recognised full citizens. As multiculturalism and the politics of recognition become popular framing devices for definitions of social problems and responses to these, it is important that those engaged in social policy development consider the potential offered by new cultural conceptions of policy and citizenship.

Constructions of difference are very powerful and are often linked to 'common-sense' assumptions about the social world. Social policy makers have an important role to play in questioning these assumptions. By taking the role of 'sceptical strangers' (Saranga, 1998: 197), we may be able to problematise representations of difference and how these are linked to the perpetuation rather than the undermining of power relations, even within social policy where redistribution and justice are important values. Debates about difference and justice provide opportunities for social policy makers to build on utopian hopes that draw on both the politics of redistribution and of recognition. This is the point where a productive dialogue can take place between social policy makers and theorists of difference.

Chapter 10

Rights and judicial activism

Gerry Whyte

Introduction

The primary engine for the formulation of social policy is the political process. Political lobbying seeks to persuade those in power to commit themselves to particular policies. However, such lobbying can be very time-consuming, with no guarantee of success. Moreover, it would appear that the effectiveness of such lobbying in Ireland often relates more to the ability of the lobby group to influence the outcome of elections (through the making of generous political donations or the mobilisation of voters), than to what might be regarded as the intrinsic merits of the group's demands. Conversely, those with least political influence would seem to be least likely to secure the adoption of social policies protecting their interests (Hardiman, 1998).

Confronted with such a process, it is hardly surprising that marginalised groups may be very tempted by the prospect of using litigation to influence the shaping of social policy (referred to hereafter as 'public interest litigation'). In particular, such public interest litigation may be perceived as giving full force to the reasoned argument behind a particular claim, which reasoned argument may not be as effective in the political process because of the claimant's weak political position.

However, while the attraction of public interest litigation may appear to be greatest for groups that are politically marginalised, it is also the case that such litigation has also been pursued by members of more mainstream groups such as farmers, landlords and married taxpayers. One possible explanation for this may be that, notwithstanding their membership of social groups generally perceived as having very good political connections, the specific claim brought by the particular litigants may not have commanded political support. This would certainly appear to have been the case in relation to the claim of married taxpayers for equity in taxation (Scannell, 2000). In addition, while litigation is neither cheap nor speedy, it is easier to organise than a political campaign and, win or lose, has an identifiable conclusion.

Certainly a feature of Irish political life during the past four decades or so has been the not infrequent recourse to the courts to address issues that could have been resolved by the political process. Such issues include access to contraception, the taxation of farmers and married couples, the decriminalisation of homosexuality, the statutory obligations of landlords and, latterly, the socio-economic rights of certain groups such as Travellers, people with learning difficulties and children at risk. This is not a new phenomenon – 200 years ago such litigation had been a feature of the campaign to abolish slavery. However, it reappeared in the 1960s against a background of growing interest, especially in the United States, in the potential of the judicial system to tackle social injustice and, domestically, received a significant boost from the judicial discovery of implied rights in the seminal case of *Ryan* v. *Attorney General* ([1965] IR 294). As we shall see presently, the latter development led directly to the identification of several new constitutional rights and no doubt encouraged lawyers and others to think in terms of invoking rights as a means of shaping public policy.

This phenomenon is not without its critics and concern has been expressed that the decision in *Ryan* v. *Attorney General* unduly expanded the power of the judiciary at the expense of that of the other organs of government, thereby undermining the democratic process. In recent times, indeed, this concern has been expressed by some senior members of the judiciary, particularly in the context of attempts to rely on the judicial process to protect socio-economic rights, and it may be that the judicial activism of the past forty years is drawing to a close.

In this chapter, I shall attempt to evaluate the role of the judiciary in shaping social policy. In particular, I shall consider whether it is legitimate, both from the point of view of constitutional law and democratic politics, for Irish judges to involve themselves in the identification of implied rights with the inevitable impact this has on public policy. Arising out of this general debate, in recent times, Ireland has witnessed various attempts to use the courts to protect socio-economic interests. In concluding, I shall consider whether such interests should be protected by justiciable rights that involve the courts in their enforcement.

In considering the legitimacy of the judicial power to identify implied rights, it seems appropriate to start with an analysis of the *fons et origo* of this power, the decisions of the High and Supreme Courts in *Ryan* v. *Attorney General* ([1965] IR 294).

Ryan *v.* Attorney General

On 31 July 1963, six days after a hearing in the High Court that lasted 65 days, Mr Justice John Kenny handed down what may fairly be described as the most seminal judgment in contemporary Irish jurisprudence. In *Ryan* v. *Attorney General* ([1965] IR 294), Mrs Gladys Ryan had challenged the constitutional validity of the Health (Fluoridation Water Supplies) Act, 1960, providing for the introduction of fluorine into drinking water. She argued that this legislation interfered with the rights of the Family under the Constitution and, in particular, with the constitutional right and duty of parents to provide, according to their means, for the religious, moral, intellectual, physical, and social education of their children. She also contended that the Act failed to respect her right to bodily integrity which, she claimed, was protected by Article 40.3 of the Constitution. That provision reads:

1° The State guarantees in its laws to respect, and, as far as practicable, by its laws to defend and vindicate the personal rights of the citizen.

2° The State shall, in particular, by its laws protect as best it may from unjust attack and, in the case of injustice done, vindicate the life, person, good name, and property rights of every citizen.

The legal significance of Mrs Ryan's third argument was its premise that the constitutional rights of the citizen were not limited to those expressly stated in the Constitution and that Article 40.3 protected implied rights, in this case, the right to bodily integrity which is nowhere mentioned in the Constitution.

Mr Justice Kenny began his treatment of this argument by emphasising that the role of the court was not to pass judgment on the wisdom of legislative or executive policy but rather to consider whether that policy contravened the Constitution, in particular, whether it infringed any constitutional right.

He then turned to the key question of whether the guarantee of personal rights in Article 40.3 was confined to those rights expressly referred to in the Constitution or whether it also embraced implied or unenumerated rights. After acknowledging that the task of identifying implied rights would seem to be a function of the legislative, rather than the judicial, branch of government, he nonetheless took the view that this task could be undertaken by the courts, noting that they had previously discharged this role during the formative period of the common law. He then gave two reasons for taking the view that constitutional protection of fundamental rights was not limited to those rights expressly listed in the Constitution.

A number of factors indicate that the guarantee is not confined to the rights specified in Article 40 but extends to other personal rights of the citizen. Firstly, there is sub-s.2 of s 3 of Article 40 . . . The words 'in particular' shows that sub-s.2 is a detailed statement of something which is already contained in sub-s.1 of the general guarantee. But sub-s.2 refers to rights in connection with life and good name and there are no rights in connection with these two matters specified in Article 40. It follows, I think, that the general guarantee in sub-s.1 must extend to rights not specified in Article 40.

Secondly, there are many personal rights of the citizen which follow from the Christian and democratic nature of the State which are not mentioned in Article 40 at all – the right to free movement within the State and the right to marry are examples of this. This also leads to the conclusion that the general guarantee extends to rights not specified in Article 40. ([1965] IR 294 at p. 313)

He then went on to hold that one of the personal rights of the citizen protected by the general guarantee is the right to bodily integrity, in the process citing from the papal encyclical, *Pacem in Terris*, in support of this conclusion, though ultimately he ruled that this right had not been infringed by the introduction of fluorine into drinking water.

On appeal, the Supreme Court agreed with Mr Justice Kenny's conclusion that the listing of personal rights in the Constitution was not exhaustive, relying however, perhaps significantly, only on the first of his two reasons for this conclusion and eschewing any reference to the 'Christian and democratic nature of the State':

> The Court agrees with Mr Justice Kenny that the 'personal rights' mentioned in s 3.1 are not exhausted by the enumeration of 'life, person, good name, and property rights' in s3.2 as is shown by the use of the words 'in particular'; nor by the more detached treatment of specific rights in the subsequent sections of the Article. To attempt to make a list of all the rights which may properly fall within the category of 'personal rights' would be difficult and, fortunately, is unnecessary in this present case. ([1965] IR 294 at p. 344).

While agreeing with the plaintiff that she enjoyed an implied right to bodily integrity, the Court ultimately dismissed her claim after concluding that the proposed fluoridation of water was harmless and, therefore, could not infringe this right.

In the decade immediately following this decision, a number of additional implied rights were recognised by the courts – the right to work and earn a livelihood, the right not to be tortured or ill-treated, the right to marital privacy, the right of access to the courts, the right to fair procedures, the right to travel, the right to marry, the rights of unmarried mothers and of their children arising out of their mutual relationship and the right to state-funded legal representation in criminal cases. Thereafter, this phenomenon tapered off and during the subsequent two decades, only six additional such rights were recognised, three – the right to communicate, the right to beget children and the right to individual privacy – during the 1980s and three more – the right to independent domicile, the right to maintenance and the right to know the identity of one's natural mother – during the past decade or so.

Criticism of Ryan

While few, if any, of these implied rights are controversial in themselves, concern has been expressed about the implications for democracy of the exercise by the courts of the power to identify implied rights. In particular, it has been argued that this type of judicial activism generates uncertainty; that it is undemocratic as it enables an unelected, unaccountable elite (the judiciary) to formulate public policy and, at times, to frustrate the wishes of elected representatives of the People; that it undermines respect for the judicial process inasmuch as judges may be perceived to be basing their decisions on their personal philosophical or social beliefs (which are often conservative and pro-individual) rather than on accessible legal principles and rules; and that it further weakens the democratic process by encouraging citizens to litigate rather than to rely on their own political power. (Gwynn Morgan, 2002; Hogan, 1990–2; Kelly, 1967).

This debate broadly mirrors a similar debate in the United States about the merits or otherwise of what is referred to as the 'originalist' approach to constitutional interpretation. Essentially this approach requires a judge to apply the Constitution according to the principles intended by those who enacted it. In the context of the United States, support for this approach is prevalent among those who advocate a restrictive role for the courts (though, as a matter of logic, an originalist approach to constitutional interpretation does not inevitably lead to an endorsement of judicial minimalism). One of the principal advocates of originalism, Robert Bork, explains this approach to constitutional interpretation as follows:

> In short, all that a judge committed to original understanding requires is that the text, structure, and history of the Constitution provide him not with a conclusion but with a major premise. That major premise is a principle or stated value that the ratifiers wanted to protect against hostile legislation or executive action. The judge must then see whether that principle or value is threatened by the statute or action challenged in the case before him. The answer to that question provides his minor premise, and the conclusion follows. (Bork, 1990: 162)

This approach has been criticised on the grounds that it amounts to a circular argument – the original understanding of the Constitution is binding because that was the original understanding – and that a proper defence of originalism requires an independent normative theory which Bork does not supply (Dworkin, 1990; Sunstein, 1993). Moreover the applicability of originalism to the Irish constitutional order has also been questioned on the grounds that the documentary evidence that might shed light on the drafters' intention is generally not available and that, given that our Constitution was directly enacted by the People (in contrast to that of the United States where the Constitution was ratified by the Constitutional Convention of 1787), the focus should be on the text itself rather than on the supposed intentions of the drafters (Kelly, 2003). However, even if the Irish courts were to adopt an originalist approach to constitutional interpretation, it does not follow that this would preclude judicial recognition of implied rights. Given the language of Article 40.3, especially the use of the phrase 'in particular' in sub-section 2, it is difficult to avoid the conclusion that the framers of the Irish Constitution did envisage that the Constitution protected rights other than those expressly listed therein and the courts would appear to be the most appropriate agency for identifying such rights.

To return to the indigenous criticism of the reasoning in *Ryan*, the first critic into the field was the doyen of Irish constitutional lawyers, the late John Kelly. In his ground-breaking work, *Fundamental Rights in the Irish Law and Constitution* (1967), he argued that Mr Justice Kenny's reasoning '[assigned] to the legislature a somewhat humbler role vis-à-vis the courts than the general tenor of the Constitution . . . envisages' and that it introduced into Irish law an element of uncertainty 'which is repugnant to the central value of the very concept of law itself' (1967: 42). He also raised question marks over the potential sources for the identification of implied rights, pointing out that natural law itself saw its propositions as subject to legislative qualification and that to rely on international instruments protecting human rights in the absence of the incorporation of such instruments into domestic law would be contrary to the spirit of Article 29.6 which provides: 'No international agreement shall be part of the domestic law of the State save as may be determined by the Oireachtas'. Kelly considered that Mr Justice Kenny's reliance on the Papal Encyclical, *Pacem in Terris*, amounted to rendering the principles of Article 45 enforceable by the courts, given the similarity between the content of that encyclical and Article 45, notwithstanding that the prefatory words to the constitutional provision clearly state that the principles in Article 45 are not to be cognisable by the courts. In sum, Kelly considered that the reasoning in *Ryan* was tantamount to elevating the courts into the role of a third House of the Oireachtas.

Support for this analysis was offered more recently by Dr Gerard Hogan who argued that there were no objective means of ascertaining the implied personal rights protected by Article 40.3 and that this seriously undermined the legal values of objectivity and certainty (Hogan, 1990–2). He contended that, with the exception of the right to travel, rights flowing from the democratic nature of the State were already expressly provided for in other provisions of the Constitution. Nor did he believe that the other limb of Mr Justice Kenny's test – the 'Christian' nature of the State – was any better fitted for this task. Even if one could assume that the State was Christian in nature, he could not see what implied rights flowed from this characterisation – freedom of religion, denominational schooling and the institution of marriage already enjoying explicit constitutional protection – unless one was to look to papal encyclicals for guidance and he was equally dismissive of natural law philosophy or the concept of the human personality as sources of objective criteria for the identification of implied rights.

Dr Hogan was compelled to concede that Mr Justice Kenny's textual analysis of Article 40.3.1 was logically faultless and that 'the language and structure of Article 40.3 and Article 45 strongly suggest that the rights protected in Article 40.3.1 are not confined to the rights expressly enumerated elsewhere in the Constitution.' (Hogan, 1990–2: 114). However, in the absence of objective criteria for the identification of such rights, he urged the judiciary to be cautious about the recognition of new implied rights in the absence of support from constitutional provisions other than Article 40.3 for such recognition. He also endorsed Kelly's earlier call for a constitutional amendment incorporating into Article 40.3 an expanded recital of specific personal rights that also detailed the standards upon which the Oireachtas could delimit such rights.

These views and this last proposal reappeared some four years later when the Constitution Review Group (of which Dr Hogan was a member) highlighted the lack of any textual basis for some of the implied rights now enjoying constitutional protection and the potential for judicial subjectivity in the identification of rights arising from the lack of objective criteria for identifying unenumerated constitutional rights (Constitution Review Group, 1996). Of equal significance, Dr Hogan's concerns about *Ryan* were also reflected in the judgment of Chief Justice Keane in *O'T* v. *B* ([1998] 2 IR 321) wherein the Chief Justice said, at pp. 369–70,

> There was no discussion in [the Supreme Court judgment in Ryan *v.* Attorney General [1965] IR 294] of the question as to whether, given that the unenumerated rights clearly existed in the contemplation of the framers of the Constitution, it was intended by them that the duty of declaring what those rights were should be the function of the judiciary rather than the Oireachtas, although that fundamental issue is referred to in the judgment of Kenny J. Nor was there any explicit endorsement of Kenny J.'s proposed criterion that they might flow from the

Christian and democratic nature of the State. This may have been because the right under discussion was conceded, on behalf of the Attorney General, to be such an unenumerated right, although not in the precise form of a right to bodily integrity.

He continued,

It would unduly prolong this judgment to consider in detail the problems that have subsequently been encountered in developing a coherent, principled juris-prudence in this area. It is sufficient to say that, save where such an unenumerated right has been unequivocally established by precedent, as, for example, in the case of the right to travel and the right of privacy, some degree of judicial restraint is called for in identifying new rights of this nature.

No implied socio-economic rights

In recent times, a number of Supreme Court judges have also signalled their opposition to attempts to read implied socio-economic rights into the Constitution. The latter half of the 1990s saw a number of cases concerning the socio-economic rights of children, in particular, come before the courts. Confronted by an apparent inability or unwillingness on the part of the executive to address the needs of certain categories of children, two High Court judges, Mr Justice Peter Kelly and Mr Justice Robert Barr, directed the State to provide, respectively, residential facilities for certain children at risk and educational facilities for certain children and adults with severe or pro-found learning disabilities but on appeal, the Supreme Court ruled that the courts did not have the authority to make such innovative orders – *T.D.* v. *Minister for Education* ([2001] 4 IR 259) and *Sinnott* v. *Minister for Education* ([2001] 2 IR 545) (Whyte (2002), ch. 5 and addendum). In both cases, the Supreme Court relied on an understanding of the constitutional doctrine of separation of powers espoused by Mr Justice Costello in an earlier case, *O'Reilly* v. *Limerick Corporation* ([1989] ILRM 181) to dismiss the claims. In that case, a group of Travellers sought damages from the State for breach of their alleged constitutional right to be provided with a certain minimum standard of basic material conditions in order to protect their dignity and freedom as humans. Invoking the Aristotelian distinction between commu-tative (or corrective) justice and distributive justice, Mr Justice Costello held that the latter is the exclusive concern of the executive.

There is an important distinction to be made between the relationship which arises in dealings between individuals (a term which includes dealings between

individuals and servants of the State and public authorities) and the relationship
which arises between the individual and those in authority in a political com-
munity (which for convenience I will call the Government) when goods held in
common for the benefit of the entire community . . . fall to be distributed and
allocated. Different obligations in justice arise from these different relationships.
Distributive justice is concerned with the distribution and allocation of common
goods and common burdens. But it cannot be said that any of the goods held in
common . . . belong exclusively to any member of the political community. An
obligation in distributive justice is placed on those administering the common
stock of goods, the common resource and the wealth held in common which has
been raised by taxation to distribute them and the common wealth fairly and to
determine what is due to each individual. But that distribution can only be made
by reference to the common good and by those charged with furthering the
common good (the Government); it cannot be made by any individual who may
claim a share in the common stock and no independent arbitrator, such as a
Court, can adjudicate on a claim by an individual that he has been deprived of
what is his due. This situation is very different in the case of commutative justice.
What is due to an individual from another individual (including a public autho-
rity) from a relationship arising from their mutual dealings can be ascertained and
is due to him exclusively and the precepts of commutative justice will enable an
arbitrator such as a Court to decide what is properly due should the matter be
disputed. This distinction explains why the court has jurisdiction to award damages
against the State when a servant of the State for whose activity it is vicariously
liable commits a wrong and why it may not get jurisdiction in cases where the
claim is for damages based on a failure to distribute adequately in the plaintiffs'
favour a portion of the community's wealth. ([1989] ILRM 181 at p. 194).

Accordingly, Mr Justice Costello held that he could not entertain the
Travellers' claim which, as he put it, must 'be advanced in Leinster House
rather than in the Four Courts'. ([1989] ILRM 181 at p. 95) (As it happens, he
subsequently changed his stance on this issue six years later in another case
involving Travellers (*O'Brien* v. *Wicklow UDC, ex tempore*, High Court, 10
June 1994), but the Supreme Court judges in *Sinnott* and *T.D.* were probably
unaware of this change of heart as *O'Brien* is not referred to in either case.)

In *T.D.*, Chief Justice Keane also questioned whether the test employed
by Mr Justice Kenny in *Ryan's* case for the identification of implied rights –
the 'Christian and democratic nature of the State' – was satisfactory for the
task and he repeated the point he had previously made in *O'T.* v. *B.* that the
Supreme Court in *Ryan* had not discussed whether the duty of identifying
implied rights should be a function of the courts rather than of the Oireachtas.
Calling for judicial restraint in this area, he said that he had 'the greatest
doubts as to whether the courts at any stage should assume the function of

declaring what are today frequently described as "socio-economic rights" to be unenumerated rights guaranteed by Article 40'. ([2001] 4 IR 259 at p.282).

Defence of Ryan

Notwithstanding the aforementioned concerns expressed about the reasoning in *Ryan*, a cogent case can be made in defence of the judicial power to recognise implied rights under the Constitution. Some commentators, including the present author, have defended the judicial power to identify implied rights against the charge of being anti-democratic on the ground that judicial activism in the protection of fundamental rights is unavoidable because of the indeterminate language used in Article 40.3 (Parker, 1997; Whyte, 1998; Whyte, 2002). As even Hogan concedes, the use of the phrase 'in particular' in Article 40.3.2 logically means that the Constitution protects unspecified rights. If such rights are to be effective and if Article 40.3 is to be given full meaning and effect, these rights will have to be identified. Where a litigant alleges that s/he enjoys a particular implied right, such a right would be denied any legal protection in the particular case if one had to await a decision of the Oireachtas as to whether or not the right existed. Thus full implementation of the intention of the People as expressed in the language of Article 40.3 would appear to require that the courts, as opposed to the Oireachtas, be entrusted with the task of identifying the implied rights clearly envisaged by the Constitution.

Moreover, given the relative ease with which the Irish Constitution may be amended, it is comparatively easy to ascertain the views of the People in relation to particular judicial decisions interpreting the Constitution, a facility that has been exercised on a number of occasions in relation to the protection of fundamental rights, specifically the right to life of the unborn – the Thirteenth and Fourteenth Amendments to the Constitution in 1992 were prompted by the Supreme Court decisions relating to the right to life of the unborn in *Attorney General (SPUC (Ireland) Ltd.)* v. *Open Door Counselling Ltd.* [1988] IR 593; [1988] ILRM 19 and *Attorney General* v. *X* [1992] 1 IR 1; [1992] ILRM 401 and the People also rejected, in 1992 and 2002, two proposals to modify constitutional policy on abortion as enunciated in *Attorney General* v. *X* [1992] 1 IR 1; [1992] ILRM 401 – and the right to bail – the Sixteenth Amendment to the Constitution in 1996 set aside the Supreme Court decision in *The People (A.G.)* v. *O'Callaghan* [1966] IR 501; (1968) 102 ILTR 45 concerning the availability of bail. Accordingly, it would seem that concerns about the undemocratic nature of the judicial power to identify implied rights might be overstated in the Irish context.

As for the argument that the exercise of this power increases legal uncertainty, one might well question to what extent legal certainty is ever attainable

(Brady, 1973). Moreover, even if legal certainty is attainable, it does not follow that this goal should be more highly prized than the goal of affording legal protection to important interests by classifying them as implied rights. For the parents of a child with severe or profound learning difficulties, introducing some uncertainty into the law may well be a price worth paying for securing appropriate educational or health facilities for their child.

Penultimately, in response to the contention that judicial activism undermines the political process by encouraging citizens to rely on the courts in preference to their elected politicians, this concern is arguably based on the questionable premise that a judicial decision pre-empts any subsequent role for politicians and/or administrators in addressing the issue in hand. In fact, my research on the use of the courts to effect social change suggests that judicial decision making usually stimulates political activity rather than resolving the issue *tout court* (Whyte, 2002). Legislation may be necessary to implement fully the judicial decision or, at the other end of the spectrum of responses, to modify or, indeed, nullify that decision. Thus far from emasculating the political process, public interest litigation will often provoke it into action.

Finally, in a response to Hogan's critique of *Ryan*, Humphreys has defended judicial reliance on natural law as a source for the identification of implied rights on the grounds both that it is constitutionally mandated, the language of various provisions of the Constitution acknowledging the existence of natural law rights, and that natural law rights provide a more secure basis for the enforcement of rights than positivism (Humphreys, 1993–5). He further argues that reliance on natural law affords the judiciary access to both international and comparative legal principles as a resource for the identification of implied fundamental rights.

However, while it is relatively easy to defend the concept of judicially identified implied constitutional rights, it does seem unlikely that there will be any significant expansion in the corpus of such rights for the foreseeable future. In the first place, as we have already noted, leading members of the present Supreme Court appear committed to a policy of judicial restraint. Second, the case law of the past thirty years or so may have exhausted, or at least diminished, the potential of the Constitution to yield up any further implied rights. Thus it is probable that, in the medium term, at any rate, social policy will be less influenced by judicial decision making than may have hitherto been the case.

Socio-economic rights and justiciability

A particular application of the debate on the legitimacy or otherwise of the judicial power to read implied rights into the Constitution concerned the issue of socio-economic rights. While the Supreme Court has resolutely set its face against the judicial implication of such rights into the Constitution, a debate has developed in recent years about the appropriateness of framing socio-economic interests in terms of justiciable rights, i.e. rights enforceable by the courts. This debate initially focused on the status of socio-economic rights within the constitutional order, though given the opposition of the current Supreme Court to the judicial implication of socio-economic rights into the Constitution, the focus for this debate has recently shifted from the Constitution to legislation. A particular context for the debate is anticipated legislation concerning the rights of people with disabilities and, indeed, a failure to provide for such justiciable rights in an earlier version of this legislation attracted considerable criticism that ultimately persuaded the government to revisit this issue.

A case for justiciable socio-economic rights may be made on the basis of the need to address the failure of the political system to protect adequately the needs of marginalised groups. Thus a vision of politics as a means of maximising human good, as distinct from an understanding of politics as a means of achieving selfish, sectoral preferences, may justify judicial intervention in cases of egregious neglect of the socio-economic interests of a disadvantaged group by the political system (Quinn, 2001; Whyte, 2002). In addition, one can also argue that the logic of Ireland's international obligations requires the State to provide for justiciable socio-economic rights (Irish Commission for Justice and Peace, 1998).

However, in making the case for a judicial role in relation to the protection of socio-economic rights, it is important to be realistic about what can be achieved through litigation in this context. One should be cautious about the judicial role in promoting social inclusion for a number of reasons. First, there are good institutional reasons for looking initially to the legislature and executive for protection of socio-economic rights – both of these branches of government have access to more expertise and are capable of formulating more sophisticated policies than the judiciary. Perhaps even more significantly, both of these branches of government effectively determine how public resources are to be allocated and without an appropriate allocation of such resources, the characterisation of a socio-economic right as justiciable may represent only the opening gambit in a process for securing the effective protection of that right rather than the culmination of such a process. As Daly points out in her analysis of the barriers impeding access to social rights, access to such rights cannot be assumed from the legal status of the right; the legal position has to be considered in conjunction with key aspects of the structure and design of social programmes, together with the capabilities and resources available to the individual that will enable him or her to assert social rights. Indeed, improving the legal basis of entitlement to social rights is only one of seven recommendations made by Daly for improving access to social rights (Daly, 2002).

Second, there are risks attendant on reliance on the courts to enforce socio-economic rights – the courts may refuse to accede to the claim presented, thereby reinforcing the status quo; gains secured in court are susceptible to reversal by the enactment of subsequent legislation; securing judicial endorsement of a claim may result in the diversion of resources from other areas of need to meet that claim; such litigation reinforces the dependency of marginalised people on middle-class professionals; and the procedural rules governing litigation impede the formulation of comprehensive and sophisticated policies. In the light of these factors, therefore, the courts should only be used as a last resort when it is clear that the political process has been guilty of egregious neglect of an important socio-economic interest.

Third, the ability of the judiciary to resolve social problems is limited. In the first place, not every social problem is susceptible to judicial resolution. But, as we have already noted, even where litigation is an option, experience in a number of discrete areas in which the courts were called upon to enforce socio-economic rights shows that, in the majority of cases such litigation did not authoritatively resolve the issue in hand but rather provoked a response from the political system (Whyte, 2002). In some cases, this response nullified the judicial decision; in other cases, it modified existing policy in response to the decision. In all cases, however, even where the litigation is based on constitutional principles, the judicial decision is always susceptible to nullification or modification. It follows that rendering socio-economic rights justiciable will not render the political process redundant and will not convert the judiciary into a corps of latter-day Platonic guardians. At most, the existence of such rights will require the political process to engage with the beneficiaries of such rights rather than, as happens at present in some cases at least, ignore them. It equally follows, of course, that supporters of such rights should not expect too much from the judicial system and should always be prepared to have to work the political process in defence of their interests.

Opposition to, or at least scepticism about, the concept of justiciable socio-economic rights falls broadly into two camps. Some participants in this debate oppose justiciable socio-economic rights because of the perceived negative impact of such rights on the politico-legal order, without addressing, explicitly at any rate, the underlying concerns about the ability of our political system to address issues of social disadvantage. I would list here the Report of the Constitution Review Group and the comments of the Minister for Justice, Equality and Law Reform, Michael McDowell, TD. In contrast, both the National Economic and Social Council and Professor Brian Nolan of the Economic and Social Research Institute have produced critiques that might be considered more sensitive to the need to promote social inclusion but which query the efficacy of justiciable socio-economic rights in securing this objective.

(i) Report of the Constitution Review Group

In 1996 a majority of the Constitution Review Group came out against the insertion of justiciable socio-economic rights in the Constitution on the ground that this would amount to a distortion of democracy, requiring the judges to rely on their own subjective appraisal of what constituted poverty and depriving the legislature and executive of any power to determine the cost of implementing such rights (Constitution Review Group, 1996). This reasoning has been criticised on a number of grounds. First, the assertion that the recognition of socio-economic rights is a 'distortion of democracy' is arguably based on one particular political vision, classical liberal democracy, and thus not convincing to those who do not subscribe to this particular philosophy (Whyte, 1998; Murphy, 1998). Moreover, it has also been argued that the insertion of a clause guaranteeing socio-economic rights into the Constitution could hardly distort democracy, given that such a move would require the approval of the People voting directly on the issue in a referendum (Irish Commission for Justice and Peace, 1998).

Second, the Review Group Report would appear to be inconsistent in some aspects of its reasoning on socio-economic rights. Thus among the arguments cited by the Review Group in support of its opposition to the inclusion of justiciable socio-economic rights in the Constitution is the view that, in any event, judicial vindication of the rights to life and to bodily integrity offer ultimate protection to anyone who might fall below a minimum level of subsistence so as to suffer from a lack of food, shelter or clothing. If this is so, then it is difficult to see what possible objection there could be to recognising, for example, an explicit right to shelter, enforceable by the courts, as an alternative to requiring the courts to infer such a right from the rights to life and bodily integrity. Moreover, in its treatment of constitutional policy on education, the Report of the Review Group calls for explicit recognition of the right of every child to free primary education and for possible extension of this right to cover second-level education. Yet the Review Group does not explain why a right to education should receive constitutional protection in this way while other, more basic (and sometimes less expensive) socio-economic rights, such as the right to shelter, are kept outside the constitutional pale. The Review Group's rejection of a judicial role in this context has also led to charges of inconsistency given that the Review Group accepts the inevitability of subjective judicial appraisal of the guarantee of private property in Article 40.3 and 43 (Irish Commission for Justice and Peace, 1998).

Third, the Review Group's understanding of the nature of socio-economic rights has been challenged in two respects. According to the Irish Commission for Justice and Peace, the Group's concern about uncontrollable costs resulting from judicial intervention 'appears to assume that there is no middle way between stating socio-economic rights in a totally open-ended manner, or excluding them from the Constitution altogether' (Irish Commission for Justice and Peace, 1998: 11). However, it is possible to frame rights, including socio-economic rights, in a manner which allows considerations of practicability to limit the extent of the State's obligations (Murphy, 1998; Irish Commission for Justice and Peace, 1998) and the Review Group itself recognises that in relation to the constitutional guarantees of the personal and property rights of the individual. The Irish Commission for Justice and Peace also accuses the Review Group of assuming a dichotomy between civil-political and socio-economic rights for which there does not appear to be any justification and which also ignores developments in international law. It is sometimes suggested that socio-economic rights cannot be compared to civil and political rights on the ground that the exercise of the former has resource implications and, moreover, requires the State to take positive action in their defence (as opposed to simply desisting from wrongfully interfering with rights). However, while it is the case that the exercise of many civil and political rights does not involve public expenditure, that is not always the case. If the State wishes to vindicate effectively the right to liberty, it has to fund the criminal court system to ensure that innocent people are not wrongly convicted of criminal charges. Even the exercise of the right to vote requires the State to fund the collection and counting of votes. Thus one cannot rely on the fact that the exercise of a right may involve public expenditure as a basis for excluding such a right from the remit of the courts. By the same token, as may be seen from the foregoing examples, an adequate vindication of some civil and political rights requires the State to take positive steps and not merely refrain from wrongful interference. As for the developments in international law, the Commission point out that Ireland has, through ratifying a variety of international treaties, made itself subject to the scrutiny of a number of international bodies, including the European Court of Human Rights, in relation to its performance on socio-economic matters and so the Commission suggests that it is somewhat anomalous to deny a similar role to the Irish courts (Irish Commission for Justice and Peace, 1998: 13–16).

Perhaps understandably, given the terms of reference of the Review Group, its focus in opposing justiciable socio-economic rights was primarily on how such rights might impact adversely on the existing constitutional order and it did not address the underlying concerns about the perceived failure of the political system to protect adequately the interests of disadvantaged groups. Yet the case for justiciable socio-economic rights is unlikely to go away until these concerns are allayed. A similar failure to address this underlying problem is also a feature of the criticisms of justiciable socio-economic rights advanced by the Minister for Justice, Equality and Law Reform, Mr Michael McDowell, TD.

(ii) Position of Michael McDowell, TD

Minister McDowell has publicly opposed the insertion of justiciable socio-economic rights in the Constitution on a number of occasions. The fullest statement of his opposition may be found in a paper he delivered at St Patrick's College, Drumcondra in April 2003, though he had previously covered some of the same ground in his address to the Annual Conference of the Irish Social Policy Association in September 2002. In the more recent paper, the Minister noted that Article 45 of the Constitution precluded the judicial enforcement of most socio-economic rights, with the notable exception of the right to free primary education and argued that the protection and achievement of policy values in the social and economic spheres were more properly the concern of the executive and/or legislature than of the judiciary. He also contended that fundamental differences existed between civil and political rights, on the one hand, and socio-economic rights on the other.

> The fundamental difference between classical civil and political rights such as the right to vote, freedom of expression, etc. and economic and social rights is, in the language of economists, that civil and political rights are 'public goods' and economic and social rights are 'private goods'. My exercising of my right to vote or my right to free speech does not prevent anyone else from exercising that right at the same time. Rights to housing, healthcare and higher education, for example, because of resource constraints and because of the nature of the goods involved are different. If I get a kidney transplant, no one else can get the same kidney. The exercise of these rights must therefore be rationed, by queuing, or price or by some other mechanism. Such decisions are . . . the stuff of politics and not at all appropriate to be decided by the Courts. (McDowell, 2003: 10)

He went on to defend the division of functions in relation to policy formation as between the legislature and executive, on the one hand, and the judiciary, on the other, arguing that societies that respect this separation of powers enjoy great social progress coupled with the vindication of civil and political liberties. He was also concerned that the transformation of disputes about social values into conflicts of rights would diminish and belittle democratic and political debate in our society and would politicise the judiciary in the carrying out of their functions. Minister McDowell also expressed disquiet about the impact of justiciable socio-economic rights on the performance of the economy, arguing that the rights-based approach could threaten economic prosperity and endanger those qualities – flexibility, choice, dynamism and freedom – that provide the climate for change, growth, wealth creation and social and cultural innovation. Finally, it should be noted that on a subsequent occasion, the Minister was reported to have linked the concept of justiciable socio-economic rights to an undermining of the idea of personal responsibility and a diminution of the 'can-do' self-reliant spirit (*The Irish Times*, 24 May 2003).

Responding to the various arguments raised by the Minister, it is worth noting, first of all, that, the terms of Article 45 notwithstanding, the Constitution does not, in fact, erect an impenetrable barrier between civil and political rights, on the one hand, and socio-economic rights, on the other. As the Minister himself concedes, the Constitution explicitly protects the right to free primary education (casting it as an obligation imposed on the State by Article 42.4). In addition, Article 42.5 also obliges the State, in exceptional cases, to look after those children whose parents, for physical or moral reasons, have failed in their parental duties. (In passing, it is also worth noting that, in the past, various High Court judges relied on the provisions of Article 45 in order to identify implied rights protected by Article 40.3. To date, however, the Supreme Court has not pronounced on the legitimacy of this use of Article 45, though one might infer from the stance adopted in *Sinnott* and *T.D.* that the present Court is unlikely to look on it with favour.) Thus justiciable socio-economic rights are already to be found in the Constitution and so, strictly speaking, the debate is really about whether or not this corpus of rights should be expanded.

As for his insistence that socio-economic rights are qualitatively different from civil and political rights, as we have already noted, some civil and political rights have resource implications and may require the State to take active steps for their vindication. So when the Minister suggests that the exercise of a socio-economic right may preclude someone else from exercising his or her socio-economic right, the same point can be made in respect of, for example, the right of an impoverished individual facing a criminal charge to be provided with State funded legal representation, yet such a right is constitutionally protected (*The State (Healy)* v. *Donoghue* [1976] IR 325). Indeed, even where a criminal defendant pays for his or her own legal representation, the State still has to finance the criminal justice system (employ judges and other officials, acquire and maintain court premises, feed and, occasionally, accommodate juries) in order to vindicate the right to liberty. Thus one cannot rely on the fact that the exercise of a right may involve public expenditure as a basis for excluding such a right from the remit of the courts.

With regard to the Minister's concerns about the impact of justiciable socio-economic rights on the economy, it would appear at least arguable that a commitment to socio-economic rights may not necessarily result in an overall increase in public expenditure. When one factors in the direct benefits of such commitment, such as having more people in the labour force and fewer people dependent on social welfare, together with possible indirect benefits in falling crime rates and improved general health, it must surely be at least arguable that improved protection for socio-economic rights is not a zero sum game in terms of public expenditure (though it may be in terms of social status). (Ultimately, of course, I would base the case for enforceable socio-economic rights not on such a crude economic calculation, but rather on the belief that each individual has an intrinsic worth and that the majority of people are only capable of realising their full potential in society which should, accordingly, structure itself so as to facilitate participation in community by every person to the full extent of his or her abilities.)

With regard to his concern about the potential of justiciable socio-economic rights to erode the individual's sense of self-reliance, the validity of this concern ultimately depends on the extent of the rights in question or, put another way, on the extent of the disadvantage and social exclusion experienced by the individual. Certainly when one considers the facts of some of the cases concerning children at risk coming before the High Court – such as *D.H.* v. *Minister for Health* (*The Irish Times*, 19 October 2000) involving a 16-year-old girl who was sexually abused at the age of 10, engaged in prostitution and substance abuse, twice tried to hang herself and once tried to set herself on fire, or *S.C.* v. *Minister for Education* ([1997] 2 ILRM 134) involving an 11-year-old boy from a dysfunctional family, diagnosed at the age of 10 as suffering from attention deficit disorder and all of whose siblings were in State care or *D.T.* v. *Eastern Health Board* (High Court, 24 March 1995), concerning a 12-year-old girl with suicidal tendencies and of such unruly disposition that she was deemed to be in need of confinement – it would appear unrealistic to expect that a 'can-do self-reliant' spirit could cope with the extent of the challenge facing the litigant.

But perhaps the most serious criticism one can make of the Minister's position relates to a core element of his argument, namely, the impact that the insertion of justiciable socio-economic rights into the Constitution might have on the democratic system. In attempting to depict this impact, it could be said that the Minister paints with a very broad brush indeed. Thus he characterises the debate to date as 'unbalanced and unsatisfactory', involving, on the one hand, those who argue for a rights-based approach to entire fields of social policy and, on the other, conservative forces who highlight issues of practicality, affordability and pragmatism. He assumes that providing for justiciable socio-economic rights in the Constitution will somehow completely pre-empt any role for the executive or legislature in this area, thereby entailing the abandonment of the doctrine of separation of powers. Perhaps more significantly, he would appear to assume that our present model of democratic politics is working well, claiming to detect among its critics 'an impatience with or contempt for the democratic process'. Finally, in common with the Constitution Review Group, he appears to consider that socio-economic rights must be stated in absolutist terms or not at all.

Many of these assumptions are arguably suspect. We have already noted that it is possible to formulate socio-economic rights in such a way as to limit the extent of the State's obligations by reference to considerations of practicability (Murphy, 1998; Irish Commission for Justice and Peace, 1998). And it is certainly possible to make a much more nuanced case in favour of justiciable socio-economic rights in the Constitution than the Minister would appear to allow, one that arguably bolsters, rather than undermines, the democratic process. Quite apart from these points, however, what is striking about the Minister's contribution to this debate is his failure to address the argument that the political process is generally unresponsive to the needs of those on the margins of society. The Minister does make it clear that he believes passionately in politics as the means for conducting and resolving social and economic issues and it may be that he also believes that our current political system is adequate to the task of promoting social inclusion. However, he does not explicitly say so and certainly does not address the concerns of those who believe otherwise. This, in my opinion, is a surprising omission for it is this argument that is arguably at the root of the call for justiciable socio-economic rights and until it is addressed, the demand for such rights will continue to be heard.

In contrast to the views of both the Constitution Review Group and Minister McDowell, the recent critiques of justiciable socio-economic rights that have emanated from the National Economic and Social Council (NESC) and Professor Brian Nolan of the Economic and Social Research Institute (ESRI) are arguably more concerned about the efficacy of justiciable socio-economic rights in promoting social inclusion than about any possible negative impact on the politico-legal order.

(iii) Contribution from NESC

One section of the NESC Report, *An Investment in Quality, Services, Inclusion and Enterprise* (2003) examines the role of rights in policies on poverty and exclusion. In its earlier *Strategy Report* (1999), the NESC noted that citizenship rights embrace social, economic and cultural rights as well as civil and political rights. However it also considered that social inclusion was not based on a set of specific justiciable rights but rather referred to equal access to those social benefits and services taken for granted in society and equal participation in decision making. Moreover the Council also pointed out that the identification of rights without standards against which progress could be measured was an empty exercise.

In its more recent Report, the Council identified very different views and expectations of social, economic and cultural rights and the potential for a 'rights-based approach' in social policy. Thus some consider that the declaration of a right is a key to securing it while others shelter behind the separation of powers in the face of urgent social problems. In order to improve the quality of this debate, the Council argues that there should be some recognition of the complex issues involved and some exploration of the relation between rights and public policy and institutions.

The Council identifies a range of complex philosophical, political, legal and practical issues inherent in the debate about the role of rights in social policy, a number of which can be recorded without further comment. Thus, with regard to the relationship between socio-economic rights and civil/political rights, the Council suggests that the argument that a strong distinction exists between both types of right and the opposing contention that there is a direct connection between the two have not proven very robust and that there is now a more nuanced view of the relation between the two which includes recognition of the fact that each requires the positive establishment and maintenance of costly administrative frameworks. The Council also points out that, with regard to the relationship between rights and duties, it is not always the case that the recognition of a right inhering in one person implies a duty imposed on another and that it is possible to state a determinate socio-economic right without specifying a determinate duty incumbent on some particular person or agency. It follows that the assertion of a right may only be a first step in ensuring that a particular need is met. The Council also stresses the need to distinguish between moral rights and legal rights, noting that there are many ways in which something may be secured legally for someone, without them having a *legal* right to it. 'A socio-economic right – such as that to a standard of living, health or housing – may or may not emerge as a specific or legal constitutional guarantee.' (2003: 360–1). This is unexceptionable if one makes allowance for the semantic point – albeit one whose clarification might facilitate further debate on this topic – that the phrase 'socio-economic right' in the above quotation probably refers to 'socio-economic interest' rather than a 'right', *strictu sensu*. Lastly, the Council suggests that the efficacy of socio-economic rights depends on their widespread acceptance among society at large and that there is a need to build public consensus on those goods, services and procedures to which people may be considered to be entitled. The Council later make the valid point that such a consensus may precede the emergence of a recognised right, rather than vice versa, and that the link between rights, institutions and commitments is 'a loop, not a line'.

A number of other issues identified by the Council prompt further comment. Thus the Council considers that the case for specific socio-economic rights cannot be regarded as self-evident. According to the Council, where the case for a socio-economic right is widely considered to be virtually self-evident, this is usually because it is stated at a high level of generality, such as a right to adequate shelter or education. The case for a particular interpretation of such a general right, for a more specific socio-economic right, cannot be taken as self-evident and may require different and additional arguments from those that support civil and political rights. That specific socio-economic rights cannot be taken as self-evident is undoubtedly true but this is also a feature of many civil and political rights. Thus, for example, while many people would accept the validity of the right to privacy, there is unlikely to be consensus as to whether such a right should embrace, for example, a right to an abortion or a right to physician-assisted suicide. Nor is it clear that socio-economic rights necessarily require different and additional arguments from those that support civil and political rights. In my opinion, an understanding of the individual as an end in him- or herself, rather than as a means to an end, and a resulting commitment to protect the dignity of the person provides an adequate philosophical premise upon which to base both civil/political rights and socio-economic rights. However it is unquestionably true that the mere assertion of a right, of whichever variety, is not necessarily enough to secure its protection and that it is often necessary to go further by adducing arguments as to why the right in question should be recognised.

The Council also considers that a rights-based approach may be imbued with an absolutist approach that appears to preclude any qualification or restriction of the rights in question. It is certainly the case that concern has been expressed in the US about a tendency to employ 'rights-speak' as a trump card that precludes any further discussion (see, for example, Glendon, 1991) and one should always be mindful of this risk in an Irish context. That said, at least some aspects of the Irish experience with rights support the view that such an absolutist approach to the making of claims is not inevitable. Thus statutory social welfare entitlements, for example, are not infrequently reduced and, occasionally, abolished. Indeed, as we have already noted, even certain constitutional rights – the right to liberty of every citizen and the right to life of the unborn – have been modified in the light of changing circumstances, the latter right in 1992 in the context of freedom to travel and freedom to obtain information about abortion services abroad and the former right in 1996 in the context of the availability of bail to persons charged with serious criminal offences. Thus even the explicit constitutional recognition of a right does not preclude its subsequent qualification or modification.

The Council also refers to the tension that exists between the operation of democratic politics and the recognition of constitutional rights. Again, we have already alluded to this point in the context of our consideration of the role of the judiciary in identifying implied rights but the point is worth repeating. In the Irish context, it is relatively easier to amend our Constitution than it is to amend, for example, that of the United States, even where, as we have just noted in the preceding paragraph, fundamental rights are an issue. All that is required is a simple majority of those voters participating on the day in a referendum. Moreover, if needs must, the Constitution may be changed relatively quickly and in the case of the Tenth Amendment of the Constitution in 1987 (concerning ratification of the Single European Act), the Constitution was amended within six weeks of the Supreme Court identifying a constitutional problem in *Crotty* v. *An Taoiseach* ([1987] IR 713). It may be thought, therefore, that concerns expressed by the Council about the loss of ability 'to evolve a free and flexible discourse of politics' and the 'disabling of the legislator (and other institutions) from their normal functions of revision, reform and innovation in the law and public policy' are overstated in the Irish context.

This point may also address, at least in part, the additional concern voiced by the Council that the specification of socio-economic rights in the Constitution may limit the involvement of the affected people in the definition and vindication of their rights. If, as I argue, the constitutionalisation of a principle does not render it immune to further change emanating from the political process, then the beneficiaries of that principle are not precluded from further involvement in debate as to its content. But perhaps the more fundamental point to make in this context is to question whether, in fact, the political system does facilitate the participation of those members of society who would typically benefit from the creation of justiciable socio-economic rights. I suspect that the impulse towards the creation of such rights stems from the perception of those affected that they cannot participate effectively in democratic politics. In the same way, while the Council is correct to say that a commitment to socio-economic rights does not necessarily entail a commitment to making such rights justiciable (i.e. enforceable by the courts, as distinct from other agencies such as administrative tribunals or an ombudsman), the push for justiciability probably stems from a perception that the judicial process places more weight on the force of argument behind a claim (ignoring completely the claimant's lack of political influence) than does the political process. Certainly concerns about the apparent lack of responsiveness of democratic politics in Ireland to marginalised groups should also be addressed if we are to obviate the need for justiciable socio-economic rights.

The Council also cautions participants in this debate about justiciable socio-economic rights to 'think carefully about the ability of rights claims to secure the social outcomes we seek in the most effective ways' (2003: 365), drawing on the writings of Simone Weil and Raimond Gaita in this context. Both of these philosophers question the efficacy of rights claims in certain types of social conflict. However, these conflicts appear to be ones in which one protagonist denies the full humanity of his or her opponent as, for example, in the case of the denial of legal protection to the interests of Australian Aborigines in the land of Australia by the common law doctrine of *terra nullius*. According to Gaita, that common law doctrine 'effectively denied [Aborigines] their full human status because it denied the depth of moral and spiritual being which alone makes dispossession such a terrible affliction and, thereby, a terrible injustice' (Gaita, 2000: 78). It is 'the expression of the kind of racism that finds literally unintelligible the thought that its victims could seriously be wronged' (2000: 79). But while the stakes in the debate over justiciable socio-economic rights may be high, the debate does not call into question the essential humanity of the putative beneficiaries of such rights. Gaita distinguishes between acts of justice and forms of fairness, observing that 'Acknowledgement of someone as fully human is an act of justice of a different kind from those acts of justice which are rightly described as forms of fairness. Fairness is at issue only when the full human status of those who are protesting their unfair treatment is not disputed' (2000: 81). In these terms, the call for justiciable socio-economic rights is a call for certain 'forms of fairness' between individuals, all of whom are acknowledged to be fully human, rather than a call to elevate the putative beneficiaries of such rights from some sub-human status. Consequently the relevance to the debate about socio-economic rights of the scepticism of Weil and Gaita about rights in the latter type of situation is questionable.

That said, in defending justiciable socio-economic rights as a means of promoting social inclusion, it is important not to overstate their capabilities and two further points made by the Council highlight the limitations of such rights. First, the creation of justiciable socio-economic rights cannot avoid problems resulting from scarcity of resources, compromises and, indeed, conflict between rights themselves. Acknowledging this, participants in this debate such as the Irish Commission for Justice and Peace have called for the State to commit itself legally to the *progressive realisation* of certain socio-economic rights, thus allowing considerations of practicality to limit the extent of the State's obligations. Second, a system of justiciable rights is not necessarily the most appropriate one for formulating social policy, a point that I have considered in more detail elsewhere (Whyte, 2002, ch. 2). Moreover, in addition to both of these points, it is important to reiterate, yet again, that making rights justiciable, even within the constitutional order, cannot ultimately preclude modification of such rights by the political system which, in the last analysis, is the primary mechanism for formulating social policy.

(iv) Views of Professor Brian Nolan

In his contribution to the debate on justiciable socio-economic rights, Professor Brian Nolan calls for clarification of the relationship between rights and resources and of the relationship between rights and justiciability. In relation to the first of these relationships, he notes that the view that justiciable socio-economic rights only obliges the State to secure their progressive realisation through an effective use of existing resources rather than necessarily an increase in those resources is not shared by all of the participants in the debate. It is clearly not the understanding of socio-economic rights adopted by the majority of the Constitution Review Group (or Minister McDowell, for that matter) but neither is it shared by all proponents of the rights approach, some of whom would regard this graduated approach to the protection of socio-economic rights as negating the value of explicit recognition of the right in the first place. In this context, it is worth noting that Article 42.4 of the Constitution, which imposes an obligation on the State to provide for free primary education and which was at the heart of the cases taken by people with learning difficulties, is not qualified by reference to available resources. According to Nolan, clarification of the relationship between rights and resources is very important.

> It is one thing to assign the courts a role in assessing whether transparent and fair *systems* are in place for the use of resources currently being devoted to, for example, education or health care – which is seen by some of those arguing for the rights approach as a core benefit. It is very different if the courts are being asked to adjudicate on whether independent standards of adequacy are being met and by extension whether resources being devoted by the State are sufficient (Nolan, 2003b: 15).

Related to this point is how Irish courts might interpret an obligation to secure the progressive realisation of socio-economic rights and whether rights framed in such a manner would be of any value.

With regard to the relationship between rights and justiciability, Nolan points out that, at the conceptual level, rights need not necessarily be justiciable, i.e. enforceable by the courts, and that there may be alternative enforcement mechanisms for the enforcement of socio-economic rights. It follows that the case for justiciability has to be argued on its merits rather than taken for granted *a priori*.

Looking specifically at the area of disability, Nolan notes how the rights-based approach to the issue of disability was linked to the change in attitude towards disability that has occurred since the 1960s. Up to that time, disability was essentially seen as a medical problem and the focus was on trying to cure or minimise the consequences flowing from the disability experienced by the individual so as to enable him or her to conform to the norm set by people without disabilities. Since that time, however, a new perspective on disability has emerged that sees disablement as stemming from the environment and the manner in which society is organised. Now the focus is on changing society so that it can accommodate the needs of the person with the disability, rather than on 'curing' the disability.

> The human rights perspective on disability continues to locate the main problem outside the person, in society and in its lack of responsiveness to difference, but

emphasises that persons with a disability should have autonomy and enjoy the same economic, social and cultural rights as others (Nolan, 2003b: 20).

This rights-based approach is central to the contemporary debate in Ireland about a proposed Disability Bill and underpins the position of the Disability Legislation Consultation Group, an umbrella group representing the disability sector in the consultation process undertaken by the Government in relation to the proposed legislation. The DLCG has called for the proposed Bill to provide for the independent assessment of the needs of individuals with disabilities and for the services identified by the assessment to be made available as a right, ultimately enforceable by the courts. The Group does accept that, in the event of the services not being available, the State should be afforded the opportunity of putting in place a programme of measures for the provision of such services within an established framework. Testing this proposal against comparative experience in the US, Australia, New Zealand, Sweden and the UK, Nolan noted that it was unique and that none of the countries surveyed entrusted decisions about service provision and resource allocation to professionals and the courts, without reference to Parliament and unconstrained by the availability of resources.

In the concluding chapter of his report, Nolan makes the following important points: First, a rights-based approach to social policy for people with disabilities can embrace a variety of approaches to delivering services, framing entitlements and instituting enforcement mechanisms. Second, rights need not necessarily be justiciable, i.e. enforceable by the courts, and may be adequately protected by alternative enforcement mechanisms. Given the political opposition to justiciable socio-economic rights, he then proposes a possible alternative whereby the State would set out clearly the level of service provision the current level of resource is intended to underpin; people with disabilities would be informed as to what this level of service provision was at individual level and would have an entitlement to those services with associated enforcement mechanisms; and the State would set out in concrete terms how services would be improved over time as more resources became available.

On the assumption that the level of service provision set out by the State addressed in a meaningful way the needs of people with disabilities and subject to one specific point in relation to justiciability, these proposals seem entirely sensible and worthwhile. In relation to justiciability, it is very unlikely that legislation could oust the High Court's traditional power of judicial review (permitting that Court to examine the decisions of inferior courts and tribunals on the grounds of whether such bodies had the lawful authority to act as they did and whether they followed fair procedures in their decision-making process) in the light of Article 34.3.1 of the Constitution which provides for, inter alia, a 'High Court invested with full original jurisdiction in and power to determine all matters and questions whether of law or fact, civil or criminal'. This power, it should be noted, enables the High Court to strike down an administrative decision that 'plainly and unambiguously flies in the face of fundamental reason and common sense' – *The State (Keegan)* v. *Stardust Victims' Compensation Tribunal* ([1986] IR 642) – though the Court is likely to be cautious in the exercise of this jurisdiction. It is certainly the case that legislation could not preclude recourse to the courts where issues of constitutional rights were at stake. Thus some role for the courts, however limited, would appear to be inevitable.

However, I agree with Nolan and the NESC that recourse to the courts is not necessarily the only way in which one can effectively protect socio-economic rights. In a recent book (Whyte, 2002), I argued in favour of a limited judicial role in the enforcement of socio-economic rights essentially as a corrective mechanism to our present model of democratic politics which, as I have suggested above, appears to be unresponsive to the needs of those on the margins of political life. The context in which I developed my argument was one in which, at the time, the High Court was being asked to protect the socio-economic rights of certain disadvantaged groups, such as children at risk, people with learning difficulties and Travellers and my focus was specifically on *the role of the courts* in the promotion of social inclusion, rather than with the most effective way of forging a more inclusive society. Accordingly, I did not consider whether socio-economic rights could be better protected by non-judicial bodies, though I did accept that the judicial role here was limited and that one could not afford to ignore the political process. Addressing this point now, a major attraction of public interest litigation to marginalised groups is the independence of the courts from the political system and the imperviousness of judges to factors such as wealth and influence that are so important in the political sphere. However, this characteristic is not exclusive to the courts and has been manifested by other agencies such as, for example, the office of the Ombudsman. I would certainly accept, therefore, that the protection of socio-economic rights does not necessarily require recourse to the courts in the first instance and that such rights could be adequately protected by independent, administrative agencies, though, as I have pointed out above, to remove such agencies from the ambit of the High Court's power of judicial review might be constitutionally problematic.

In essence, I consider justiciable socio-economic rights to be a last resort, necessitated by the failure of the political system to address in a meaningful way different aspects of social exclusion. However, to the extent to which the political system commits itself to the effective protection of socio-economic rights, there may be no need to involve the courts, as distinct from other independent agencies, in this area (other than through the High Court's supervisory power of judicial review). In the absence of such a commitment, however, those who feel ignored by the political system are likely to be tempted by the prospect of obtaining protection for their interests through the courts. Thus the debate on justiciable socio-economic rights should be seen as inextricably linked to the larger debate about the nature of Irish politics.

Conclusion

Since the mid-1960s, increasing recourse has been made to the courts in relation to different aspects of Irish social policy. While the initial response of the courts did not discourage this phenomenon, in the very recent past senior members of the Supreme Court have evinced a marked hostility to judicial activism, especially in the area of socio-economic rights. Thus it is probable that, for the foreseeable future, Irish courts may play a less prominent role than hitherto in the shaping of public policy.

However, it is arguable that the earlier activist role of the courts was, at least in part, a symptom of a malaise rather than a malaise in itself. Certainly in the area of socio-economic rights, and probably in other contexts as well, the use of litigation to promote rights was invariably a reaction to the lack of any response from the political system to the pressing needs of particular groups. In this context, judicial intervention may be seen as a mechanism for promoting what Perry refers to as 'deliberative, transformative politics', i.e. 'politics in which questions of human good, of what way or ways of life human good consists in, are not marginalized or privatized but, instead, have a central public place' (Perry, 1998: 103).

The eschewing by the courts of an activist role will not resolve the problem posed by the not infrequent failure of our political system to tackle difficulties confronted by various minorities in our society. Indeed it may very well have exacerbated it for arguably the most significant feature of public interest litigation was not that it authoritatively resolved particular issues of social policy, removing them from the remit of the political system, but rather that it required that system to take those issues seriously. If so, this new era of judicial restraint, inspired by a desire to protect parliamentary democracy, may paradoxically weaken our political system by reinforcing the sense of alienation from politics that some, perhaps many, in Ireland experience.

References

Abrahamson, P. (1999) 'The Scandinavian model of welfare', in *Comparing Social Welfare Systems in Europe.* Vol. 4. Paris: MIRE-DREES, pp. 31–60.

Ackerlof, G. A. (1998) 'Men without children', *Economic Journal* 108 (447), pp. 287–389.

Akenson, D. H. (1991) *Small Differences: Irish Catholics and Protestants 1815–1922.* Dublin: Gill & Macmillan.

Alber, J. (1983) 'Some causes of social security expenditure developments in western Europe 1949–1977', in Loney, M., Boswell, D., Clarke, J. (eds), *The Development of Welfare States in Europe and America.* New Jersey: Transaction Books.

Alcock, P. et al. (2001) *Welfare and Well-being: Richard Titmuss's Contribution to Social Policy.* London: Policy Press.

Allen, K. (1999/2003) 'The Celtic Tiger, inequality and social partnership', in Fanning, B. and MacNamara, T. (eds), *Ireland Develops: Administration and Social Policy 1953–2003.* Dublin: IPA, pp. 119–39.

Allen, K. (2000) *The Celtic Tiger: The Myth of Social Partnership in Ireland.* Manchester: Manchester University Press.

Anthias, F. (1999) 'Theorising identity, difference and social divisions', in O'Brien, M., Penna, S. and Hay, C. (eds), *Theorising Modernity: Reflexivity, Environment and Identity in Giddens' Social Theory.* Harlow: Longman, pp. 156–78.

Balanda, K. (2001) *Inequalities in Mortality: A Report on All-Ireland Mortality Data, 1989–1999.* Dublin: Institute of Public Health in Ireland.

Bales, K. and Robbins, P. T. (2000) 'No one shall be held in slavery or servitude; a critical analysis of international slavery agreements', unpublished paper. Cited in O'Byrne, J. (2003) *Human Rights: An Introduction.* Essex: Pearson Education, pp. 1–17

Barrington, R. (1987) *Health, Medicine and Politics in Ireland 1900–1970.* Dublin: IPA.

Barrington, R. (1998) 'The future political, legislative and social framework of the health services' in Leahy, A. L. and Wiley, M. (eds), *The Irish Health System in the 21st Century.* Dublin: Oak Tree, pp. 83–101.

Barry, B. (1998) 'Social exclusion, social isolation and the distribution of income', *Case Paper 12, Centre for Analysis of Social Exclusion.* London: LSE.

Barry, F. (2002) 'The Celtic Tiger era: delayed convergence or regional boom?', in McCoy, D., Duffy, D., Bergin, A., Eakins, J., Hore, J. and MacCoille, C. (eds), *Quarterly Economic Commentary,* summer 2002, pp. 84–91.

Barry, J., Sinclair, H., Kelly, A., O'Loughlin, R., Handy, D. and O'Dowd, T. (2001) *Inequalities in Health in Ireland: Hard Facts.* Dublin: Trinity College, Department of Community Health and General Practice.

Bartley, B. (1999) 'Spatial poverty and planning in North Clondalkin', in Pringle, D., Walsh, J. and Hennessy, M (eds), *Poor People, Poor Places: A Geography of Poverty and Deprivation in Ireland.* Dublin: Oak Tree, pp. 225–59

Bauman, Z. (1998a) *Globalization: The Human Consequences.* Cambridge: Polity.

Bauman, Z. (1998b) *Work, Consumerism and the New Poor.* Buckingham: Open University Press.

Bauman, Z. (1999) *In Search of Politics.* London: Polity.

Beck, U. (1992) *Risk Society: Towards a New Modernity.* London: Sage.

Beck, U. and Beck-Gernsheim, E. (2002) *Individualization.* London: Sage.

Beck-Gernsheim, E. (2000) 'Health and responsibility: from social change to technological change and vice versa', in Adam, B. et al. (eds), *The Risk Society and Beyond: Critical Issues for Social Theory.* London: Sage, pp. 122–35.

Beere, T. (2003) 'Commission on the Status of Women: Progress report', in Fanning, B. and McNamara, T. (eds), *Ireland Develops: Administration and Social Policy 1953–2003.* Dublin: IPA, pp. 240–57.

Bellah, R. (1995) 'Community properly understood: a defence of 'democratic communitarianism', *The Responsive Community,* 6 (1) http://www.gwu.edu/~icps/bellah.html.

Bellah, R., Madsen, R., Sullivan, W. M., Swidler, A. and Tipton, S. M. (2002) 'Habits of the heart: individualism and commitment in American life', in Hess, A (ed.), *American Social and Political Thought: A Reader.* New York: New York University Press, pp. 275–80.

Bellamy, R. (1990) *Victorian Liberalism: Nineteenth Century Political Thought and Practice.* London: Routledge.

Benhabib, S. (1996) 'Towards a deliberative model of democratic legitimacy', in Benhabib, S. (ed.), *Democracy and Difference.* Princeton: Princeton University Press, pp. 17–34.

Benn, M. (1998) *Madonna and Child: Towards a New Politics of Motherhood.* London: Jonathan Cape.

Bergman, H. and Hobson, B. (2002) 'Compulsory fatherhood: the coding of fatherhood in the Swedish welfare state', in Hobson, B. (ed.), *Making Men into Fathers: Men, Masculinities and the Social Politics of Fatherhood.* Cambridge: Cambridge University Press, pp. 92–124

Blank, R. H. (1997) *The Price of Life: The Future of American Health Care.* New York: Columbia University Press.

Blankenhorn, D. (1995) *Fatherless America, Confronting Our Most Urgent Social Problem.* New York: Basic Books.

Bock, G. and Thane, P. (1991) *Maternity and Gender Policies, Women and the Rise of the European Welfare States 1880s–1950s.* London: Routledge.

Bocock, R. and Thompson, K (1998) (eds) 'Consumption and lifestyles', in Bocock, R. (ed), *Sociological and Cultural Forms of Modernity.* London: Polity.

Bocock, R. and Thompson, K. (1998) (eds), *Sociological and Cultural Forms of Modernity.* London: Polity.

Booth, A (1999) 'Causes and consequences of divorce: reflections on recent research, in Thompson, R. A. and Amato, P. R. (eds), *The Post-Divorce Family: Children, Parenting and Society,* London: Sage, pp. 29–48.

Bork, R. (1990) *The Tempting of America: The Political Seduction of the Law.* New York: Free Press.

Born, A. and Jensen, P. H. (2002) 'A second order reflection on the concepts of inclusion and exclusion' in Andersen, J. G. and Jensen, P. H. (eds), *Changing Labour Markets, Welfare Policies and Citizenship.* Bristol: Policy Press, pp. 257–79.

Bottero, W. and Irwin, S. (2003) 'Locating difference: class, 'race' and gender, and the shaping of social inequalities', *Sociological Review* 51 (4), pp. 463–83.

Bourdieu, P. (1974) 'The schools as a conservative force' in Eggleston, J. (ed.), *Contemporary Research in the Sociology of Education.* London: Methuen.

Bourdieu, P. (1984) *Distinction; A Social Critique of the Judgement of Taste.* London; Routledge & Kegan Paul.

Bourdieu, P. (2001) *Masculine Domination.* London: Polity.

Boyce, D. George. (1992) *Ireland 1892–1923: From Ascendancy to Democracy.* Oxford: Oxford University Press.

Boyce, D. George and O'Day, A. (1996) 'Revisionism and the revisionist controversy', in Boyce, D. George and O'Day, A. (eds), *Modern Irish History: Revisionism and the Revisionist Controversy.* London: Routledge, pp. 1–14.

Brady, J. (1973) 'Legal certainty: the durable myth', *Irish Jurist* (n.s.) 8, p. 18.

Brah, A. (1992) 'Black women and 1992', in Ward, A., Gregory, J. and Yuval-Davis, N. (eds), *Women and Citizenship in Europe: Borders, Rights and Duties,* London: Trentham Books for the European Forum of Socialist Feminists, pp.19–35.

Brah, A. (1996) *Cartographies of Diaspora: Contesting Identities.* London: Routledge.

Brandth, B. and Kvande, E. (2003) 'Home alone fathers', *NIKK Magazine, The Power of Gender* 3, pp. 22–5.

Breathnach, P. (2002) 'Social polarisation in the post-fordist informational economy; Ireland in international context', *Irish Journal of Sociology* 11: pp. 3–22.

Breen, R., Hannan, D. F., Rottman, D. B. and Whelan, C. T. (1990) *Understanding Contemporary Ireland: State, Class and Development in the Republic of Ireland.* Dublin: Gill & Macmillan.

Breuilly, J. (1994) *Labour and Liberalism in Nineteenth-Century Europe: Essays in Comparative History.* Manchester: Manchester University Press.

Brown, P (2000) Augustine of Hippo, London: Faber & Faber.

Brudell, P. (1998) *The Delivery of Quality Services for Children in Areas of High Long-term Unemployment.* Dublin City Partnership

Burke, H. (1987) *The People and the Poor Law in 19th Century Ireland.* Dublin: Women's Education Bureau.

Bussemaker, J. and Voet, R. (1998) 'Citizenship and gender: theoretical approaches and historical legacies', *Critical Social Policy* 18 (3), pp. 277–308.

Byrne, A. and Lentin, R. (2000) *(Re)searching Women: Feminist Research Methodologies in Social Sciences in Ireland.* Dublin: IPA.

Byrne, A. and Leonard, M. (1997) (eds), *Women in Irish Society: A Sociological Reader.* Belfast: Beyond the Pale.

Byrne, D. (1999) *Social Exclusion.* Buckingham: Open University Press.

Cancer Consortium (2001) *All-Ireland Cancer Statistics, 1994–1996: A Joint Report on Incidence and Mortality for the Island of Ireland.* Belfast/Dublin: Cancer Consortium, Ireland–Northern Ireland National Cancer Institute.

Cantillon, B. (1998) 'The challenge of poverty and exclusion', in *Family, Market and Community – Equity and Efficiency in Social Policy.* Paris: OECD, pp. 115–61

Casey, Patricia (2002): 'Casualties of unbridled social change are being ignored', *The Irish Times,* 28 October 2002.

Cassell, E. J. (2001) 'Forces affecting caring by physicians', in Leighton, E. C. and Buislock, R. H. (eds), *The Lost Art of Caring: A Challenge to Health Professionals, Families, Communities and Society.* Baltimore: Johns Hopkins University Press, pp. 104–23.

Castles, S. and Miller, M. J. (2003) *The Age of Migration: International Population Movements in the Modern World.* Basingstoke: Macmillan.

Cerny, P. G. (1999) 'Globalising the political and politicising the global: concluding reflections on international political economy as a vocation', *New Political Economy,* 4 (1), pp. 147–62.

Cerny, P. G. (2000a) 'Restructuring the political arena: globalization and the paradoxes of the competition state', in Germain, R. D. (ed.), *Globalization and its Critics: Perspectives from Political Economy.* Basingstoke: Macmillan, pp. 117–38.

Cerny, P. G. (2000b) 'Structuring the political arena: public goods, states and governance in a globalizing world', in Palan, R. (ed.), *Global Political Economy: Contemporary theories.* London: Routledge, pp. 21–35.

Chubb, B. (1993) *The Government and Politics of Ireland.* London: Longman.

Clancy, P. (1995) *Access to College: Patterns of Continuity and Change.* Dublin: Higher Education Authority.

Clancy, P. (2003) *College Entry in Focus: A Fourth National Survey of Access to Higher Education.* Dublin: Higher Education Authority.

Clarke, J. (1998) 'Consumerism', in Hughes, G. (ed.), *Imagining Welfare Futures.* London: Routledge, pp. 14–54.

Clarke, J. (2001) 'Oppression and Caring: A Feminist Ethnography of Working to Improve Patient Care in Ethiopia', Unpublished PhD thesis, Trinity College, Dublin: University of Dublin.

Clinch, P., Convery, F. and Walsh, B. (2002) *After the Celtic Tiger: Challenges Ahead.* Dublin: O'Brien.

Coakley, A. (1997) 'Gendered citizenship; the social construction of mothers in Ireland', in Byrne, A. and Leonard, M. (eds), *Women in Irish Society: A Sociological Reader.* Belfast: Beyond the Pale, pp. 181–95.

Coakley, A. (1999) 'Poverty and Social Inclusion', PhD thesis. Dublin: University of Dublin.

Coakley, A. (2004) 'Mothers and poverty', in Kennedy, P. (ed.), *Motherhood in Ireland: Creation and Context.* Cork: Mercier Press, pp. 207–17.

Cochrane, A. and Clarke, J. (1993) *Comparing Welfare States.* London: Sage.

Collins, M. and Kavanagh, C. (1998) 'For richer, for poorer: the changing distribution of household income in Ireland, 1973–94', in Healy, S. and Reynolds, B. (eds), *Social Policy in Ireland.* Dublin: Oak Tree, pp. 163–92.

Combat Poverty Agency (2000a) *The Role of Community Development in Tackling Poverty.* Dublin: Combat Poverty Agency.

Combat Poverty Agency (2000b) *Planning for a more Inclusive Society: An Initial Assessment of the National Anti-Poverty Strategy.* Dublin: Combat Poverty Agency.

Combat Poverty Agency (2002a) *Poverty Briefing No. 13. Poverty in Ireland – The Facts.* Dublin: Combat Poverty Agency.

Combat Poverty Agency (2002b). *Poverty and Policy; Submission on Budget 2003 to the Minister for Social and Family Affairs.* Dublin: Combat Poverty Agency.

Combat Poverty Agency (2003), *Pre-Budget Submission,* Dublin: Combat Poverty Agency

Commaille, J. and de Singly, F. (1998) *The European Family.* Dordrecht: Kluwer.

Commission on the Family (1998) *Strengthening Families for the Future.* Dublin: Stationery Office.

Commission on Financial Management and Control Systems in the Health Service (Brennan Report) (2003), Dublin: Stationery Office.

Commission on Itinerancy (1963) *Report of the Commission on Itinerancy.* Dublin: Stationery Office.

Commission on Nursing (1998), Dublin: Stationery Office.

Conference of the Representatives of the Governments of the Member States (1996) *The European Union Today And Tomorrow: A General Outline For A Draft Revision Of The Treaties* http://wwww.irlgov.ie/iveagh/eu/state/treaty_rev/index.html

Connolly, L. (1997) 'From revolution to devolution: mapping the contemporary women's movement in Ireland', in Byrne, A. and Leonard, M. (eds), *Women in Irish Society: A Sociological Reader*. Belfast: Beyond the Pale, pp. 552–73.

Connor, S. (2001) *Postmodernist Culture: An Introduction to Theories of the Contemporary*. Oxford: Blackwell.

Conroy, P. (1998) 'Lone mothers: the case of Ireland', in Lewis, J. (ed.), *Lone Mothers in European Welfare Regimes – Shifting Policy Logics*. London: Jessica Kingsley, pp. 76–95.

Conroy, P. (1999) 'From the fifties to the nineties: social policy comes out of the shadows', in Kiely, G., O'Donnell, A., Kennedy, P. and Quin, S. (eds), *Irish Social Policy in Context*. Dublin: University College Dublin Press, pp. 33–50.

Conroy Jackson, P. (1993) 'Managing the mothers: the case of Ireland', in Lewis, J. (ed.), *Women and Social Policies in Europe: Work, Family and State*. Aldershot: Edward Elgar, pp. 72–91.

Constitution Review Group (1996) *Report of the Constitution Review Group*. Dublin: Stationery Office (Pn.2632).

Cook, G. and McCashin, A. (1997) 'Male breadwinner: a case study of gender and social security in the Republic of Ireland', in Byrne, A. and Leonard, M. (eds), *Women in Irish Society, A Sociological Reader*. Belfast: Beyond the Pale, pp. 167–80.

CORI (Conference of Religious in Ireland) (1993) *Growing Exclusion*. Dublin: CORI.

CORI Justice Commission (1999) *Socio-Economic Review 2000: Resources and Choices Towards a Fairer Future*. Dublin: Conference of Religious in Ireland.

CORI Justice Commission (2003) *Ireland in 2003: The Context*. CORI website.

Coulter, C. (2003) 'The end of Irish history?', in Coulter, C. and Coleman, S. (eds), *The End of Irish History?: Critical Reflections on the Celtic Tiger*. Manchester: Manchester University Press, pp. 1–33

Coulter, C. and Coleman, S. (eds) (2003) *The End of Irish History? Critical Reflections on the Celtic Tiger*. Manchester: Manchester University Press.

Cousins, M. (1992) 'Pregnancy and maternity benefits: a case study of Irish social welfare provision', *Administration* 4 (3), pp. 220–33.

Cousins, M. (2003) *Report on Consultation for National Action Plan against Poverty and Social Exclusion, National Anti-Poverty Strategy*. Dublin: Office for Social Inclusion –Combat Poverty Agency.

Cremer-Schäfer, H., Pelikan, C., Pilgram, A., Steinert, H., Taylor, I. and Vobruba, G. (2001) *Social Exclusion as a Multidimensional Process: Sub-cultural and Formally Assisted Strategies of Coping with and Avoiding Social Exclusion*. Brussels: European Commission. Targeted Socio-Economic Research (TSER) SOE1–CT98–2048.

Cronin, M. (2002) 'Speed limits: Ireland, globalisation and the war against time', in Kirby, P., Gibbons, L. and Cronin, M. (eds), *Reinventing Ireland: Culture, Society and the Global Economy*. London: Pluto, pp. 54–66.

Crotty, R. (1986) *Ireland in Crisis: A Study In Capitalist Colonial Underdevelopment*. Dingle: Brandon.

Crowley, N. (1999) 'Travellers and Social Policy', in Quin, S., Kennedy, P., O'Donnell, A. and Kiely, G. (eds), *Contemporary Irish Social Policy*. Dublin: University College Dublin Press, pp. 243–65.

Crowther, T. (1993) 'Euthanasia', in Clark, D. (ed.), *The Future of Palliative Care: Issues of Policy and Practice*, Milton Keynes: Open University Press, pp. 111–31.

CSO (Central Statistics Office) (2003) 2002 Census. http://www.cso.ie.

Curran, C. E. (2002) *Catholic Social Teaching 1891–Present: A Historical, Theological and Ethnical Analysis*. Washington: Georgetown University Press.

Curry, J. (2003) *The Irish Social Services*, 4th edn. Dublin: IPA.

Curtin, C., Jackson, P. and O'Connor, B. (1987) *Gender in Irish Society*. Galway: Galway University Press.

Daly, M. (1978) *Gyn /Ecology: The Metaethics of Radical Feminism*. Boston: Beacon Press.

Daly, M. (1984) *Pure Lust: Elemental Feminist Philosophy*. London: Beacon Press.

Daly, M. (2000) *The Gender Division of Welfare: The Impact of the British and German Welfare States*. Cambridge: Cambridge University Press.

Daly, M. (ed.) (2001) *Care Work: The Quest for Security*. Geneva: International Labour Office.

Daly, M. (2002) 'Access to social rights in Europe', in Lavan, A. (ed.), *Social Rights and Social Cohesion*. Dublin: EISS/IEA/Department of Social and Family Affairs.

Daly, M. and Leonard, M. (2002) *Against All Odds: Family Life on a Low Income in Ireland*. Dublin: Combat Poverty Agency.

Daly, M. and Lewis, J. (1998) 'Introduction: conceptualizing social care in the context of welfare state restructuring', in Lewis, J. (ed.), *Gender, Social Care and Welfare State Restructuring in Europe*, Aldershot: Ashgate.

Daly, M. and Standing, G. (2001) 'Introduction', in Daly, M. (ed.), *Care Work: The Quest for Security*. Geneva: International Labour Office, pp. 1–9.

Daykin, N. and Naidoo, J. (1995) 'Feminist critiques of health promotion', in Bunton R. et al. (eds), *The Sociology of Health Promotion: Critical Analyses of Consumption, Lifestyle and Risk*. London: Routledge, pp. 56–69.

Deacon, B. (1999) 'Social policy in a global context', in Hurrell, A. and Woods, N. (eds), *Inequality, Globalization, and World Politics*. Oxford: Oxford University Press, pp. 211–47.

Delanty, G (2000) *Citizenship in a Global Age*, Buckingham: Open University Press.

Deloitte and Touche (2001) *Audit of the Irish health system for value for money*. Dublin: Department of Health and Children.

Delphy, C. and Leonard, D. (1992) *Familiar Exploitation, New Analysis of Marriage in Contemporary Western Societies*. Cambridge: Polity.

Department of Health (1994) *Shaping a Healthier Future: A Strategy for Effective Healthcare in the 1990s*. Dublin: Stationery Office.

Department of Health and Children (2001a) *Quality and Fairness: A Health System for You*. Dublin: Stationery Office.

Department of Health and Children (2001b) *The Health of Our Children*. Annual Report of the Chief Medical Officer. Dublin: Stationery Office.

Department of Health and Children (2002) *Strategic Task Force on Alcohol: Interim Report*. Dublin: Stationery Office.

Department of Justice, Equality and Law Reform (2002) *Towards a National Plan Against Racism*. Dublin: Stationery Office.

Department of Justice, Equality and Law Reform (2003) *Report of the Consultative Group on Male/Female Wage Differentials.* Dublin: Stationary Office.

Department of Social, Community and Family Affairs (1999) *Statistical Information on Social Welfare Services.* Dublin: Stationery Office.

Department of Social, Community and Family Affairs (2001) *Building an Inclusive Society: Review of the National Anti-Poverty Strategy.* Dublin: Stationery Office.

Department of Social, Community and Family Affairs (2002) *Study to Examine the Future Financing of Long-term Care in Ireland,* Dublin. Stationery Office.

Department of Social, Community and Family Affairs (**Date**) *National Action Plan Against Poverty and Social Exclusion, 2003–05.* Dublin: Stationery Office.

Ditch, J., Bradshaw, J. and Eardley, T. (1997) *Developments in Family Policy in 1994.* York: European Observatory on National Family Policies, Social Policy Research Unit.

Donaghy, K. (2004) *Irish Independent,* 17 January.

Donnellan, E. (2003) 'Shortage of nurses will reach crisis in 2005, union warns', *The Irish Times,* 3 July.

Dooley, D. (1998) 'Gendered citizenship in the Irish constitution', in Murphy, T. and Twomey, P. (eds), *Ireland's Evolving Constitution.* Oxford: Hart.

Doorley, P. (1998) 'Health Status', in McAuliffe, E. and Joyce, L. (eds), *A Healthier Future? Managing Healthcare in Ireland.* Dublin: IPA, pp. 17–40.

Doyal and Gough (1991) *A Theory of Human Need.* Basingstoke, Macmillan

Doyle, A. (1999) 'Employment equality since accession to the European Union', in Kiely, G., Kennedy, P., O'Donnell, A. and Quin, S. (eds), *Irish Social Policy in Context.* Dublin: University College Dublin Press, pp. 114–54.

Drudy, S. and Lynch, K. (1993) *Schools and Society in Ireland.* Dublin: Gill & Macmillan.

Drudy, P. J. and Punch, M. (2001) 'Housing and inequality in Ireland', in Cantillon, S., Corrigan, C., Kirby, P. and O'Flynn, J. (eds), *Rich and Poor: Perspectives on Tackling Inequality in Ireland.* Dublin: Oak Tree in association with the Combat Poverty Agency, pp. 235–61.

Dworkin, A. (1981) *Pornography: Men Possessing Women.* London: Women's Press.

Dworkin, R. (1978) *Taking Rights Seriously.* London: Duckworth.

Dworkin, R. (1990) 'Bork's Jurisprudence' (1990) 57 *University of Chicago Law Review,* pp. 657.

Eardley, T. (1996) 'From safety nets to springboards? Social assistance and work incentives in the OECD countries', *Social Policy Review* 8, pp. 265–85.

Economic and Social Research Institute (ESRI) (2000) *Monitoring Poverty Trends: Results of 1998 Living in Ireland Survey.* Dublin: ESRI.

Ehrenreich, B. and Hochschild, A. R. (eds) (2003) *Global Women, Nannies, Maids and Sex Workers in the New Economy.* London: Granta.

Engels, F. (1844/1991) *The Condition of the Working Class in England.* Oxford: Blackwell.

Equality Authority (2003a) *Towards a Vision for a Gender Equal Society.* Dublin: Equality Authority.

Equality Authority (2003b) *Building an Intercultural Society.* Dublin: Equality Authority.

Esping-Andersen, G. (1990) *The Three Worlds of Welfare Capitalism.* Cambridge: Polity.

Esping-Andersen, G. (1996) (ed.), *Welfare States in Transition; National Adaptations in Global Economies.* London: Sage in association with the United Nations Research Institute for Social Development.

Esping-Andersen, G. (1999) *Social Foundations of Postindustrial Economies.* Oxford: Oxford University Press.

Esping-Andersen, G. (2002) 'The sustainability of welfare states: reshaping social protection', in Barbara Harriss-White (ed.), *Globalization and Insecurity: Political, Economic and Physical Challenges.* Basingstoke: Palgrave, pp. 218–32.

Ester, P., Halman, L., and de Moor, R. (1993) (eds), *The Individualizing Society.* Tilburg: Tilburg University Press.

Etzioni, A. (1993) *The Spirit of Community: The Reinvention of American Society.* New York: Touchstone.

Etzioni, A. (1999) 'Communitarianism', in Bullock, A. and Trombley, A. (eds), *The New Fontana Dictionary of Modern Thought.* London: HarperCollins, pp. 144–5.

European Commission (1999) *European Working Group on Fundamental Rights.* Brussels: European Commission.

European Commission (2000) *The Social Situation in the European Union 2003.* Brussels. European Commission.

European Commission (2001) *MISSOC: Social Protection in the EU Member States and the European Economic Area.* Brussels: European Commission.

European Commission (2003) *The Social Situation in the European Union.* Luxembourg: Office for Official Publications of the European Communities.

Eurostat (1999) *European Community Household Panel.* Luxembourg: European Commission

Eurostat (2000) *Key Data on Health 2000: Health in the EU under the Microscope.* Brussels: Eurostat.

Fahey, T. (1998a) 'Housing and social exclusion', in Healy, S. and Reynolds, B. (eds), *Social Policy in Ireland.* Dublin: Oak Tree, pp. 285–302.

Fahey, T. (1998b) 'The Catholic Church and social policy', in Healy, S. and Reynolds, B. (eds) *Social Policy in Ireland.* Dublin: Oak Tree, pp. 411–30.

Fahey, T. and Lyons, M. (1995) *Marital Breakdown and Family Law in Ireland.* Cork: Oak Tree.

Falk, R. (1999) *Predatory Globalization: A Critique.* Cambridge: Polity.

Fanning, B. (1999) 'The Mixed Economy of Welfare', in Kiely, G., O' Donnell, A., Kennedy, P. and Quin, S. (eds), *Irish Social Policy in Context.* Dublin: University College Dublin Press, pp. 3–18.

Fanning, B. (2002a) *Racism and Social Change in the Republic of Ireland.* Manchester: Manchester University Press.

Fanning, B. (2002b) 'The political currency of Irish racism: 1997–2002', *Studies* 91, pp. 319–27.

Fanning, B. (2003) 'The construction of Irish social policy 1953–2003', in Fanning, B. and MacNamara, T. (eds), *Ireland Develops: Administration and Social Policy 1953–2003.* Dublin: IPA, pp. 3–18.

Fanning, B., Veale, A. and O'Connor, D. (2001) *Beyond the Pale: Asylum Seeker Children and Social Exclusion in Ireland.* Dublin: Irish Refugee Council.

Farmer, P. (2003) *Pathologies of Power: Health, Human Rights and the New War on the Poor.* Berkeley: University of California Press

Faughnan, P., Humphries, N. and Whelan, S. (2002) *Patching up the System: The Community Welfare Service and Asylum Seeker.* Dublin: Social Science Research Centre.

Fennell, D. (1993) *Heresy: The Battle of Ideas in Modern Ireland.* Belfast: Blackstaff.

Ferguson, I., Lavalette, M. and Mooney, G. (2002) *Rethinking Welfare, A Critical Perspective.* London: Sage.

Ferriter, D. (1999) *A Nation of Extremes: The Pioneers in Twentieth-Century Ireland.* Dublin: Irish Academic Press.

Ferriter, D. (2003) 'Sobriety and temperance' in Kilcommins, S. and O'Donnell, I. (eds), *Alcohol, Society and Law.* Chichester: Barry Rose Law.

Fink, J (2001) 'Silence, absence and elision in "the family" in European social policy', in Fink, J., Lewis, G. and Clarke, J. (eds), *Rethinking European Welfare*, London: Sage.

Fitzgerald, Eithne (2001): 'Redistribution through Ireland's welfare and tax systems', in Cantillon, S., Corrigan, C., Kirby, P. and O'Flynn, J. (eds), *Rich and Poor: Perspectives on tackling inequality in Ireland.* Dublin: Oak Tree, pp. 151–96.

Flanagan, N. (2001) 'Born outside marriage: the social implications for Irish pre-school children', in Cleary, A., Nic Ghiolla Phadraig, M. and Quin, S. (eds), *Understanding Children Volume 2: Changing Experiences and Family Forms.* Cork: Oak Tree, 19–46.

Foucault, M (1977) *Discipline and Punish: The birth of the Prison*, London: Allen Lane.

Foucault, M (1979) *The History of Sexuality, Vol. 1, An Introduction.* London: Allen Lane.

Fraser, N. (1995) 'From redistribution to recognition: dilemmas in justice in a post-socialist age', *New Left Review* 212, pp. 68–93.

Fraser, N. (1997) *Justice Interruptus: Critical Reflections on the 'Postsocialist' Condition.* New York: Routledge.

Friedman, M. (1997) 'Autonomy and social relationships: rethinking the feminist critique', in Meyers, D. T. (ed.), *Feminists Rethink the Self.* Boulder, CO: Westview, pp. 40–61.

Frommel, D. (2002) 'Exporting health', *Le monde diplomatique*, May.

Gaita, R. (2000) *A Common Humanity: Thinking about Love and Truth and Justice.* London: Routledge.

Galbraith, J. K. (1992) *The Culture of Contentment.* London: Pelican.

Galbraith, J. K. (1998) 'The rich drive by', *Guardian*, 9 September 1998.

Gallagher, L. A., Doyle, E. and O'Leary, E. (2002) 'Creating the Celtic Tiger and sustaining economic growth: a business perspective', in McCoy, D., Duffy, D., Bergin, A., Eakins, J., Hore, J. and MacCoille, C (eds), *Quarterly Economic Commentary*, Spring, pp. 63–81.

Garavan, R., Winder, R., McGee, H. M. (2001) *Health and Social Services for Older People.* Report No 64. Dublin: National Council on Ageing and Older People.

Garrett, G. (2000) 'Shrinking states: globalization and national autonomy', in Woods, N. (ed.) *The Political Economy of Globalization.* Basingstoke: Palgrave, pp. 107–46.

Garvin, T. (1998) 'The strange death of clerical politics in University College Dublin', *Irish University Review* 28 (2), pp. 308–14.

Garvin, T. (2004, forthcoming) *Preventing the Future.* Dublin: Gill & Macmillan.

Gavanas, A. (2004) *Fatherhood Politics in the United States.* Illinois: University of Illinois Press.

George, V. and Wilding, P. (2002) *Globalization and Human Welfare.* Basingstoke: Palgrave.

Giddens, A. (1998) *The Third Way.* Cambridge: Polity.

Ginsburg, N. (1997) 'Sweden: the Social Democratic case', in Cochrane, A. and Clarke, J. (eds), *Comparing Welfare States.* London: Sage, pp.173–204.

Glendon, Mary Ann. (1991) *Rights Talk: The Impoverishment of Political Discourse.* New York: Free Press.

Goodbody Economic Consultants (2001) *Review of the National Anti-Poverty Strategy: Framework Document.* Dublin: Goodbody Economic Consultants.

Goodbody (2003) *Eurovision 2007.* Dublin: Goodbody Stockbrokers.

Gould, A. (1993) *Capitalist Welfare Systems.* London: Longman.

Government of Ireland (1997) *National Anti-Poverty Strategy: Sharing in Progress.* Dublin: Stationery Office.

Government of Ireland (2000) *The National Children's Strategy: Our Children – Their Lives.* Dublin: Stationery Office.

Government of Ireland (2002) *Building an Inclusive Society: Revised National Anti-Poverty Strategy.* Dublin: Stationery Office.

Government of Ireland (2003) *Sustaining Progress: Social Partnership Agreement 2003–2005.* Dublin: Stationery Office.

Gray, A. and Jenkins, B. (1999) 'Public expenditure decision-making', in Baldock, J., Manning, N., Millar, S. and Vickerstaff, S. (eds), *Social Policy.* Oxford: Oxford University Press, pp. 218–49.

Gray, J. (1998) *False Dawn.* London: Granta.

Greater Blanchardstown Response to Drugs (2003) www.west15.com

Green, D. (1990) *Equalizing People.* Choice in Welfare Series, No. 4. London: Institute of Economic Affairs.

Grogger, J. (2003) 'The effects of time limits, the eitc, and other policy changes on welfare use, work and income among female-headed families', *Review of Economics and Statistics* 85 (2), pp. 394–408.

Gwynn Morgan, D. (2001) *A Judgment Too Far? Judicial Activism and the Constitution.* Cork: Cork University Press.

Hardiman, N. (1998) 'Inequality and the representation of interests', in Crotty, W. and Schmitt, D. (eds), *Ireland and the Politics of Change.* London: Addison Wesley Longman, pp. 122–43.

Hatland, A. (2001) 'Changing family patterns: a challenge to social security', in Kautto, M., Fritzell, J., Hvinden, B., Kvist, J. and Uusitalo, H. (eds), *Nordic Welfare States in the European Context.* London: Routledge, pp. 116–36

Hayek, F. A. (1993) *Law, Legislation and Liberty.* Vol. 1. London: Routledge.

Healy, S. and Reynolds, B. (1993) 'Work, jobs and income: towards a new paradigm', in Healy, S. and Reynolds, B. (eds), *New Frontiers For Full Citizenship.* Dublin: Conference of Major Religious Superiors, pp. 40–85.

Healy, S. and Reynolds, B. (eds) (1998) *Social Policy in Ireland.* Dublin: Oak Tree.

Held, D, and McGrew, A. (2000) 'The great globalization debate: an introduction', in Held, D. and McGrew, A. (eds), *The Global Transformations Reader.* Cambridge: Polity, pp. 1–53.

Held, D. and McGrew, A. (2002) *Globalization/Anti-Globalization.* Cambridge: Polity.

Held, D., McGrew, A., Goldblatt, D. and Perraton, J. (1999) *Global Transformations: Politics, Economics and Culture.* Cambridge: Polity.

Helleiner, J. (1995) 'Gypsies, Celts and tinkers: colonial antecedents and anti-Traveller racism in Ireland', *Ethnic and Racial Studies* 18 (3), pp. 532–54.

Helleiner, J. (1997) '"Women of the itinerant class": gender and anti-Traveller racism in Ireland', *Women's Studies International Forum* 20 (2), pp. 275–87.

Henderson, M., Charter, D. and Frean, A. (2004) 'Sperm donor children win right to trace their fathers', *The Times*, 17 January.

Hervey, T. and Shaw, J. (1998) 'Women, work and care: women's dual role and double burden in EC sex equality law', *Journal of European Social Policy* 8 (1), pp. 43–63.

Hess, A. (2000) *American Social and Political Thought: A Precise Introduction*. New York: New York University Press.

Hillman, J. (1996) *The Soul's Code: In Search of Character and Calling*. New York: Random House.

Hirst, P. and Thompson, G. (1999): *Globalization in Question*, 2nd edn. Cambridge: Polity.

Hobson, B. and Morgan, D. (2002) 'Introduction: making men into fathers', in Hobson, B. (ed.), *Making Men Into Fathers: Men, Masculinities and the Social Politics of Fatherhood*. Cambridge: Cambridge University Press.

Hochschild, J. P. (2002) *The Principle of Subsidiarity and the Agrarian Ideal*. http://www.nd.-edu/~ndphilo/Philo/Papers/Subsidiarity.html

Hogan, G., (1990–2), 'Unenumerated personal rights: *Ryan's* case re-evaluated', *Irish Jurist* (n.s.) 25–7, p. 95.

Horton, R. (2003) *Second Opinion: Doctors, Diseases, and Decisions*. London: Granta.

Humphreys, R. (1993–5) 'Interpreting Natural Rights', *Irish Jurist* (n.s.) 28–30, p. 221.

IDA (2003) 'Ireland remains a top location for investment', press release, www.ida.ie/news, downloaded 20 September 2003.

Illich, I. (1996) 'Brave new biocracy: a critique of health care from womb to tomb', in Chesworth, J. (ed.), *The Ecology of Health*. London: Sage, pp. 17–29

Immigrant Council of Ireland (2003) *Labour Migration into Ireland: Study and Recommendations on Employment Permits*. Dublin: Immigrant Council of Ireland.

Inglis, T. (1998) *Moral Monopoly: The Rise and Fall of the Catholic Church in Modern Ireland*, 2nd edn. Dublin: University College Dublin Press.

Iredale, R. (1999) 'Public consultation and participation in policy making', in Kiely, G., O'Donnell, A., Kennedy, P. and Quin, S. (eds), *Irish Social Policy in Context*. Dublin: University College Dublin Press, pp. 178–94.

Irish Commission for Justice and Peace (1997) *Refugees and Asylum Seekers: A Challenge to Solidarity*. Dublin: Irish Commission for Justice and Peace.

Irish Commission for Justice and Peace (1998) *Re-Righting the Constitution: The Case for New Social and Economic Rights: Housing, Health, Nutrition, Adequate Standard of Living*. Dublin: Irish Commission for Justice and Peace.

Isin, E. F. and Wood, P. K. (1999) *Citizenship and Identity*. London; Sage.

Jackson, P. (1984) 'Women in nineteenth-century Irish emigration', *International Migration Review* XVIII (4), pp. 1004–20.

Jensen, A. M. (1994) 'The feminization of childhood', in Qvortup, J., Bardy, M., Sgritta, S. and Wintersberger, H. (eds), *Childhood Matters, Social Theory, Practice and Politics*. Aldershot: Averbury, pp. 59–76.

Jorgensen, P. (1991) 'The family with dependant children in Denmark', in Kiely, G. and Richardson, V. (eds), *Family Policy: European Perspectives*. Dublin: Family Studies Centre, pp. 89–104.

Kaim-Caudle, P. (1967) *Social Policy in the Irish Republic*. London: Routledge & Kegan Paul.

Kallianes, V. and Rubenfeld, P. (1997) 'Disabled women and reproductive rights', *Disability and Society* 12 (2), pp. 203–21.

Kavanagh, J. (1966) *The Manual of Social Ethics.* Dublin: Gill & Macmillan.

Kearney, A. T. (2002): 'Globalization's last hurrah?' *Foreign Policy,* January/February, pp 38–51.

Kearney, A. T. (2003): 'Measuring globalization: who's up, who's down?', *Foreign Policy,* January/February, pp 60–72.

Kelly, J.M. (1967) *Fundamental Rights in the Irish Law and Constitution,* 2nd edn. Dublin: Figgis.

Kelly, J. M. (2003) *The Irish Constitution,* 4th edn. Dublin: LexisNexis Butterworths.

Kennedy, A. (1997) *Swimming Against the Tide: Feminist Dissent on the Issue of Abortion.* Dublin: Open Air.

Kennedy, P. (2002) *Maternity in Ireland: A Woman-Centred Perspective.* Dublin: Liffey Press.

Kennedy, P. (2004) *Motherhood in Ireland: Creation and Context.* Cork: Mecier.

Kennedy, P. and Murphy Lawless, J. (2002) *The Maternity Needs of Refugee and Asylum Seeking Women.* Dublin: Women's Health Unit, Northern Area Health Board.

Kennedy, P. and Murphy-Lawless, J. (2003) 'The maternity care needs of refugee and asylum-seeking women in Ireland', *Feminist Review* 73, pp. 39–53.

Kennett, P. (2001) *Comparative Social Policy.* Buckingham: Open University Press.

Kenny, M. (1997) 'Who are they, who are we? Education and Travellers', in Crowley, E. and Mac Laughlin, J. (eds), *Under the Belly of the Tiger: Class, Race, Identity and Culture in the Global Ireland.* Dublin: Irish Reporter, pp. 61–70.

Kiely, G. (1995) 'Fathers in families', in McCarthy, I. C. (ed.), *Irish Family Studies: Selected Papers.* Dublin: Family Studies Centre, University College Dublin. 147–58.

Kiely, G., O' Donnell, A., Kennedy, P. and Quin, S. (1999) *Irish Social Policy in Context.* Dublin: University College Dublin Press.

Kirby, P. (2003a) *Introduction to Latin America: Twenty-First Century Challenges.* London: Sage.

Kirby, P. (2003b) *Macroeconomic Success and Social Vulnerability: Lessons for Latin America from the Celtic Tiger,* Serie financiamiento del desarrollo, No. 129, UN Economic Commission for Latin America and the Caribbean, Santiago: ECLAC.

Kirby, P. (forthcoming) 'The Irish state and the Celtic Tiger: a "flexible developmental state" or a competition state?', in Harrison, G. (ed.), *Global Encounters: International Political Economy, Development and Globalisation.* Basingstoke: Palgrave Macmillan.

Kirby, P., Gibbons, L. and Cronin, M. (2002) (eds), *Reinventing Ireland: Culture, Society and the Global Economy.* London: Pluto.

Kirby, Peadar (2002a): *The Celtic Tiger in Distress: Growth with Inequality in Ireland,* Basingstoke: Palgrave.

Kirby, Peadar (2002b): 'The world bank or Polanyi: markets, poverty and social well-being in Latin America', *New Political Economy* 7 (2), pp. 199–219.

Kukathas, C. (1990) *Hayek and Modern Liberalism.* Oxford: Clarendon.

Kvist, J. and Meier Jaeger, M. (2003) 'Pressures on post-industrial societies: Better is more or less state welfare?', 4th International Research Conference on Social Security, Antwerp, 5–7 May.

Labour Party (2002) *Election Manifesto: Part 2, A Better Quality of Life.* Dublin: Labour Party.

Laffan, B. and O'Donnell, R. (1998) 'Ireland and the growth of international governance', in Crotty, W. and Schmitt, D. E. (eds), *Ireland and the Politics of Change.* Harlow: Longman, pp. 156–77.

Lalor, S. (1996/2003) 'Planning and the Civil Service', in Fanning, B and MacNamara, T. (eds), *Ireland Develops: Administration and Social Policy 1953–2003.* Dublin: IPA, pp. 89–104.

Langan, M. (1998) 'The restructuring of health care', in Hughes, G. and Lewis, G. (eds), *Unsettling Welfare: the Reconstruction of Social Policy*. London: Routledge, pp. 81–115.

Lee, J. J. (1989) *Ireland 1912–1985: Politics and Society*. Cambridge: Cambridge University Press.

Lewis, E. (1954) *Medieval Political Ideas*. London: Routledge & Kegan Paul.

Lewis, G., Gewirtz, S. and Clarke, J. (2000) *Rethinking Social Policy*. London: Sage.

Lewis, J. (1987) *Women's Welfare, Women's Rights*. London: Croom Helm.

Lewis, J. (1992) 'Gender and the development of welfare regimes', *Journal of European Social Policy* 2 (3), pp. 159–73.

Lewis, J. (1993) (ed.), *Women and Social Policies in Europe: Work, Family and the State*. New York: Edward Edgar.

Lewis, J. (1997) (eds), *Lone Mothers in European Welfare Regimes, Shifting Policy Logics*. London: Jessica Kingsley.

Lewis, J. (2001) 'Legitimizing care work and the issue of gender equality', in Daly, M. (ed.), *Care Work: The Quest for Security*. Geneva: International Labour Office, pp. 57–75.

Lister, R (1997) *Citizenship: Feminist perspectives*. London: Macmillan.

Lister, R. (2002) 'Citizenship and Changing Welfare States', in Andersen, J. G. and Jensen, P. H. (eds), *Changing Labour Markets, Welfare Policies and Citizenship*. Bristol: Policy Press, pp. 39–57.

Ludmerer, K. M. and Fox, R. (2001) 'Caring and Medical Education', in Leighton, E. C. and Buislock, R. H. (eds), *The Lost Art of Caring: A Challenge to Health Professionals, Families, Communities and Society*. Baltimore: Johns Hopkins University Press, pp. 125–35.

Lynch, J. W., Smith, G. D., Kaplan, G. A. and House, J. S. (2000) 'Income inequality and mortality: importance to health of individual income, psychosocial environment, or material conditions', *British Medical Journal* 320, pp. 1200–4.

Lynch, K. and McLaughlin, E. (1995) 'Caring labour and love labour', in Clancy, P., Drudy, S., Lynch, K. and O'Dowd, L. (eds), *Irish Society: Sociological Perspectives*. Dublin: IPA, pp. 250–92.

MacLachlan, M. and O'Connell, M. (2000) *Cultivating Pluralism: Psychological, Social and Cultural Perspectives on a Changing Ireland*. Dublin: Oak Tree.

MacSharry, R. and White, P. (2000) *The Making of the Celtic Tiger: The Inside Story of Ireland's Boom Economy*. Cork: Mercier.

Marmot, M. and Wilkinson, R. G. (2001) 'Psychosocial and material pathways in the relation between income and health; a response to Lynch et al.', *British Medical Journal* 322, pp. 1233–36.

Marshall, T. H. (1950) *Citizenship and Social Class*, Cambridge, Cambridge University Press.

Marshall, T. H. (1969) *Class, Citizenship and Social Development*. New York: Anchor.

McCashin, T. (1999) 'The tax/welfare treatment of households', in *Report of the Working Group Examining the Treatment of Married, Cohabiting and One-Parent Families under the Tax and Social Welfare Codes*. Dublin: Stationery Office, Appendix 2. pp. 1–13..

McCreevy, C. (1999) *Budget 2000. Dublin:* Department of Finance.

McDowell, M. (2002) *Address to Annual Conference of the Irish Social Policy Association*. (12 September, available on Department of Justice, Equality and Law Reform website).

McDowell, M. (2003) *Address to Conference on Irish Culture and the Law*, St Patrick's College, Drumcondra, Dublin, 5 April.

McKeown, K. (2000) *A Guide to What Works in Family Support Services For Vulnerable Families*. Dublin: Stationery Office.

McKeown, K. (2001) *Fathers and Families: Research and Reflection on Key Questions*. Dublin: Stationery Office.

McKeown, K., Ferguson, H. and Rooney, D. (1998) 'Fathers: Irish experience in an international context – an abstract of a report to the Commission on the Family', *The Commission on the Family Final Report to the Minister for Social Community and Family Affairs – Strengthening Families for Life*. Dublin: Stationery Office. pp. 404–59.

McKeown, K. and Fitzgerald G. (1997) *Developing Childcare Services in Disadvantaged Areas: Evaluation of the Pilot Childcare Initiative 1994–1995*. Dublin: ADM Ltd.

McKeown, K., Pratschke, J. and Haase, T. (2003) *Family Well-Being: What Makes a Difference. Study based on a representative sample of parents and children in Ireland – Report to T he Ceifin Centre, County Clare – Insights and Initiatives for a Changing Society*. Clare: Ceifin Centre.

McKeown, K. and Sweeney, J. (2001) *Family Well-being and Family Policy: A Review of Research on Benefits and Costs*. Dublin: Stationery Office.

McLanahan, S. S. (1997) 'Parents' absence or poverty: which matters more?', in Duncan, G. J. and Brooks Gunn, J. (eds), *Consequences of Growing Up Poor*. New York: Russell Sage Foundation.

McLaughlin, E. (1993) 'Ireland: Catholic corporatism' in Cochrane, A. and Clarke, J. (eds), *Comparing Welfare States*. London: Sage, pp. 205–38.

McLaughlin, E. (1999) 'Economic independence and individualisation', in *Report of the Working Group Examining the Treatment of Married, Cohabiting and One-Parent Families under the Tax and Social Welfare Codes* (1999). Dublin: Stationery Office, Appendix 2.

McLaughlin, J. (1995) *Travellers in Ireland: Whose Country, Whose History?* Cork: Cork University Press.

Mac Laughlin, J. (ed.) (1997) *Under the Belly of the Tiger: Class, Race, Identity and Culture in the Global Ireland*. Dublin: Irish Reporter, pp. 61–70.

Mac Laughlin, J. (1999) 'Nation building, social closure and anti-traveller racism in Ireland', *Sociology* 33 (1), pp. 129–51.

Micklewright, J. and Stewart, K. (1999) 'Is the well-being of children converging in the European Union', *Economic Journal* 109 (459), pp. 692–714

Millar, J. and Warman, A. (1996) *Family Obligations in Europe*. London: Family Policy Studies Centre.

Miller, D. (1987) *Material Culture and Mass Consumption*. Oxford: Blackwell.

Millotte, M. (1997) *Banished Babies*. Dublin: New Island.

Mintz, S. (1998) 'From patriarchy to androgyny and other myths: placing men's family roles in historical perspective', in Booth, A. and Crouter, A. C. (eds), *Men in Families: When Do They Get Involved: What Difference Does It Make?* New Jersey: Lawrence Erblaum, pp. 3–30

Mishra, R. (1999) *Globalization and the Welfare State*. Cheltenham: Edward Elgar.

Montanari, I. (2000) 'From family wage to marriage subsidy and child benefits; controversy and consensus in the development of family support', *Journal of European Social Policy* 10 (4), pp. 307–33.

Moore, R. (2004) 'Lambegs and bodhrans: religion, identity and health in Northern Ireland', in Kelliher, D. (ed.) *Identity and Health.* London: Palgrave.

Moroney, R. (1991) *Social Policy and Social Work: Critical Essays on the Welfare State.* New York: Aldine De Gruyter.

Morris, J. (1991) *Pride Against Prejudice: Transforming Attitudes Towards Disability,* London: Women's Press.

Morris, J. (1997) '"Us" and "them"? Feminist research, community care and disability', in Taylor, D. (ed.), *Critical Social Policy.* London: Sage, pp. 77–94.

Murphy, G. (1999/2003) 'Towards a corporate state: Sean Lemass and the realignment of interest groups in the policy process 1948–64', in Fanning, B. and MacNamara, T. (eds), *Ireland Develops: Administration and Social Policy 1953–2003.* Dublin: IPA, pp. 105–18.

Murphy, T. (1998) 'Economic Inequality and the Constitution', in Murphy, T. and Twomey, P. (eds), *Ireland's Evolving Constitution 1937–1997: Collected Essays.* Oxford: Hart, pp. 163–81.

Murphy-Lawless, J. (2002) *Fighting Back: Women and the Impact of Drug Use on Families and Communities.* Dublin: Liffey.

Murray, C. (1984) *Losing Ground: American Social Policy 1950–1980.* New York: Basic Books.

Mustard, J. F. (1999) 'Health, health care and social cohesion', in Drache, D and Sullivan, T. (eds), *Health Reform: Public Success, Private Failure.* London: Routledge, pp. 329–350.

Myrdal, G. (1945) *Nation and Family: The Swedish Experiment in Democratic Family and Population Policy.* London: Keegan Paul.

(NAPS) National Anti-Poverty Strategy (1997) *Sharing in Progress: National Anti-Poverty Strategy.* Dublin: Stationery Office.

(NAPS) National Anti-Poverty Strategy (2001) *Social Inclusion Strategy.* Annual Report of the Inter-Departmental Committee 2000/2001. Dublin: NESF.

(NAPS) National Anti-Poverty Strategy (2003) *Conference Report.* Dublin: NESF.

Narayan, D. (2000) *Can Anyone Hear Us?* New York: Oxford University Press for the World Bank.

National Children's Strategy (2000) *Our Children – Their Lives.* Dublin: Stationery Office.

National Development Plan / Community Support Framework (2003) *Evaluation of the Equal Opportunities Programme 2000–06.* Dublin: CSF Unit.

(NESC) National Economic and Social Council (1999) *Opportunities, Challenges and Capacities for Choice.* Report No. 105. Dublin: NESC.

(NESC) National Economic and Social Council (1999) *Strategy Report.* Dublin: NESC.

(NESC) National Economic and Social Council (2003) *An Investment in Quality, Services, Inclusion and Enterprise.* (Pn.12312) Dublin: NESC.

(NESF) National Economic and Social Forum (1996) *Equality Proofing Issues.* Dublin: NESF.

(NESF) National Economic and Social Forum (2000a) *National Anti-Poverty Strategy; Forum Opinion No. 8.* Dublin: NESF.

(NESF) National Economic and Social Forum (2000b) *Social and Affordable Housing and Accommodation; Building the Future.* Forum Report No. 18. Dublin: NESF.

(NESF) National Economic and Social Forum (2001) *Lone Parents.* Forum Report No. 20. Dublin: Stationery Office.

(NESF) National Economic and Social Forum (2003a) *Inaugural Meeting on 30 January 2003 of the NAPS Social Inclusion Forum, Conference Report.* Dublin: NESF.

(NESF) National Economic and Social Forum (2003b) *The Policy Implications of Social Capital: NESF Report 28*. Dublin: Stationery Office.

Newman, J. (1998) 'Managerialism and social welfare', in Hughes, G. and Lewis G. (eds), *Unsettling Welfare: The Reconstruction of Social Policy*. London: Routledge, pp. 333–74.

Nic Ghiolla Phádraig (1994) 'Daycare – adult interest versus children's need? A question of compatability', in Qvortrup, J. (ed.), *Childhood Matters*. Aldershot: Avebury.

Nolan, B. (2000) *Child Poverty in Ireland*. Dublin: Combat Poverty Agency.

Nolan, B. (2003a) 'Income inequality during Ireland's Boom', *Studies* 92 (366), pp. 132–50.

Nolan, B. (2003b) *On Rights-Based Services for People with Disabilities*. Dublin: ESRI.

Nolan, B. (n.d.) 'Trends in the distribution of earnings in Ireland', unpublished paper, ESRI.

Nolan, B. and Callan, T. (1994) *Poverty and Policy in Ireland*. Dublin: Gill & Macmillan.

Nolan, B., Gannon, B., Layte, R., Watson, D. and Williams, J. (2002) *Monitoring Poverty Trends in Ireland; Results from the 2000 Living in Ireland Survey*. Dublin: ESRI.

Nolan, B., Maitre, B., O'Neill, D. and Sweetman, O. (2000) *The Distribution of Income in Ireland*. Dublin: Combat Poverty Agency/Oak Tree.

Nolan, B., O'Connell P. J. and Whelan, C. T., (2000) (eds) *Bust to Boom: The Irish Experience of Growth and Inequality*. Dublin: IPA.

Nolan, B and Watson, D. (1999) *Women and Poverty in Ireland*. Dublin: Oak Tree/Combat Poverty Agency.

Nolan, B. and Whelan, C. T. (1999) *Loading the Dice? A study of Cumulative Disadvantage*. Dublin: Oak Tree/ Combat Poverty Agency.

North West Inner City Area Network (1999) *Meeting the Challenge: Area Action Plan 1999–2004*. Dublin: NWICN.

O'Brien, M. (1981) *The Politics of Reproduction*. London: Routledge & Kegan Paul.

O'Brien, M. and Penna, S. (1998) *Theorising Welfare Enlightenment and Modern Society*. London: Sage.

O'Byrne, J. (2003) *Human Rights: An Introduction*. Essex: Pearson.

Ó Cinnéide, S. (1998) 'Democracy and the constitution', *Administration* 46 (4), winter 1998–9, pp 41–58.

Ó Cinnéide, S. (2003) 'Democracy and the constitution', in Fanning, B. and MacNamara, T. (eds), *Ireland Develops: Administration and Social Policy 1953–2003*. Dublin: IPA, pp. 326–40

O'Cinnéide, S (1970) *A Law for the Poor: A Study of Home Assistance in Ireland*. Dublin: IPA.

O'Connell, M. (2003) *Right-wing Ireland? The Rise of Populism in Ireland and Europe*. Dublin: Liffey.

O'Connor, J. (1993) 'Gender, class and citizenship in the comparative analysis of welfare state regimes; theoretical and methodological issues', *British Journal of Sociology* 44 (3), pp. 501–18.

O'Connor, J. S., Orloff, A. S. and Shaver, S. (1999) *States, Markets, Families, Gender, Liberalism and Social Policy in Australia, Canada, Great Britain and the United States*. Cambridge: Cambridge University Press.

O'Donnell, R. (2000): 'The new Ireland in the new Europe', in Rory O'Donnell (ed.), *Europe: The Irish Experience*, Dublin: IEA, pp. 161–214.

O'Donnell, R. (2002) *The Economic Dimension*. Dublin: IEA.

Office for Social Inclusion (n.d.) *National Action Plan against Poverty and Social Exclusion 2003–2005*, Dublin: Stationery Office.

O'Hearn, D. (1998) *Inside the Celtic Tiger: The Irish Economy and the Asian Model.* London: Pluto.

O'Hearn, D. (2000) 'Globalization, "New Tigers", and the end of the developmental state? The case of the Celtic Tiger', *Politics & Society* 28 (1), pp 67–92.

O'Hearn, D. (2001) *The Atlantic Economy: Britain, the US and Ireland.* Manchester: Manchester University Press.

O'Hearn, D. (2003) 'Macroeconomic policy in the Celtic Tiger: a critical reassessment', in Coulter, C. and Coleman, S. (eds), *The End of Irish History? Critical Reflections on the Celtic Tiger.* Manchester: Manchester University Press, pp. 34–55.

Ohlander, A. S. (1991) 'The invisible child? The struggle for a social democratic family policy in Sweden, 1900–1960s', in Bock, G. and Thane, P. (eds), *Maternity and Gender policies: Women and the Rise of the European Welfare State 1880s–1950s.* London: Routledge, pp. 60–72.

Ohmae, K. (2000) *The Invisible Continent: Four Strategic Imperatives of the New Economy.* New York: Harper Business.

Olah, L. S. Z., Bernhardt, E. M. and Goldscheider, F. K. (2002) 'Coresidential paternal roles in industrial countries: Sweden, Hungary and the United States', in Hobson, B. (ed.), *Making Men into Fathers: Men, Masculinities and the Social Politics of Fatherhood.* Cambridge: Cambridge University Press, pp. 25–60.

Oliver, M. (1996) *Understanding Disability: From Theory to Practice.* London: Macmillan.

O'Neill, B. and Sweetman, O. (2000) 'Female Labour Force Participation and Household Income Inequality in Ireland', in Nolan, B., Maitre, B., O'Neill, D., and Sweetman, O. (eds), *The Distribution of Income in Ireland,* pp. 79–88.

O'Regan, E. (2003) 'Wealthy have "best health service and least illness"', *Irish Independent,* 19 December.

Ó Riain, S. (2000) 'The flexible developmental state: globalization, information technology and the "Celtic Tiger"', *Politics & Society* 28 (2), pp. 157–93.

Orloff, A. S. (1993) 'Gender and the social rights of citizenship; the comparative analysis of gender relations and welfare states', *American Sociological Review* 58 (June), pp. 303–28.

Orloff, A. S. and Monson, R. (2002) 'Citizens, workers or fathers? Men in the history of US Social Policy', in Hobson, B. (ed.), *Making Men into Fathers: Men, Masculinities and the Social Politics of Fatherhood.* Cambridge: Cambridge University Press, pp. 61–91

O'Sullivan, T. (2003) 'Consumerism in the Health Services', in Fanning, B. and McNamara, T. (eds), *Ireland Develops: Administration and Social Policy 1953–2003.* Dublin: IPA, pp. 219–30.

O'Toole, F. (2003) *After the Ball.* Dublin: TASC/New Ireland.

O'Toole, J. (2002), Book Review: McKeown, K. and Sweeney, J. (2001) 'Family well-being and family policy: a review of research on benefits and costs', *Irish Journal of Sociology* 11 (1), pp. 127–9.

O Tuathaigh, G. (1991) 'The Irish-Ireland Idea: rationale and relevance', in Longley E (ed.), *Culture in Ireland: Division or Diversity.* Belfast: Institute of Irish Studies, pp. 56–65.

Owusu-Bempah, J. and Howitt, D. (1997) 'Socio-genealogical connectedness, attachment theory and childcare practice', *Child and Family Social Work,* 2, pp. 199–207.

Pahl, J. (1999) 'The family and the production of welfare', in Baldock, J., Manning, N., Millar, S. and Vickerstaff, S. (eds), *Social Policy.* Oxford: Oxford University Press, pp. 154–87.

Pang, T., Lansang, M. A. and Haines, A. (2002) 'Brain drain and health professionals', *British Medical Journal* 324 (2), pp. 499–500.

Parekh, B. (2000) *Rethinking Multiculturalism: Cultural Diversity and Political Theory.* Basingstoke: Macmillan.

Parker, W. (1997) 'Must constitutional rights be specified? Reflections on the proposal to amend Article 40.3.1', *Irish Jurist* (n.s.) 32, p. 102.

Parreñas, R. (2003) 'The care crisis in the Philippines: Children and transnational families in the new global economy', in Ehrenreich, B. and Hochschild, A. R. (eds), *Global Woman: Nannies, Maids and Sex Workers in the New Economy.* London: Granta.

Pateman, C. (1988) 'The patriarchal welfare state', in Gutman, A. (ed.), *Democracy and Welfare State.* Princeton: Princeton University Press.

Pearson, M, (2003) 'Targeting social expenditure', paper at seminar on Irish Social Expenditure in a Comparative International Context, Dublin, 16 September.

Pearson, M. (2003) 'Social expenditure and poverty in Ireland; a comparative perspective', *Poverty Today*, 3.

Peillon, M. (1982) *Contemporary Irish Society.* Dublin: Gill & Macmillan.

Peillon, M. (1994) 'Placing Ireland in a comparative perspective', *Economic and Social Review* 25 (2), pp. 179–95.

Peillon, M. (1995) 'Interest groups and the state', in Clancy, P., Drudy, S., Lynch, K. and O'Dowd, L. (eds), *Sociological Perspectives.* Dublin: IPA, pp. 358–78.

Peillon, M. (2001) *Welfare in Ireland: Actors, Resources and Strategies.* London: Praeger.

Perry, M. (1988) *Morality, Politics and Law.* Oxford: Oxford University Press.

Phillips, A. (1991) *Engendering Democracy: From Inequality to Difference: A Severe Case of Displacement?* Cambridge: Polity.

Phillips, A. (1997) 'From inequality to difference: a severe case of displacement?', *New Left Review* 224, pp. 143–53.

Pierce, M. (2003) *Minority Ethnic People with Disabilities in Ireland.* Dublin: Equality Authority.

Pingle, D., Walsh, J., and Hennessy, M. (1999) *Poor People, Poor Places: A Geography of Poverty and Deprivation in Ireland.* Dublin: Oak Tree.

Polanyi, K. (1957 [1944]) *The Great Transformation: The Political and Economic Origins of our Time.* Boston: Beacon Press.

Powell, F. (1992) *The Politics of Irish Social Policy 1600–1990.* Lampeter: Edwin Mellen.

Powell, F. and Guerin, D. (1997) *Civil Society and Social Policy.* Dublin: A. and A. Farmer.

Preston, M. (1998) 'Discourse and hegemony: race and class in the language of charity in nineteenth century Dublin', in Foley, T. and Ryder, S. (eds), *Ideology and Ireland in the Nineteenth Century.* Dublin: Four Courts, pp. 100–12.

Pringle, D. G. (1999) 'Something old, something new; lessons to be learnt from previous strategies of positive territorial discrimination', in Pringle, D. G., Walsh, J. and Hennessy, M. (eds), *Poor People, Poor Places: A Geography of Poverty and Deprivation in Ireland.* Dublin: Oak Tree, pp. 263–78.

Pringle, D. G., Walsh, J. and Hennessy M. (eds) (1999)

Putnam, R. D. (2000) *Bowling Alone: The Collapse and Renewal of American Community.* New York: Touchstone.

Quin, S., Kennedy, P., O'Donnell, A. and Kiely, G. (1999) (eds), *Contemporary Irish Social Policy.* Dublin: University College Dublin Press.

Quinn, G. (2001) 'Rethinking the nature of economic, social and cultural rights in the Irish legal order', in Costello, C. (ed.), *Fundamental Social Rights: Current European Legal Protection and the Challenge of the EU Charter of Fundamental Rights.* Dublin: Irish Centre for European Law, pp. 35–54.

Raftery, M. and O'Sullivan, E. (1999) *Suffer Little Children: The Inside Story of Ireland's Industrial Schools.* Dublin: New Island.

Rathzel, N. (1992) 'Racism in Europe, a case for socialist feminists?', in Ward, A., Gregory, J. and Yuval-Davis, N. (eds), *Women and Citizenship in Europe: Borders, Rights and Duties.* London: Trentham Books for the European Forum of Socialist Feminists, pp. 25–36.

Rawls, J. (1973) *A Theory of Justice.* Oxford: Oxford University Press.

Report of the Task Force on Violence Against Women (1997). Dublin: Stationery Ofice

Report of the Working Group Examining the Treatment of Married, Cohabiting and One-Parent Families under the Tax and Social Welfare Codes (1999). Dublin: Stationery Office.

Reynolds, P. (2003) *Sex in the City, the Prostitution Racket in Ireland.* London: PAN.

Rich, A. (1977) *Of Women Born, Motherhood as Experience and Institution.* London: Virago.

Rich, A. (1980) *On Lies, Secrets And Silence, Selected Prose 1966–1978.* London: Virago.

Richardson, V. (2001) 'Legal and Constitutional Rights of Children in Ireland', in Cleary, A., Nic Ghiolla Phadraig, M. and Quin, S. (eds), *Understanding Children* Vol. 1: *State, Education and Economy.* Cork: Oak Tree Press, pp. 21–44

Ritzer, G. (1992) *Sociological Theory,* 3rd edn. New York: McGraw Hill.

Ritzer, G. (1996) *Sociological Theory,* 4th edn. New York: McGraw Hill.

Roche, W. K. and Cradden, T. (2003) 'Neo-corporatism and social partnership', in Adshead, M. and Millar, M. (eds), *Public Administration and Public Policy in Ireland: Theory and Methods,* London: Routledge, pp. 69–87.

Room, G. (2000) 'Trajectories of social exclusion; the wider context for the third and first worlds' in Gordon, G. and Townsend, P. (eds), *Breadline Europe.* Bristol: Policy Press, pp. 407–39.

Rorty, R. (1994) *Objectivism, Relativism and Truth.* New York: Cambridge.

Rose, H. (2000) 'Risk, trust and scepticism in the age of the new genetics', in Adam, B. et al. (eds), *The Risk Society and Beyond: Critical Issues for Social Theory.* London: Sage, pp. 63–77.

Ruhama Annual Report 2001–02.

Ruhama Philosophy and Values, March 2003.

Ruhs, M. (2003) *Emerging Trends and Patterns in the Immigration and Employment of Non-EU Nationals in Ireland: What the Data Reveal.* Dublin: Working Paper Series, Policy Studies Institute, Trinity College, Dublin.

Rush, M. (1999) 'Social partnership in Ireland' in Kiely, G., O' Donnell, A., Kennedy, P. and Quin, S. (eds), *Irish Social Policy in Context.* Dublin: University College Dublin Press, pp. 155–77.

Rush, M. (2003a) *Children, Diversity and Childcare,* Waterford: Waterford City Childcare Committee.

Rush, M (2003b) *Including Children – Childcare Audit 2003: Diversity, Disability and Additional Needs.* Waterford: Waterford County Childcare Committee.

Rush, M. (2003c) Book Review: Peillon, M. (2001) 'Welfare in Ireland: actors, resources and strategies', *Irish Journal of Sociology* 12 (1), pp. 98–100.

Sabel, Charles (1998) 'Foreword', in Peadar Kirby and David Jacobson (eds), *In the Shadow of the Tiger: New Approaches to Combating Social Exclusion*. Dublin: Dublin City University Press, pp. xi–xiii.

Sachs, J. D. (1997) 'Ireland's growth strategy: lessons for economic development', in Alan W. Gray, (ed.), *International Perspectives on the Irish Economy*. Dublin: Indecon, pp 54–63.

Sainsbury, D. (1996) *Gender Equality and Welfare States*. Cambridge: Cambridge University Press.

Sainsbury, D. (1999) (ed.), *Gender and Welfare State Regimes*. Oxford: Oxford University Press.

Saranga, E. (1998) 'Review', in Saranga, E. (ed.), *Embodying the Social: Constructions of Difference*. London: Routledge, pp. 189–206.

Scannell, Y. (2000) 'The taxation of married women. *Murphy* v. *Attorney General* (1982)', in O'Dell, E. (ed.), *Leading Cases of the Twentieth Century*. Dublin: Round Hall/Sweet & Maxwell, pp. 327–52.

Scharpf, F. W. (2000) 'The viability of advanced welfare states in the international economy: vulnerabilities and options', *Journal of European Public Policy* 7 (2), pp. 190–228.

Schmitt, D. (1973) *The Irony of Irish Democracy*. Massachusetts: Lexington.

Schneir, M (1994) *Feminism: The Essential Historical Writings*. New York: Vintage Books.

Seltzer, J. A. (1998) 'Men's contribution to children and social policy', in Booth, A. and Crouter, A. C. (eds), *Men in Families: When Do They Get Involved: What Difference Does It Make*. New Jersey: Lawrence Erblaum, pp. 303–14.

Sen, A. (1985) *Commodities and Capabilities*. North Holland: Amsterdam.

Sennett, R. (2004) *Respect: The Formation of Character in an Age of Inequality*. London: Penguin.

Shaver, S (1994) 'Body rights, social rights and the liberal welfare state', *Critical Social Policy* 39, pp. 66–93.

Sheinfeld, G. S. and Arnold, J. (1998) *Health Promotion Handbook*. St Louis: Mosby

Simonnews (2003) 'New homeless figures do not tell the whole story', in *Simonnews*, No. 6, June.

Sjoberg, G. (1999) 'Some observations about bureaucratic capitalism: knowledge about what and why', in Abu-Lughod, J. (ed.), *Sociology for the Twenty-first Century: Continuities and Cutting Edges*. Chicago: University of Chicago Press, pp. 43–64.

Sklair, L. (2002) *Globalization: Capitalism and its Alternatives*, Oxford: Oxford University Press.

Skrabanek, P. (1994) *The Death of Humane Medicine and the Rise of Coercive Healthism*. Dublin: Social Affairs Unit.

Slattery, L.(2003) 'Save Euros and lose pounds in health club price war', *The Irish Times*, 7 November.

Smyth, A (1993) (ed.), *Irish Women's Studies Reader*, Dublin: Attic Press.

Smyth, E. and Hannan, D. F. (2000) 'Education and inequality', in Nolan, B., O'Connell, P. J. and Whelan, C. T. (eds), *Bust to Boom? The Irish Experience of Growth and Inequality*. Dublin: IPA, pp. 109–26.

Sommestad, L. (1997) 'Welfare state attitudes to the male bread winning system: the United States and Sweden in comparative perspective', in Janssens, A. (ed.), *The Rise and Decline of the Male Breadwinner Family*. Cambridge: Cambridge University Press, pp. 153–74

St Leger, F. and Gillespie, N. (1991) *Informal Welfare in Belfast: Caring Communities*. Aldershot: Avebury.

Standing, G. (2001) 'Care work overcoming insecurity and neglect', in Daly, M. (ed.) *Care Work, the Quest for Security*. Geneva: ILO.

Stevenson, Nick (2003) *Cultural Citizenship: Cosmopolitan Questions*. Maidenhead: Open University Press.

Stier, M. (1998) 'How much communitarianism is left (and right)?', in Lawler, P. A. and McConkey, D. (eds), *Community and Political Thought*. Westport: Praeger, pp. 40–52.

Stoesz, D. (2002) 'The American welfare state at twilight', *Journal of Social Policy* 31 (3), pp. 487–503.

Sunday Tribune Property Supplement (2004) 1 February.

Sunstein, C. (1993) *The Partial Constitution*. Cambridge MA: Harvard University Press.

Swank, D. (2002) *Global Capital, Political Institutions, and Policy Change in Developed Welfare States*. Cambridge: Cambridge University Press.

Sweeney, P. (1990) *The Politics of Public Enterprise and Privatisation*. Dublin: Tomar.

Sweeney, P. (1999) *The Celtic Tiger: Ireland's Continuing Economic Miracle*. Dublin: Oak Tree.

Task Force on the Travelling Community (1995) *Report*. Dublin: Stationery Office.

Tawney, R. H., (1926) *Religion and the Rise of Capitalism*. London: Pelican.

Taylor, G. (1995/2003) 'The politics of conviviality: voluntary workfare and the right to useful unemployment', in Fanning, B. and McNamara, T. (eds), *Ireland Develops: Administration and Social Policy 1953–2003*. Dublin: IPA, pp. 309–25.

Taylor, G. (2002): 'Hailing with an invisible hand: a "cosy" political dispute amid the rise of neoliberal politics in modern Ireland', *Government and Opposition* 37 (4), pp. 501–23.

Taylor-Gooby, P. (1991) 'Welfare state regimes and welfare citizenship', *Journal of Social Policy* 1 (20), pp. 93–105.

Taylor-Gooby P. (1997) 'European welfare futures: the views of key influentials in six European countries on likely developments in social policy', *Social Policy and Administration* 31 (1), pp. 1–19.

Tighe, C. A. (2001) 'Working at disability: a qualitative study of the meaning of health and disability for women with physical impairments', *Disability and Society* 16 (4), pp. 218–28.

Timonen, V. (2003) *Irish Social Expenditure in a Comparative International Context*. Dublin: IPA.

Titmuss, R. M. (1943) *Birth, Poverty, and Wealth*. London: Hamish Hamilton.

Touraine, A. (2000) *Can We Live Together? Equality and Difference*. Cambridge: Polity.

Tovey, H. (1999) 'Rural poverty: a political economy perspective', in Pringle, D. G., Walsh, J. and Hennessy, M. (eds), *Poor People, Poor Places: A Geography of Poverty and Deprivation in Ireland*. Dublin: Oak Tree, pp. 97–121.

Tovey, H. and Share, P. (2000) *A Sociology of Ireland*. Dublin: Gill & Macmillan.

Townsend, P. (1979) *Poverty in the United Kingdom: A Survey o f Household Resources and Standards*. Harmondsworth: Penguin.

Troeltsch, E. (1931) *The Social Teaching of the Christian Churches: Vol. II*. London: Allen & Unwin.

Turner, B. (1999) *Religion and Social Theory*. London: Sage.

Turner, B. S. (1994) 'Postmodern culture? Modern citizens', in Steenbergen, B. V. (ed.), *The Condition of Citizenship*. London: Sage, pp. 153–68.

Twine, F. (1994) *Citizenship and Social Rights; the Interdependence of Self and Society*. London: Sage.

Udry, C. A. (2004) 'Brazil: the challenges of a new political period', *International Socialist Tendency, Discussion Bulletin* 4, pp. 2–6.

Van den Akker, P. (1993) 'Primary relations in western societies', in Ester, P., Halman, L., and de Moor, R. (eds), *The Individualizing Society*. Tilburg: Tilburg University Press, pp. 97–127.

Van Kersbergen, K. (1995) *Social Capitalism: A Study of Christian Democracy and the Welfare State*. London: Routledge.

Viney, L. L. (1983) *Images of Illness*. Florida: Robert E. Krieger.

Wainwright, H. (2003) *Reclaim the State: Experiments in Popular Democracy*. London: Verso.

Waite, L. J. (1995) 'Does marriage matter?' *Demography* 32 (4), pp. 483–507.

Walsh, J. (1999) 'The role of area-based programmes in tackling poverty', in Pringle, D. G., Walsh, J. and Hennessy, M. (eds), *Poor People, Poor Places: A Geography of Poverty and Deprivation in Ireland*. Dublin: Oak Tree, pp. 279–309.

Walsh, J. (2002) 'Area Programmes; an effective strategy for tackling poverty?', *The Adult Learner, Journal of Adult and Community Education in Ireland*, Dublin: Aontas. pp. 27–33.

Ward, A, Gregory J and Yuval-Davis N (eds) (1992) *Women and Citizenship in Europe: Borders, Rights and Duties*. London: Trentham Books for the European Forum of Socialist Feminists.

Waters, M. (1995) *Globalization*. London: Routledge.

Watson, S. (2000) 'Foucault and the study of social policy', in Lewis, G., Gewirtz, S. and Clarke, J. (eds), *Rethinking Social Policy*. London: Sage/OU Press, pp. 66–77.

Weber, M. (1904/1969) 'The Protestant sects and the spirit of capitalism' in Gerth, H. H. and Wright Mills, C. (eds), *From Max Weber: Essays in Sociology*. New York: Oxford University Press, pp. 302–22.

Whelan, C. T., Layte, R., Maitre, B., Gannon, B., Nolan, B., Watson, D. and Williams, J. (2003) (eds), *Monitoring Poverty Trends in Ireland: Results from the 2001 Living in Ireland Survey*. Policy Research Series Number 51, Dublin: ESRI.

Whitty, G. (1998) 'Education, economy and national culture', in Bocock, R. and Thompson, K. (eds), *Sociological and Cultural Forms of Modernity*. London: Polity.

(WHO) World Health Organisation (2000) The World Health Report 2000.

Whyte, G. (1998) 'Discerning the philosophical premises of the Report of the Constitution Review Group: An analysis of the recommendations on fundamental rights', *Contemporary Issues in Irish Law and Politics*, pp. 216–38.

Whyte, G. (2002) *Social Inclusion and the Legal System: Public Interest Law in Ireland*. Dublin: IPA.

Whyte, J. (1971) *Church and State in Modern Ireland 1923–1970*. Dublin: Gill & Macmillan.

Wilensky, H. (1975) *The Welfare State and Equality: Structural and Ideological Roots of Public Expenditure*. Berkeley: University of California Press.

Wilkinson, R. G. (1999) 'Putting the picture together: prosperity, redistribution, health and welfare', in Marmot, M. and Wilkinson, R. G. (eds), *Social Determinants of Health*. Oxford: Oxford University Press, pp. 256–79.

Williams, F. (1996) 'Postmodernism, feminism and the question of difference', in Parton, N. (ed.), *Social Theory, Social Change and Social Work*. London: Routledge, pp. 61–76.

Williams, F. (1999) 'Good enough principles for welfare', *Journal of Social Policy* 28 (4), pp. 667–87.

Williams, F. (2002) 'The presence of feminism in the future of welfare', *Economy and Society*, 31 (4), pp. 503–32.

Wren, M-A. (2003) *Unhealthy State: Anatomy of a Sick Society*. Dublin: New Island.

Yeates, N. (1997) 'Gender and the development of the Irish social welfare system', in Byrne, A. and Leonard, M. (eds), *Women in Irish Society: A Sociological Reader*. Belfast: Beyond the Pale, pp. 145–66.

Yeates, N. (2000) *Globalization and Social Policy*. London: Sage.

Yeates, P. and Stoltz, P. (1995) *Unequal status, Unequal treatment: The Gender Restructuring of Welfare: Ireland*. Dublin: working paper of the Gender and European Welfare Regimes research of the Human Capital Mobility programme of DGXII of the European Commission. Dublin: WERRC.

Young, I. M. (1990) *Justice and the Politics of Difference*. Princeton: Princeton University Press.

Yuval-Davis, N. (1991) 'The citizenship debate: women, ethnic processes and the state', *Feminist Review* 39, pp. 58–68.

Yuval-Davis, N. (1992) 'Women as citizens' in Ward, A., Gregory, J. and Yuval-Davis, N. (eds), *Women and Citizenship in Europe: Borders, Rights and Duties*. London: Trentham Books for the European Forum of Socialist Feminists, pp.11–17.

Zappone, K. E. (2001) *Charting the Equality Agenda: A Coherent Framework for Equality Strategies in Ireland, North and South*. Dublin: Equality Authority.

Index